PROBLEM SOLVING
ACROSS
THE DISCIPLINES
Preliminary Edition

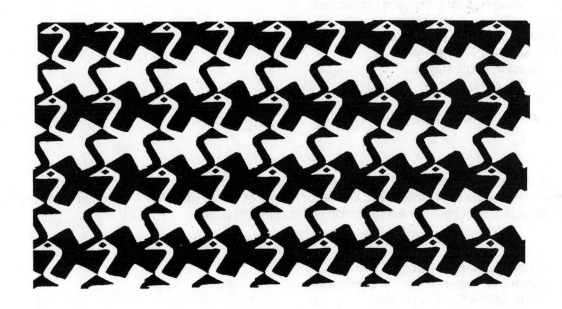

R.R. KADESCH
University of Utah

D1377244

PRENTICE HALL
Upper Saddle River, NJ 07458

Acquisitions Editor: Sally Denlow
Editorial Assistant: Joanne Wendelken
Assistant Editor: Audra I. Walsh
Editorial Director: Tim Bozik
Editor-in-Chief: Jerome Grant
Assistant Vice President of Production and Manufacturing: David W. Riccardi
Editorial/Production Supervision: Robert C. Walters
Managing Editor: Linda Mihatov Behrens
Executive Managing Editor: Kathleen Schiaparelli
Manufacturing Buyer: Alan Fischer
Manufacturing Manager: Trudy Pisciotti
Marketing Assistant:Jennifer Pan
Creative Director: Paula Maylahn
Art Manager: Gus Vibal
Art Director: Jayne Conte
Cover Designer: Bruce Kenselaar

Title page photo: A superposition of nine pillow cover designs, each drawn by A. Pertschuk, from *Symmetries of Culture* by Washburn and Crowe. University of Washington Press. All other photo credits appear on page x and constitute a continuation of this copyright page.

Printed in the United States of America
10 9 8 7 6 5 4 3 2 1

ISBN 0-13-654187-9

PRENTICE-HALL INTERNATIONAL (UK) LIMITED, LONDON
PRENTICE-HALL OF AUSTRALIA PTY. LIMITED, SYDNEY
PRENTICE-HALL CANADA INC. TORONTO
PRENTICE-HALL HISPANOAMERICANA, S.A., MEXICO
PRENTICE-HALL OF INDIA PRIVATE LIMITED, NEW DELHI
PRENTICE-HALL OF JAPAN, INC., TOKYO
SIMON & SCHUSTER ASIA PTE. LTD., SINGAPORE
EDITORA PRENTICE-HALL DO BRASIL, LTDA., RIO DE JANEIRO

CONTENTS

Preface

When a new problem is encountered knowledge relevant to that problem must be applied along with an appropriate problem solving strategy for attacking it. This process has been said to involve "critical thinking" by some, "reflective thinking" by others, or simply "problem solving." Classically, the cognitive domain consists of a hierarchy of six cognitive skill levels (upper of the two accompanying figures). The lowest level in this hierarchy is **Knowledge**. The next higher level, the lowest level of understanding, is **Comprehension**. This denotes the understanding of what is being communicated without necessarily relating this to other material. Third is **Application** involving the use of general ideas and methods in particular situations. Next there is **Analysis** in which things are broken down into their constituent parts and the relationships among these parts understood. Level five is **Synthesis** where elements and parts are put together to form a whole. Finally there is the level of **Evaluation** in which judgments are made about the value of methods and materials and the extent to which they satisfy certain criteria.

HIERARCHY OF INTELLECTUAL SKILLS
- Bloom -

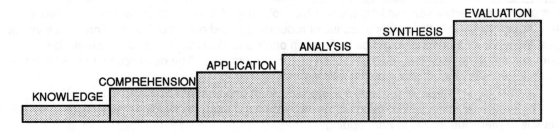

PROBLEM SOLVING STAGES

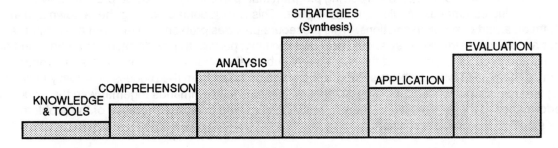

All of these same cognitive levels appear in problem solving situations with only a slight change in labeling and sequencing (lower of the two accompanying figures). Here, for the sake of making things more explicit, the lowest problem solving level is divided into two parts, **Knowledge** and **Tools**. The label "Tools" simply indicates a background knowledge of various approaches to solving problems. Next comes **Comprehension**, as before, but following that in a typical problem solving sequence of operations comes **Analysis** in which all the elements of a problem, both explicit and implicit, are identified and understood. Once the pieces of a problem are understood these, together with new elements, are put together in some new arrangement to form one or more **Strategies** for solving a problem. This is clearly the operation of Synthesis. Next comes the process of **Application** to the problem of selected elements of both knowledge and tools together with an identified problem solving strategy. Referring to the hierarchy of problem solving skills, it is seen that Application generally requires a lower level of skill than either the process of Analysis or that of devising a Strategy. It is at this point, however, that problem solvers may realize that they have failed to produce a satisfactory solution to a problem. For this reason a section entitled **Help** may be inserted following the Application section. The skill level required here may range over the full extent of the cognitive hierarchy depending upon the nature of the help required. Finally, the problem together with its solution is subjected to a critical **Evaluation**. Whether Strategies (synthesis) or Evaluation stands higher in the hierarchy of problem solving skills depends on the particular problem situation. Some would insist that the term "critical thinking" be reserved only for these highest two levels. Devising or inventing a new combination or rearrangement of elements (synthesis) may require creativity of the highest order. On the other hand, evaluation may involve making critical judgements about the extent to which certain criteria are satisfied. In such cases this might involve the highest level of cognitive skill.

Problem solving COMMANDS (heuristics) are those things problem solvers tell themselves to do in seeking solutions to problems before they actually do them. They are self-instructions, i.e., "commands" that are given to oneself in order to solve a problem. These are then followed by the execution of those commands. At every level in the cognitive hierarchy there are commands appropriate to that level of cognitive activity. Commands consist of key words and phrases that suggest what might be done at a particular stage in solving a problem. Command examples include IDENT RELEV KNOWLEDGE, CLARIFY PROB, and EVAL PROB SOLUTION. These are the tips, hints, cues, and suggestions problem solvers often give themselves that help them solve problems. A list of such commands, or heuristics, is given in Appendix C. It is the author's list, full of redundancy, and quite extensive. This list serves only to suggest the kinds of items that might be included in one's personal repertoire. It is actually best for problem solvers to develop their own collection of such commands. The development of skills in the use of such heuristics is characterized by the following:

    a) the transferability of problem solving skills from one academic discipline to another,

    b) greater efficiency in learning achieved by problem analysis that is as applicable to sociology as it is to medicine as it is to anthropology,

    c) greater permanence in learning because of the generalized nature of the problem solving commands,

    d) the applicability of the command structure to unforeseen future problems.

It is the thesis of this problem solving program that, particularly for novice problem solvers, problem solving commands should be made explicit. This is best done by writing these down and including them as a part of problem solutions. This procedure provides problem solvers with a constant reminder as to what instruction they should now be executing; permits the modification of a command at any time and even its rejection and the subsequent substitution of an alternative command; properly separates the plan of what problem solving steps are to be taken from the process of actually taking those steps; and results in a written problem solution that contains the commands together with the work done in performance of those instructions, thereby resulting in a more complete narrative of the problem solver's path to the problem solution.

It is strongly recommended that beginning problem solvers keep a journal of problem solving heuristics (commands) that they, and others, have found useful. As this journal grows in size, so grows one's ability to grapple with new problems. The journal entries provide a reminder of past experience upon which future problem solving will rest. The precise words that are used to describe individual problem solving commands are not important. What is important is that commands be made explicit while remaining sufficiently general to have wide application.

Chapter I is an introduction to the skill, and the art, of problem solving. It contains twenty-six "warmup" problems designed to get one's collective feet wet in the subject. With no particular background available at this point, individuals are made aware that good problem solving is often a matter of simply using one's head. In Chapter II probabilistic problems are encountered. Notions of probability are found almost everywhere and have applications in the fields of medicine, law, economics, management, and biology, to name a few. Problems presented in Chapter III involve decision making strategies together with the ever present decision trees. Decision making is found in most disciplinary areas, for example in history, social work, writing, sports, geology, medicine, and law.

Next, in Chapter IV, dilemma "games" are treated, games in Von Neuman's sense of competition with one or more adversaries. Although Von Neuman's games were in the field of economics, application is now made to such fields as international politics, ethics, sociology, history, law, and biology. Graphs are the subject of Chapter V. Such graphs are not the kind we learned about in our first algebra class, but are simply networks of lines, called *edges,* drawn between points, called *vertices*. These graphs are important in that they denote relationships and impose a structure that is helpful in many problem situations. Graph theory is important in anthropology, sociology, systems engineering, political science, and management. Chapter VI deals with problems involving patterns and visual thinking. Patterns appear in linguistics, music, dance, art, architecture, theater, geography, meteorology, and elsewhere. Many of the characteristics of ordinary reasoning are presented in Chapter VII, entitled Plausible Reasoning. There is of course the problem of illogical thinking. Such considerations are particularly important in rhetoric, advertising, marketing, philosophy, and writing. Problem solving disabilities, both real and imagined, and problem solutions, both rational and irrational, are the subject of Chapter VIII. There are a far greater number of ways to flounder in attempting to solve problems than there are useful ways to proceed. In Chapter IX ten problems in ethics in the professions are presented. Important problems such as these are so often extremely difficult ones. Perhaps no "solution" as such is possible in many cases, and one may have to be satisfied with a modest amount of headway. Problems in ethics stand in contrast to those more direct and simpler problems treated earlier. Are the problem solving heuristics brought to bear on these more difficult problems the same as for the more straightforward problems, or are we now on a radically different playing field? Finally, four advanced problem solving topics are presented in Chapter X. Each is an extension of an earlier activity.

Robert R. Kadesch

Note to the Student:

Each of the chapters in this manual except the first and the last two are divided into four parts:

Introductory Problems
Background
Introductory Problem Solutions
Additional Problems

The Introductory Problems are intentionally placed before the Background section to encourage you to see how far you can proceed toward a solution without special instruction in the discipline in which the problem is found. The purpose here is to encourage you, the problem solver, to rely strongly upon your native intellect without any special instruction. In so-called context lean problems your native thinking ability may be all that is needed. On occasion however, special background work to supplement your basic intelligence may be required before you will be able to proceed toward a problem solution. The section entitled Background includes, not only subject matter knowledge, but in addition knowledge of certain problem solving strategies and methods. You will gradually accumulate both subject matter knowledge and problem solving skills as your experience in problem solving deepens. Having mastered the background material you are then better prepared to return to the Introductory Problems and renew your attack on those problems. Your efforts can then be compared to the solutions presented in the Introductory Problem Solutions section. You should now be better equipped to handle the Additional Problems, problems designed to give you further experience in problem solving. Those marked with an asterisk have brief solutions given in Appendix A. Your instructor may assign as homework any of the problems in the Additional Problems section. Don't expect all of the problems presented in this manual to arise directly from everyday experience. Some are of the nature of mental "calisthenics," and as such, important to the achievement of problem solving skills in general.

If you do not already own one, you will want to purchase a pocket calculator to help you make the calculations important to the kind of problem solving found in several of the chapters. Two so-called Self Tests for Chapters II-VIII are to be found at the end of those chapters. One of these "tests" calls for familiarity with four or five of the Additional Problems. The second probes more deeply into a single aspect of the problem work or the background material for the chapter. Solutions to these tests are given in Appendix B. These are brief exercises that can be completed in about fifteen minutes or so. They serve to exemplify the kind of "open book" in-class quiz that your instructor may wish to give over each chapter.

Credits

I. GETTING STARTED IN PROBLEM SOLVING

Problem Solving Across the Disciplines

Types of Problems

Problem Solving for Non-Experts

Example Problems with Solutions

        MIXING MARBLES
        THE ESSENTIAL BOYS
        THE FIRST ACE
        DOLLHOUSE TABLE

Warmup Problems

1. A CHICKEN AND A HALF
2. TWO TRAINS AND A BEE
3. THE BLACK AND WHITE HATS
4. THE OLDEST HAS RED HAIR
5. WHERE DO THEY LIVE?
6. MARVIN AND THE SUBWAY
7. CRYPTARITHMETIC
8. WEIGHING WITH FOUR WEIGHTS
9. THE NOTCHED CHECKERBOARD
10. SLICING A CUBE
11. HOW MANY LIARS?
12. MENDING A CHAIN
13. DAVE'S DILEMMA
14. EXCHANGING KNIGHTS
15. WHAT HAPPENED TO THE TWO DOLLARS?
16. YES OR NO MEANS LIFE OR DEATH
17. WHERE ARE YOU?
18. HOW MUCH GOLD?
19. WHAT IS THE FRONT VIEW?
20. PAPER BAGS OR PLASTIC
21. SEARCH ROUTINE
22. NUMBER PATTERS
23. THE BUICK SALE
24. BIDDING TO MAKE DECISIONS
25. PRO CHOICE OR PRO LIFE?
26. EMERGENCY ROOM PROBLEM

I. GETTING STARTED IN PROBLEM SOLVING

Problem Solving Across the Disciplines

This is a program in problem solving strategies, or heuristics. Problem solving heuristics are tips, cues, suggestions, and hints to help solve problems. Remarkably, many heuristics are as applicable to problems in medicine as they are to those in international politics, as useful in designing routes for postmen as they are in the field of management. The language individuals may use in solving problems in the choreography of modern dance will differ from that employed by a lawyer in attempting to apply points of law. However, many of the strategies and techniques employed are the same. The background knowledge a biologist should have before launching an attack on problems in evolution is naturally quite different from that of an anthropologist studying the exchange of goods in the island cultures off New Guinea. In spite of such differences there remains a significant body of problem solving expertise common to all disciplines, skills that are as readily and effectively employed in one discipline as in another. Modes of thought are held to be characteristic of the human intellect, not of specialized academic areas. What does vary from one area to the next is the background knowledge needed to understand a problem and a specialized vocabulary of modest size.

The approach to be employed in this program emphasizes problem solving skills using examples from various disciplines only as contexts in which to learn such skills. Capabilities in problem solving readily transfer to other academic disciplines and will persist long after the specialized facts of the subject matter settings in which problems are presented and solved are forgotten. This program thus stresses thinking skills as opposed to knowledge for its own sake.

Types of Problems

Problems come in all flavors. They may be context rich, as in much of the sciences, or context lean, as in puzzle problems to be found in newspapers and popular magazines. Context rich means that there often are fairly heavy demands made on the problem solver as regards the background knowledge and tools needed before launching an attack on a problem. Context lean means that only a little background knowledge if any is required. Problems may be relatively straightforward or they may be highly complex, they may be probabilistic or deterministic, qualitative or quantitative, important or mundane. Problems may be those associated with decision making or with answering some question. Problems may entail the resolution of some issue. Problems may involve matters of ethics. A problem may be a member of a large network of related problems. There are problems of persuasion. There are personal problems and there are societal problems. Some problems are so difficult that the best one can expect to do, perhaps, is to chip away slowly toward some sort of solution that may prove in the end to be only marginally satisfactory. A few problems don't have a solution at all. For example, consider the following: In a certain town there is one barber. He shaves everyone who does not shave himself. Who shaves the barber? There is no answer to this question because the problem statement contains a contradiction.

For the most part we will be dealing here with relatively straightforward problems for which some sort of a solution is expected. It is undoubtedly better to deal first with such problems. Later, when one's problem solving skills are more fully developed, it will be more appropriate to deal with larger, more complex, even "wicked" problems. Many very important problems fall into this latter category. Take, for example, problems surrounding such issues as capital punishment, sexual harassment, gun control, pornography, abortion rights, animal and human experimentation, genetic engineering, drug abuse, gun control, racism, welfare reform, health care reform, environmental concerns, assisted suicide, nuclear power, and world hunger.

Problem Solving for Non-Experts

The one thing that we can be sure of that distinguishes expert problem solvers from neophytes is that experts have solved a great many problems and neophytes haven't. The most important single piece of advice that can be given beginners is to solve a large number of problems. But one can do better than this. One can become a student of problem solving. This means looking for general strategies that can be used in many different problems, not just one, strategies that can be used in a variety of disciplines, not just one. This means developing the habit of carrying on a dialog with oneself to bring to the upper-most level of consciousness what is going on, or should be going on, in one's mind as problem solving activity proceeds. It means being able to state the problem in one's own words, to be able to clarify or even simplify the problem before proceeding. It means making explicit certain assumptions and conditions that were initially implicit. It means developing a tidy mind in which the elements of a problem are organized. It means constantly reminding oneself of where the problem started and where one wants it to go. It means to cultivate the ability to identify and then acquire, if necessary, knowledge that is relevant to the problem at hand. It means examining alternative strategies for solving a problem and alternative routes toward a problem solution. It means acquiring the skill to use pictorial and mathematical language as well as one's native language. It means to question. It means the ability to get oneself out of a problem impasse should one occur. It means to analyse and evaluate a problem solution once obtained. It means the vision to look ahead to determine what problems might now be more readily solved than was the case before the present problem was completed. It means all this and a whole lot more!

Equipped with the kinds of skills described above, one is better prepared to grapple with problems that might arise from any quarter. Competence in problem solving minimizes learning effort. Problem solving in one discipline need not be learned all over again when considering problems in other areas. It cannot be emphasized too strongly that learning problem solving strategies involves the analysis of one's own thinking. The best tactic for doing this that has as yet been found is for the problem solver to think aloud. Yes, think aloud! When a record is made of such talk these transcriptions are called think-aloud protocols. A person might use an audiotape recorder to help analyse what is going on in one's mind and hopefully, to do something to improve matters. If one cannot speak aloud for fear of disturbing others it is permissible to move one's lips, if necessary, while thinking through a problem. A procedure in which the recording of problem analysis is deferred is less effective than making a record of one's thinking at the time one is actually solving a problem. Think aloud protocols have been found to be important in math and science education research, and more recently, in research into the nature of the writing process.

Each of the four example problems that follow employ certain heuristics (commands) that serve as an aid in the search for a problem solution. Each of these is underlined to focus attention on its use. When working on a problem it is preferable to write these down rather than attempting to keep them stored in one's mind. An opportunity to employ such hints, cues, tips, and suggestions for problem solvers is provided by the twenty-six warmup problem that follow the examples. Although these vary as to level of difficulty all may be classified as context lean. What is required is the ability and the willingness to use one's head, your chief tool in all problem solving activity. Try each of these problems before looking at the given solution. It is relatively easy to agree with the printed solution, but more challenging and more interesting to see what you can do on your own. You may learn that you can actually be successful in many cases. You will of course have to think. Your thinking skills are almost sure to be greater than you give yourself credit for.

1. **MIXING MARBLES.** There are 1000 red marbles in one barrel and 1000 clear marbles in another barrel. A blindfolded person transfers 100 red marbles from the first barrel to the second barrel, mixes the marbles in this barrel, and transfers 100 of these marbles back to the first barrel. Are there now more clear marbles in the first barrel than red marbles in the second barrel, or more red marbles in the second barrel than clear marbles in the first barrel, or is the number of red marbles in the second barrel the same as the number of clear marbles in the first barrel?

Solution. __DRAW A DIAGRAM__

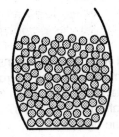 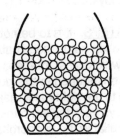

1000 red marbles   1000 clear marbles

__JUMP TO A CONCLUSION.__ After the two transfers of marbles there are still 1000 marbles in each barrel. Whatever number of red marbles there are in the second barrel, these have displaced the same number of clear marbles that were there initially. The displaced clear marbles must now be in the first barrel. Therefore, there are just as many red marbles in the second barrel as there are clear marbles in the first barrel.

__USE NUMERICAL EXAMPLE.__ To confirm this conclusion consider a numerical example in which 100 marbles are transferred in each direction. After the first transfer of 100 marbles to the second barrel there are now 900 red marbles in the first barrel and 1100 marbles in the second barrel, 1000 of these being clear and 100 red. Suppose that of the 100 marbles of this mixture that are transferred back to the first barrel, 20 are red and 80 are clear. Now we have 920 red marbles in the first barrel along with 80 clear marbles. In the second barrel, which had 1000 clear marbles and 100 red marbles before the second transfer, in this transfer it lost 80 clear and 20 red leaving 920 clear marbles and 80 red marbles. The fact that there are now 80 clear marbles in the first barrel and 80 red marbles in the second confirms the conclusion that was jumped to above.

__MODIFY PROB.__ Instead of transferring 100 marbles from the first barrel to the second, suppose a fistful is transferred. After mixing the marbles in the second barrel, another fistful is transferred back to the first barrel making sure that this fistful contains the same number of marbles as the first fistful. In this case the number of clear marbles in the first barrel will also be the same as the number of red marbles in the second barrel.

2. THE ESSENTIAL BOYS. Nine men and two boys want to cross a river using an inflatable raft that will carry either one man or the two boys. How many times must the raft cross the river in order to accomplish this goal? (A round trip equals two crossings.)

Solution. <u>MAKE A DIAGRAM</u>.
For the first crossing of the river it is obvious that the two boys must go first so that one of them can then return to the left bank of the river to help the men cross the river. After this is done there will be 9 men and 1 boy on the left bank (as shown on the diagram). It is clear than one of these men can now cross the river to the right bank where we now have 1 man and 1 boy. The boy can return the raft to the left bank where there are now 8 men and 2 boys.

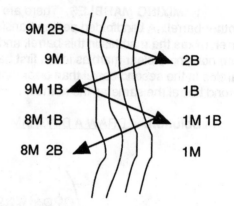

<u>IDENT PROBLEM STEPS</u>. It is to be noted that with 8 men and 2 boys on the left bank, the situation now is the same as the one with which we started except that 1 man has been transported to the right bank. Four river crossings have been required to this point. Eight more groups of crossings of this kind will transport the rest of the men to the right bank making a total of 36 crossings. One more crossing is required to transport the 2 boys from the left bank to the right bank making 37 crossings in all. The two boys have indeed been essential to the river crossing for the nine men.

3. **THE FIRST ACE.** Shuffle an ordinary deck of 52 playing cards containing four aces. Then turn up cards from the top of the deck one at a time until the first ace appears. On average, how many cards are required to produce the first ace?

Solution.   <u>VISUALIZE PROBLEM SITUATION</u>.   <u>CONSIDER AN EXAMPLE</u>.

A particular example of the location of the four aces in a well-shuffled deck is illustrated below. The location of the aces is shown by the cards in heavier lines. The first ace happens to be card #6, the second ace card #24, the third ace card # 31, and the fourth ace card #41. These locations divide the deck into five sections as shown above the cards. These sections contain 5, 17, 6, 9, and 11 cards which total 48 cards since the aces themselves are excluded.

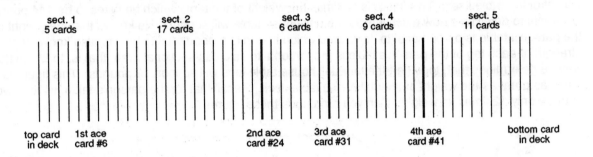

No doubt advanced techniques in solving probabilistic problems together with considerable effort could be successfully applied to problems of this sort. Instead, try a simpler strategy that may also lead to a solution.

<u>USE SYMMETRY</u>. With every shuffle, the numbers of cards in the five sections into which the deck is divided by the four aces change. Think of shuffling the deck many times and counting, after each shuffle, the numbers of cards in section #1, in section #2, in section #3, in section #4, and in section #5. There appears to be no particular reason why the average number of cards in any section should be different from the average number in any other section.

<u>CONCLUSION</u>. *By symmetry*, then, we can say that each section is the same (in this sense) as the others. This sameness hasn't been *proved*, but its simplicity makes it a very attractive supposition. Five sections divided by 48 cards gives 9.6 cards per section on average. The first ace will then be, on average, the 10.6th card in the deck.

4. DOLLHOUSE TABLE. A young father has decided to build a table for his daughter's doll house. She wants a table just like the parson's table that the family uses for a dining table (shown below), only smaller. The top of the parson's table is 6 feet long (call this the dimension L) and its width, thickness, and the leg measurements are as drawn to scale in the figure. Dad decides to make the doll house table of the same material and change every dimension in feet for the parson's table into inches for the doll house table, i.e., scale the parson's table down by a factor of 1/12. The length of the top of the doll house table will therefore be 6 inches which is 1/12 of L. Every other linear measurement of the doll house table will also be 1/12 of the corresponding measurement for the parson's table.

Because dad is an engineer he is concerned with the strength of the doll house table legs. He figures that the four parson's table legs will support a maximum load of 1728 pounds which includes the weight of the table itself. This figure is 12 times the weight of the table which he takes to be 144 pounds. He wants to determine how much weight the doll house table will support. He knows that the weight of the parson's table is proportional to its volume which in turn is proportional to L^3. He also knows that the strength of each leg of the parson's table is proportional to its cross-sectional area, that is, to L^2. In this way he determines that, together, the four doll house table legs will support 12 pounds. This figure is 144 times as great as the weight of the doll house table itself. Recall that for the parson's table, its legs would support only 12 times its weight. Can you reproduce these figures?

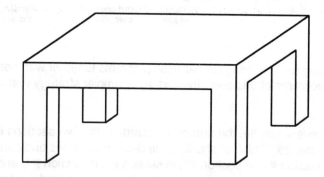

Out of pure curiosity, dad wonders what a giant's table would be like, one made of the same material as the parson's table and whose every dimension is 12 times larger. He learns that this table would weigh 248,832 pounds and would support only its own weight of 248,832 pounds, nothing more. What does all this mean for four-legged animals? Let a brown bear correspond to the parson's table, a fox to the doll house table, and an elephant to the giant's table. Compared to the bear, what do you suppose the legs of these other animals are like?

Solution. <u>GIVEN</u> (in the form of a table):

	Parson's table	dollhouse table
length of table top	L = 6 ft.	ℓ = 1/12 L = 0.5 ft.
weight of table	W = 144 lb	w =
max. load (incl. weight of table)	LOAD = 1728 lb	load =
strength of one leg	S = 1/4 LOAD = 432 LB	s =

<u>WANTED</u>. The three unknown quantities in the dollhouse table column, viz., the weight w of the dollhouse table, the load it will support, and the strength "s" of one of the dollhouse table legs.

<u>IDENT REL RELATIONSHIPS</u>. Let capital letters refer to the parson's table and lower case letters to the dollhouse table, then:

$$\text{any length } \ell = 1/12 \text{ times the corresponding length L}$$
$$\text{any area } a = (1/12)^2 \text{ of the corresponding area A}$$
$$\text{any volume } v = (1/12)^3 \text{ of the corresponding volume V}$$

the wanted quantities become:

$$w = (1/12)^3 W = 1/12 \text{ lb}$$
$$s = (1/12)^2 S = 3 \text{ lb}$$
$$\text{load} = 4s = 12 \text{ lb} = 144 \, w$$

<u>ALSO WANTED</u>: A response to the question: Compared to a brown bear, what do you suppose the legs of these other animals (fox and elephant) are like?

An elephant is something like the giant's table, the brown bear like the parson's table, and the fox like the dollhouse table. Each animal must support its own weight and more. We learn that the elephant should have leg bones with a quite large cross-sectional area, the bear should have modest size leg bones, and the fox ought to be able to get along quite well with leg bones that are quite spindly compared to larger animals. Surely these animals bear out these prescriptions, at least approximately.

WARMUP PROBLEMS

1. A CHICKEN AND A HALF. A chicken and a half lays an egg and a half in a day and a half. How many eggs does one chicken lay in one day?

2. TWO TRAINS AND A BEE. Two trains 100 miles apart are on the same track heading toward each other at 50 miles per hour. At this moment a bee moving at 75 miles per hour flies from the front of one train to the front of the other. After landing he immediately reverses course heading for the first train. He repeats this back and forth motion going a shorter and shorter distance with each trip from train to train until he is crushed in the collision of the two trains. How far did the bee fly?

3. THE BLACK AND WHITE HATS. Three blindfolded people, Abe, Beth, and Chuck, each take one hat from a barrel containing three black and two white hats. Abe and Beth remove their blindfolds and can then see the hats on the heads of the other two, but not the hat on their own head. Abe says: "I cannot tell what color my hat is." Upon hearing this, Beth says: "I cannot tell the color of my hat either." Hearing these two statements, Chuck, who is still blindfolded, says: "Now I know what color my hat is." How did he know, and what was the color of his hat?

4. THE OLDEST HAS RED HAIR. The following conversation takes place between two friends A and B, who have not seen each other for a long time.

A: I have three sons.
B: How old are they?
A: The product of their ages is 36.
B: That is not enough information to answer my question. Can you give me another clue?
A: Yes, their ages are integer numbers whose sum is the same as the number you see on the store across the street.
B: Give me a few minutes to work it with pencil and paper.
B: (a few minutes later) I have almost got the answer but I need another clue.
A: O.K. The oldest one has red hair.
B: I have got it.

What are the ages of the three sons?

5. WHERE DO THEY LIVE? Alice, Bob, Chuck, David, and Elsa live in five different houses that are numbered 101, 102, 103, 104, and 105, along a street that runs from south to north, with 105 being farthest north.

Alice does not live in 105.
Bob does not live in 101.
Chuck does not live in either 101 or 105.
David lives in a house farther north than Bob.
Elsa does not live in a house adjacent to Chuck.
Chuck does not live in a house adjacent to Bob.

Identify the occupants of the five houses.

6. MARVIN AND THE SUBWAY. Marvin leaves work at random times between 3 and 5 P.M. His mother lives uptown; his girl friend lives downtown. Uptown and downtown trains arrive at his station with equal frequency. He takes the first subway that comes in either direction and eats dinner with the one he is first delivered to. His mother complains that he hardly ever comes to dine with her, but he says it's a 50-50 chance. He has had dinner with her twice in the last 20 working days. Explain.

7. CRYPTARITHMETIC. In the following problem each letter stands for a different digit.

$$\begin{array}{r} \text{DONALD} \\ + \text{GERALD} \\ \hline \text{ROBERT} \end{array}$$

Given that D = 5, what digits are represented by the other letters?

8. WEIGHING WITH FOUR WEIGHTS. Using a balance scale, show that only four weights are required to weigh objects with integer weights from 1 to 40 pounds. Note: weights may be placed on the pan that carries the object to be weighed as well as on the opposite side.

9. THE NOTCHED CHECKERBOARD. You are given a checkerboard and 32 dominoes. Each domino covers exactly two adjacent squares on the board. Thus, 32 dominoes can cover all 64 squares of the checkerboard. Now suppose two squares are cut off at diagonally opposite corners of the board. Is it possible to place 31 dominoes on the board so that all of the 62 remaining squares are covered? If possible, show how it can be done. If not possible, give a convincing reason for this conclusion.

10. SLICING A CUBE. You are working with a power saw and wish to cut a wooden cube 3 inches on a side into 27 1-inch cubes. You can do this by making six cuts through the cube keeping the pieces together in the cube shape. Can you reduce the number of necessary cuts by rearranging the pieces after each cut?

11. HOW MANY LIARS? The country of Marr is inhabited by two types of people, liars and truars (truth tellers). Liars always lie and truars always tell the truth. Inhabitants of Marr know who are truars and who are liars. As the newly appointed United States ambassador to Marr, you have been invited to a cocktail party. While consuming some of the local libations, you are engaged in conversation with three of Marr's most prominent citizens: Joan Landill, Shawn Farrar, and Peter Gant. At one point in the conversation Joan remarks that Shawn and Peter are both liars. Shawn vehemently denies that he is a liar, but Peter replies that Shawn is indeed a liar. From this information can you determine how many of the three are liars and how many are truars?

12. MENDING A CHAIN. You are given four separate pieces of chain that are each three links in length. It costs $2 to open a link and $3 to close a link. All links are closed at the beginning of the problem. Your goal is to obtain a single closed chain, using all twelve links. What is the least cost for doing the job?

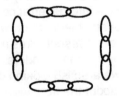

13. DAVE'S DILEMMA. Each day, Dave either walks to work and rides his bicycle home, or rides his bicycle to work and walks home. Either way, the round trip takes one hour. If he were to ride his bicycle both ways, it would take 30 minutes. How long would a round trip take if Dave walked both ways?

14. EXCHANGING KNIGHTS. A three by three chessboard has two black knights on adjacent corners of the board. Two white knights occupy the other two corners. A knight can only move to an unoccupied square that lies one square in one direction and two squares in a direction at right angles to the first direction. It is desired to interchange the two black with the two white knights. What is the least number of moves required to accomplish this?

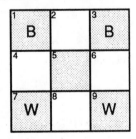

15. WHAT HAPPENED TO THE TWO DOLLARS? Three ladies go to a concert. Tickets for the main floor are $20 each, so the ladies paid a total of $60. When they arrive at the concert they learn that no main floor seats remain. They receive instead less expensive balcony seats and the manager refunds them $10 which is given to an usher to return. The usher returns $6 to the ladies but keeps $4 for himself. So each lady pays, in effect, $18 for her seat. Three times $18 is $54, and with $4 for the usher the total is $58. What happened to the other two dollars?

16. YES OR NO MEANS LIFE OR DEATH. You are being detained by the authorities in the country of Xanadu. There are, however, two doors. One of these, you know not which, leads to freedom and the other to execution. In front of each door there is a guard. All you know is that one of these guards always tells the truth and the other always lies. Of course the guards know which door is which and which of them is a liar and which always tells the truth. You are permitted to ask one of the guards a simple yes-no question and then to pass through the door of your choice. After much deliberation you ask one of the guards the following question: "If I were to ask the other guard whether he stands in front of the door to freedom would he answer 'yes' ?" Will the answer to this question guarantee that you can choose the door to freedom? Explain.

17. WHERE ARE YOU? If, after walking one mile south from some point on the earth's surface, one mile east, and another mile back north, you end up exactly where you started, where would you be? Assume the earth to perfectly spherical with no hills or valleys. Consider the possibility that there may be more than one starting point.

18. HOW MUCH GOLD? Two identical cubical boxes contain spheres of gold. The first box contains 8 spheres (two layers of 4 spheres) which just fit inside the box. The second box contains 64 spheres (four layers of 16 spheres), and these too fit perfectly inside their box. Thus, each of the smaller spheres in the second box has half the radius of the larger spheres in the first box. The question is: Which box is more valuable, that is, which box contains more gold?

19. WHAT IS THE FRONT VIEW? A hollow metal cylinder cuts through a glob of modeling clay forming a cylindrically shaped piece of clay that came from the inside of the metal cylinder. This same metal cylinder is now used to cut at right angles through the cylinder of clay made by the first cut. A small piece of clay can now be found inside the metal cylinder. The problem is simply this: What does this piece of clay look like? Referring to the figure below we see that if we visualize two cylindrical shapes crossing each other at right angles, with each cylinder being able to penetrate the other as if it weren't there, the final piece of clay that we're interested in has the shape of that volume of space that is inside both of these interpenetrating cylinders. In drawing this shape we use the following two rules: the margins of an object are drawn as lines and also, all sharp edges and corners are shown as lines. Such lines do not represent wires nor lines on the surface of this object. In the side view we look along the throat of one of the cylinders. From this viewpoint the object is represented by a circular outline. In the top view we are also looking down a cylinder and once again see the object as one with a circular outline. But what about the front view? What does it look like? This clearly is a problem in spatial visualization.

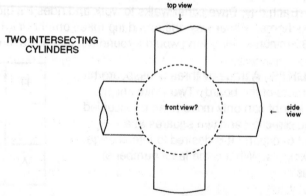

A related problem is as follows. Think now of three mutually perpendicular and interpenetrating cylinders of the same diameter. The problem is to describe the shape of the space enclosed by all three cylinders as if that space were a solid object. The object is described according to its front view, side view, and top view, *all of which appear identical*. Surely this problem is easier after having solved the first problem.

20. PAPER BAGS OR PLASTIC? When checking out of the market with several bags of groceries and produce a bagger may ask whether you want your items put in a paper bag or in a plastic bag. Once while pondering this question in my mind the checker volunteered the following observation: "It doesn't really make much difference," he said, "it's a matter of whether you want to sacrifice ancient trees or relatively new ones." I had to agree with his logic, for the plastic bags are made from petroleum products which in turn came from decaying organic matter laid down many centuries ago. The paper bags, on the other hand, are made from wood pulp that was part of a living tree not too long ago. The problem of choice between paper and plastic is not quite so simple, however. First of all, it's not just my choice, it is the choice of millions of others and how they choose that can make a real difference. Secondly, as a society we want that choice to be as intelligently made as possible. The problem, then, is this: What choice should be made? To "solve" this problem simply list the factors that must be taken into account if a serious attack on the problem is to be undertaken.

21. SEARCH ROUTINE. Ron Ridley of Dallas, Texas has contributed a puzzle that is a kind of word game. In this puzzle seven letters, always in the same order, are used in each of three lines of text. In the first line they make one word; in the second line they make two words; and in the third line they make two new words. The seven letters are represented by the digits 1234567. The problem is to determine the seven letters that each of these digits represents. The three-line sentence is grammatically correct and makes sense. It is:

> The 1234567 surgeon
> was 123 4567 to operate
> because he had 12 34567.

The only reasonable way to tackle this problem is to devise a systematic search routine for the seven letters. This is an important kind of problem solving activity that is frequently encountered. Suppose we search the entire alphabet. Since there are 26 letters in the alphabet there are 26 choices to represent the digit "1". For each of these choices there are 25 possibilities for the letter represented by the digit "2". Thus the number of possibilities for the first two letters is 26 X 25 = 650. Without continuing we can easily see that if we search the entire 26-letter alphabet in this way the number of possibilities is horrendously large. There must be a better alternative. A good place to search for letter combinations that make words is in an ordinary dictionary. But here the number of words to search through is very large. The American Heritage Collegiate Dictionary, for example, has over 303,000 entries. A search effort for the seven letters we seek would still be a very large job.

Interestingly, American Heritage has developed an electronic dictionary called AHED™ that contains a software program for the computer that will conduct a very rapid search through its own dictionary. This program is called WILDCARD. In this program one enters all the known letters in some word in the positions they occupy and for the unknown letters a "?" is entered. For example, if you enter "bea?" the search through the entire 303,000 word dictionary returns only 8 possibilities. These are the words *bead, beak, beam, bean, bear, Beas, beat,* and *beau.* If you know only two letters in a four-letter word there are of course many more possibilities. If you enter "be??" the search returns the eight words given above and then continues with the words *beck, Beda, Bede, beds, beef* . . . . providing 43 four-letter words in all beginning with the two letter combination "be".

The problem is to find the seven letters represented by the digits 1234567. Assume you have access to the power of the WILDCARD program. One still faces the problem of devising a search routine to identify these digits. How would you proceed? There are a number of ways of doing this, and some of these are going to take a whole lot longer than others. The basic search strategy will be the same with or without the WILDCARD program. What is this strategy?

22. NUMBER PATTERNS. Patterns of one kind or another are found almost everywhere — in art, in language, in music, in science and engineering, in poetry, in dance, in human behavior, in history, in medicine, in the law and — in numbers. Suppose somehow we notice that

$$1 + 8 + 27 + 64 = 100$$

This looks like an interesting equation. The numbers on the left are all cubes and that on the right is a square! That is,

$$1^3 + 2^3 + 3^3 + 4^3 = 10^2$$

From this beginning one can go on to identify additional patterns that can be obtained simply by continuing the number play that has already begun. It will be helpful if you focus on the bases involved, that is, on those numbers which are both cubed and squared. It will also be a good idea to extend the sequence of terms on the left side of the above expression while noting the sequence of numbers that are then created on the right side. What about the continuing relationship between the left side and the right side? Problem: Find as many additional patterns as you can.

23. THE BUICK SALE. In Poundstone's book *Prisoner's Dilemma* he describes a problem which he calls "The Buick Sale." He states it as follows:

> In June 1949, Flood wanted to buy a used Buick from a RAND employee who was moving back East. Buyer and seller were friends. They weren't looking to cheat each other, just to agree on a fair price for the car. How should they set the price?
> As it happened, Flood and the seller knew a used-car dealer. They took the car to the dealer and asked him his selling and buying price for the car in "as is" condition. The difference, the dealer's profit, was a gain the buyer and seller could split between themselves.
> Let's say the dealer's buying price was $500, just to have a concrete figure. The seller could, if he wanted, sell the car to the dealer for that price. Likewise, the buyer could buy a car just as good as the Buick from the dealer for the dealer's selling price — say, $800. In a transaction handled by the dealer, the dealer's cut would be $300. By not going through the dealer, the buyer and seller have an extra $300 to split between themselves.

How might the $300 be split to satisfy both Flood and his friend?

24. BIDDING TO MAKE DECISIONS. In his book *Armchair Economist*, Landsburg describes a procedure whereby he and his wife make an amicable decision as to which movie to go and see. They agreed that the person with the stronger preference — expressed in dollar terms — should earn the right to select the movie. They each wrote their bid on a piece of paper. The high bidder got to choose the movie but was required to make a contribution equal to the loser's bid to another couple who were playing the same game. Of course this other couple make their contributions to the Landsburgs. Suppose it was worth exactly $8 for Landsburg to get his way. What does he hope his wife's bid will be?

25. PRO CHOICE OR PRO LIFE? One of the most hotly contested issues in today's society has to do with abortion. The advocates of pro-choice are squared off against those who stand with equal fervor for the pro-life position. How can this situation possibly be resolved to everyone's satisfaction? The two positions, it seems, are entirely incompatible. There is little if any room for compromise. Eventually the issue must be resolved or it must simply die away. The problem here hinges upon the following question. What happens to the strength of one side in this ongoing battle as the strength of the other goes down for whatever reason? Is this a societal see-saw? When the persuasive power of one side goes up, does that on the other side necessarily go down? State your reasons for either agreeing with or disputing the validity of this argument.

14

26. EMERGENCY ROOM PROBLEM. The educational series "Ethics in America" supported by the Annenberg Foundation has described problems in medical ethics having to do with the autonomy of the patient and the roles of the physician and family. One of these is the following.

An accident victim is brought in, bleeding profusely, only conscious enough to announce that she is an Apostle of God and according to her religion cannot have any blood transfusions. Only a blood transfusion will save her life.

You are a resident physician temporarily in charge of the emergency room of a city hospital. How should you handle the case described above? Comment only on its ethical aspects for there is no reason for you to be familiar with either the medical or legal aspects.

II. THE MONTY HALL AND OTHER PROBABILISTIC PROBLEMS

Introductory Problems: THE MONTY HALL PROBLEM
           BLUE AND GREEN TAXICABS
           MAMMALARY CANCER
           CASE OF THE RODEO GATECRASHERS

Background: BASIC PROBABILITY RULES
           EQUI-PROBABLE EVENTS
           CONDITIONAL PROBABILITY
           "AND'S" AND "OR'S"
           BAYES' EQUATION

Introductory Problem Solutions

Additional Problems: CHANCES FOR PAROLE
           THE TRUEL
           PROBABILITY PARADOXES
           BLASTING A HYPOTHESIS
           DIAGNOSTIC VALUE OF ACNE
           THE ROBBERY AND THE TORN COAT LINING
           X-LINKED LETHALS
           FAULTY SUSPENSION
           HEMOPHILIA
           TESTING FOR THE HIV VIRUS

Self Tests: SELECTED PROBLEMS
           THE POLLSTER

II. THE MONTY HALL AND OTHER PROBABILISTIC PROBLEMS

Probability considerations are everywhere — selecting apparel when one is going out, chances for rain, catching your bus, getting caught in traffic. Perhaps you learn when you get to work that your boss has handed you a pink slip. What are your chances for successfully stopping smoking? What is the probability that your house will have been robbed before you return home? At dinnertime will your wife tell you she's pregnant? Will the police call to tell you that your stolen car has been recovered — but with the wheels missing? Will your income tax return be audited? Will your brother die of bone cancer? What is the chance you will be hit by lightning or win $11 million in the Publisher's Clearing House lottery? You might encounter these and many other probabilistic situations on an almost daily basis. Problems involving the calculation or estimation of probabilities arise in every academic area, every workplace, and during your leisure hours as well. Given below are four introductory problems that involve notions of probability. See what you can do with them. Perhaps you can make significant headway with one or more. Or perhaps you will not be able to get started at all. After making a serious effort to handle these problems you can then remedy your deficiencies by reading the background materials that follow. Upon returning to these same introductory problems you should then fare much better!

In this problem solving program we will be dealing with three quite distinct kinds of probability. The first of these is "objective" probability, so-called because of what it's not, and it's not subjective. It is standard text book probability based upon the idea of equi-probable events. Example settings include the tossing of a coin, the throw of a pair of dice, drawing from a deck of cards, or blindly selecting colored beads from an urn. It is only because there are events with equal probability that we know that in the single toss of a coin the probability that it will come up heads is the same as for it coming up tails. For this same reason we know that every possible outcome in the throw of a pair of dice has a probability of 1/36. This makes the probability for a single outcome, say of two 6's, one in thirty-six because there is only one way to obtain this particular outcome. Similarly, the probability for drawing a Queen of Spades from a full pack of playing cards is 1/52 or for drawing any one of the four Queens in the deck 4/52. The second kind of probability may be called "sample probability." If in 1000 individuals 200 become afflicted with stomach ulcers after having taken ibuprofin for a month, we say that the "probability" for getting a stomach ulcer if one takes ibuprofin for a month is 200/1000, or 20%. Since there are considerably more individuals than 1000 taking ibuprofin, the group of 1000 individuals is but a sample. The probability value of 0.20 is likely to be fairly close to the probability figure that would be appropriate for all individuals taking ibuprofin for a month, and so we use that figure. If the size of the sample is relatively small, however, a probability figure based upon that number would of course be highly suspect. The third kind of probability is called "subjective," or personal, probability. For example, it can be used to express the probability that the earliest Americans came from Asia across a land bridge between the continents where now there is the Bering Straits. Suppose we set this probability to be 0.99. It is of course ridiculous to say that in 100 opportunities for these early Asians to cross such a bridge to America, in 99 cases they siezed the opportunity and on one occasion they did not, making the probability for crossing 0.99. Other examples of subjective probability include the probability for a horse to win a race, the probability for an incumbent to win a second term in office, and the probability for the stock market to crash this month. A more complete investigation of subjective probability will be made in a later chapter.

Introductory Problems

THE MONTY HALL PROBLEM. This problem was presented by Marilyn vos Savant in Parade Magazine. It involves the game show Let's Make A Deal hosted by Monty Hall. Monty gives a game contestant the opportunity to choose one of three closed doors. Behind one of these doors is a new automobile but behind each of the other two there is a tethered goat. The contestant gets to keep whatever is behind the door he or she selects. Let us call these doors door A, door B, and door C. With considerable "help" from the audience the contestant selects one of the doors. Suppose it is door A. Before opening this door, however, Monty opens one of the other two doors, say it is door B, to reveal a goat. At this point Monty gives the contestant an opportunity to change the original selection of door A to that of door C.

The question is a simple one. Should the contestant switch to door C or remain with the original choice of door A, or doesn't it make any difference? Of course it is not certain which of these two doors conceals the new car. It is a matter of probability. Is the probability greater to find the auto behind door A or behind door C or are the probabilities equal? It is important to recognize that although the contestant doesn't know where the new car is, Monty does.

BLUE AND GREEN TAXICABS. This problem is described by the psychologists Kahneman and Tversky in *Judgment under uncertainty: Heuristics and biases*. A cab was involved at night in a hit and run accident. In this town there are only two cab companies, the Blue with 85% of the cabs and the Green company with the remaining 15%. As it happened there was a witness to the accident who identified the hit and run cab as Blue. The case came to trial. An important part of the testimony was a test of the reliability of the eyewitness to identify a cab as being either Blue or Green under the same circumstances as those that existed the night of the accident. The result of these tests was that the witness correctly identified a blue cab as blue 60% of the time and a green cab as green 80% of the time. On the basis of the claim of the eyewitness and the tests conducted by the court, what is the probability that the cab involved in the accident was in fact Blue as the witness had claimed?

MAMMALARY CANCER. The following is a case adapted from one described by David Eddy. A physician has a patient with a breast mass. On the basis of his rather extensive experience with such patients of the same age, family history, and symptoms he is somewhat suspicious that the breast mass is cancerous. He assigns a subjective probability of ten percent to the possibility that this patient has breast cancer. The doctor orders that a mammogram be taken. In the radiologist's opinion the lesion is malignant. At this point the physician does some library research. The best evidence he could find regarding the accuracy of mammography is a study with the following results: mammography correctly diagnosed 79.2 percent of 475 lesions as malignant and correctly diagnosed 90.4 percent of 1,105 lesions as benign. On the basis of this information, taking account of the patient's mammogram, the physician revises his opinion. What probability should he now assign to the possibility of cancer?

CASE OF THE RODEO GATECRASHERS. A hypothetical case in civil law is described by Allen in *Probability and Inference in the Law of Evidence*. A thousand people are seated in the stands at a rodeo. However, only 499 tickets have been sold. Since no ticket stubs were given to any of the ticket purchasers, there is no way of telling which of the 1000 individuals in the stands bought their tickets and who "climbed over the fence." The rodeo organizers single out a particular individual, call him A, as a test case and charge him with having climbed over the fence. It would appear that the rodeo organizers are entitled to judgment against A for the admission money since, in a civil case, one needs only to show guilt by a "preponderance" of the evidence. Clearly, the probability that A is guilty is 501/1000, a value exceeding 50 percent and therefore sufficient to make the case for the rodeo organizers. The absurdity of this situation is evident since, if the price of admission can be claimed against A it can also be claimed against the other 999 people in the stands. The management would then stand to collect the price of 1000 admissions in addition to the 499 that were already paid for. Something is not quite right here, but what is it?

Background

BASIC PROBABILITY RULES. In our work we will be dealing with only two propositions at a time. Call these proposition or statement A and proposition or statement B. Understand that A and B are merely symbols that can stand for almost any kind of affirmative statement. A could be *it is raining* and

B could represent *it is cold*. Either A or B could say: *this patient has cancer,* or *the test for AIDS was negative.* We will restrict ourselves for the time being to statements that are either true or false, nothing in-between. P(A) = 0.6 means only that the fraction of times A is true is 0.6. It is recognized that this condition is quite unrealistic in the real world where propositions such as *our foreign policy in China will be successful* lurk everywhere. There are three important mathematical rules. These are:

$$P(A) + P(\bar{A}) = 1$$
$$0 \leq P(A) \leq 1$$
$$P(A) = P(A.B) + P(A.\bar{B})$$

where P($\bar{A}$) expresses the probability that proposition A is false and P(A.B) is read as the probability of A *and* B, i.e., that both are true. The first equation states that a proposition such as A must be either true or false since the probability that it is true when added to the probability that it is false must be one, the probability that it is one or the other. The second states that probability values are never negative and never greater than 1. P(A) = 0 and P(A) = 1 express, respectively, the certainty that A is false and the certainty that it is true. The third expression tells us that P(A) is the sum of the probabilities of A "anded" with each of B and $\bar{B}$, i.e., that P(A) is the probability that A is true and B is true added to the probability that A is true and B is false.

EQUI-PROBABLE EVENTS. In the roll of a pair of fair dice each possible outcome is as probable as every other outcome. One must, however, think of each die as being distinguishable from the other. That is, imagine one die as being red and the other as green. In this way a roll that yields a red 3 and a green 4 is distinct from one that yields a red 4 and a green 3. With 36 possible outcomes the probability P for each outcome is 1/36. If one wishes to know the probability for rolling a seven, one need only count the "ways" this can occur: 1 and 6, 2 and 5, 3 and 4, 4 and 3, 5 and 2, and finally, 6 and 1. With six ways, the probability P(7) becomes 6 x 1/36, or 1/6. Another equi-probable situation is found when drawing blindly from an urn which contains colored beads. Suppose an urn contains 7 red beads and 14 white beads. There are then 21 possible draws of a single bead, each of which is a likely as any other. P(red) is therefore 7/21, or 1/3, and P(white) is 14/21 = 2/3. An ordinary deck of playing cards contains 13 Spades, 13 Hearts, 13 Diamonds, and 13 Clubs making 52 cards in all. In each suit the cards are 2 through 10 followed by a Jack, Queen, King, and Ace. With the deck well shuffled and face down the probability for drawing the Queen of Spades is 1/52 since each card is as likely to be drawn as any other. The probability for drawing any Queen is 4/52 and for drawing a Heart is 13/52 = 1/4. Finally, for each toss of a fair coin the probability for tossing a head is the same as that for tossing a tail, viz., 1/2.

CONDITIONAL PROBABILITY. A conditional probability is written in the form P(A|B) and read as *the probability of A on condition that B is true.* The short vertical line between the A and the B represents the language *on condition that,* or *given that.* For example, the probability for drawing an Ace from a deck of cards on condition that another Ace has already been drawn from the deck can be written $P(A_2|A_1)$ where the subscripts indicate the second draw and the first respectively. Whether this probability equals $P(A_2)$ depends on whether the first Ace is returned to the pack before making the second draw. In drawing colored beads from an urn the probability for drawing a particular color depends on whether prior draws were or were not returned to the urn after each draw. In tossing a coin time after time the situation is similar to that for repeated throws of a pair of dice. The probability for tossing a head P(H) is 1/2 no matter what the previous throws might have been. We say that each throw is *independent* of all other throws. In the case of the woman whose physician thinks there is only one chance in ten that the lump in her breast is malignant, the quantity that is sought is the probability that the woman has cancer on condition that she has tested positive. This can be abbreviated as P(C|+). For conditional probabilities the first rule above becomes P(A|B) + P($\bar{A}$|B) = 1, and it is **not** true that P(A|B) + P(A|$\bar{B}$) = 1.

***AND'S* and *OR'S*.** Time and time again we will want to know the probability of one statement, or proposition, call it A, **and** a second proposition or statement, call it B. This is often written P(A.B), or sometimes, without the period inbetween the A and the B. This is called the conjunctive probability of A and B (recall that the word *and* is a conjunction). The probability of A or B is written P(AvB). This *or* means that either A is true or B is true or both are true. It is therefore the inclusive *or* as opposed to the exclusive *or*. The exclusive *or* means that either A is true or B is true but not both. There are rules for calculating both P(A.B) and P(AvB), a rule for each that applies in general, and a second rule for each that is used if a certain condition is met. This makes four rules in all. These are important!

and rule:

$$P(A.B) = P(A)P(B|A)$$
$$= P(B)P(A|B) \dots \quad \text{both are valid expressions in general}$$

if A and B are independent: $P(A.B) = P(A)P(B)$ since in this case $P(B|A) = P(B)$
and $P(A|B) = P(A)$

or rule:

$$P(AvB) = P(A) + P(B) - P(A.B) \dots \quad \text{valid in general}$$

if A and B are mutually exclusive:

$$P(AvB) = P(A) + P(B) \dots \quad \text{since here } P(A.B) = 0$$

In the above *independence* as applied to the *and* rule means that proposition A is in no way related to proposition B. For the *or* rule, when two propositions are mutually exclusive it means that they cannot occur together. Recall the basic probability rule

$$P(A) = P(A.B) + P(A.\bar{B})$$

Using the *and* rule this can now be rewritten as

$$P(A) = P(A|B)P(B) + P(A|\bar{B})P(\bar{B})$$

These rules will have more meaning when we see them play a role in several examples. Consider a deck of playing cards. Recall that Spades and Clubs are both colored black while Hearts and Diamonds are both red. Let us draw one card from the deck and then, <u>without replacing</u> this card in the deck, draw a second card. The probability that both of these cards are red is:

$$P(R_1.R_2) = P(R_1)P(R_2|R_1) = (1/2)(25/51)$$

since after drawing the first card there are only 25 red cards left in a pack of 51 cards. If however <u>the first card drawn is replaced</u> before the second draw the two draws are independent of each other so that

$$P(R_1. R_2) = P(R_1)P(R_2) = (1/2)(1/2) \dots \quad \text{independence}$$

To illustrate the *or* rule consider a deck of cards from which a single card is taken. The question is this: What is the probability for drawing a Queen or a Heart? Since these are not mutually exclusive possibilities, we use the *or* rule to obtain:

$$P(QvH) = P(Q) + P(H) - P(Q.H)$$
$$= 1/13 + 1/4 - (1/13)(1/4) = 4/52 + 13/52 - 1/52$$
$$= 16/52 = 4/13$$

This may appear as an odd expression for the probability for selecting in a single draw a Queen or a Heart (this *or* is the inclusive *or*). What's odd is the subtracting off of the quantity P(Q.H).

The answer, as is shown below, is that in adding the probability of a Queen to that for a Heart we have added the Queen of Hearts twice. Therefore, one of these must be subtracted. The subtraction itself is due to the fact that a Queen and a Heart are not mutually exclusive outcomes.

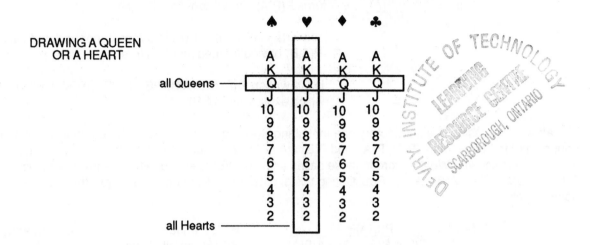

DRAWING A QUEEN
OR A HEART

all Queens

all Hearts

Another example to illustrate the "or" rule is provided by the result of tossing a coin four times in succession to obtain a sequence of heads and tails. The question can then be asked: What is the probability for tossing at least 2 Hs or at least 2 Ts in the sequence of four tosses? To examine this question it is necessary first to identify all the possible sequences that may result. There are 16 in all and these are shown below in the column at the left.

HHHH
THHH
HTHH
HHTH
HHHT

HHTT
HTHT
HTTH
THHT
THTH

TTHH
HTTT
THTT
TTHT
TTTH

TTTT

As can be observed, the sixteen sequences are arranged in five groups. At the top is the one "way" to obtain all Hs. Next there are four ways to obtain 3 Hs and 1 T. The next grouping consists of 6 ways to obtain 2 Hs and 2 Ts. After this we have a grouping of four that consists of 1 H and 3 Ts. Finally, there is the one way to obtain 4 Ts. The "or" rule tells us that the probability for obtaining at least 2 Hs or at least 2 Ts equals the probability for obtaining at least 2 Hs plus the probability for obtaining at least 2 Ts minus the probability for obtaining at least 2 Hs and at least 2 Ts. Numerically, we obtain: P(at least 2 Hs or at least 2 Ts) = 11/16 + 11/16 - 6/16 = 16/16 = 1.

Another question is the following: What is the probability for obtaining a sequence that contains 3 or more Hs or 3 or more tails? Numerically, this probability P = 5/16 + 5/16 - 0 = 10/16. This time no subtraction is necessary because the result 3 or more Hs and the result 3 or more Ts are mutually exclusive, i.e., both cannot happen at the same time in four tosses.

For an extensive listing of English language equivalents for the logical "and' and the logical "or" see Chapter VII.

BAYES' EQUATION. Bayes' Equation is one of the more important expressions in all of probability theory. For example, Bayes' Equation helps to solve the problem of MAMMALARY CANCER as well as that of the BLUE AND GREEN TAXICABS in the Introductory Problems. The Bayes' equation that we will use applies to a relationship involving two conjectures, propositions, or statements. To be perfectly general, let us call these two statements A and B. Then A can represent the statement that the hit and run taxicab was blue ($\bar{A}$ the statement that it was not blue, but green) and B the statement that the witness identified that cab as blue (with $\bar{B}$ the statement that she identified it as green). That is, P(A) represents P(blue) and P(B) represents P(ident B). Of course these two statements could be switched around. Even the statement and its negation could be switched, i.e., interchanged.

Bayes' equation is written in its simplest possible form below. Also noted below are the various roles it can play.

$$P(A|B) = \frac{P(B|A)P(A)}{P(B)}$$ . . . turns P(B|A) into its converse P(A|B)

. . . converts a prior value P(A) into a posterior updated value P(A|B) having learned that B is true

. . . is a rewritten form of P(A|B)P(B) = P(B|A)P(A), each side of which expresses P(A.B)

The above expression is a satisfactory one for finding P(A|B) provided that the three quantities on the right side of the equation, P(B|A), P(A), and P(B) are all known. But in this chapter P(B) is *not* known and P(B|$\bar{A}$) *is* known. We therefore in these cases use, not P(B) itself, but what it equals which is P(B) = P(B|A)P(A) + P(B|$\bar{A}$)P($\bar{A}$). Substituting this expression into the denominator of the expression above gives:

$$P(A|B) = \frac{P(B|A)P(A)}{P(B|A)P(A) + P(B|\bar{A})P(\bar{A})}$$ . . . Bayes' equation when P(B|A), P(A), and P(B|$\bar{A}$) are all known

Including the version of Bayes' equation written above, there are in all a total of four such expressions. It is useful to be able to write all of these correctly. The remaining three are:

P(A|$\bar{B}$) = . . . same as the above with $\bar{B}$ substituted for B everywhere

P(B|A) = . . . same as the first expression with A and B interchanged everywhere

P(B|$\bar{A}$) = . . . same as expression directly above with A replaced by $\bar{A}$ everywhere

It may be easier to remember all these expressions when one concentrates on the *pattern* exhibited by all the symbols. This pattern can perhaps be better seen if it is written in Greek:

$$P(\Psi|\Phi) = \frac{P(\Phi|\Psi)P(\Psi)}{P(\Phi|\Psi)P(\Psi) + P(\Phi|\bar{\Psi})P(\bar{\Psi})}$$ . . . Bayes' equation relating propositions Ψ and Φ

Here, Ψ can represent the proposition C that the patient has cancer, as it does in the MAMMALARY CANCER problem, and then Φ represents the proposition + indicating a positive result from a mammogram. Then, of course $\bar{\Psi}$ represents the proposition that the patient does not have cancer and $\bar{\Phi}$ the proposition that the mammogram gives a negative result.

But what about the conditionals P($\bar{A}$|B), P($\bar{A}$|$\bar{B}$), P($\bar{B}$|A), and P($\bar{B}$|$\bar{A}$)? Each of these is directly obtainable by taking, in turn, 1 minus P(A|B), P(A|$\bar{B}$), P(B|A), and P(B|A). These are relationships that are related to P(A) + P($\bar{A}$) = 1 and P(B) + P($\bar{B}$) = 1, differing only in the fact that they are conditionals.

In setting up Bayes' equation in the analysis of a problem, one needs to be sensitive to the various ways a conditional probability can be expressed. For instance, in the MAMMALARY CANCER problem one piece of data that is given is that P(+|C) = 0.792. Symbolically this is unambiguous. However, it could have been stated as *the probability for a positive result on condition that the patient has mammalary cancer*, or as, *the probability for a positive result given that the patient has mammalary cancer*, or as, *the probability for a positive result if the patient has mammalary cancer*. Also, things could be turned around by stating that *if the patient has cancer the probability for a positive result is 0.792*, or as, *given that the patient has cancer the probability for a positive result is 0.792*, or as, *on condition that the patient has cancer the probability that the test will be positive is 0.792*. Finally, one could say that *the probability is 0.792 that a patient with cancer will receive a positive test*.

THE MONTY HALL PROBLEM. <u>DRAW TREE</u>. A decision tree for the Monty Hall problem is given below. It is assumed that the producers of the television show select at random the door behind which the automobile is to be placed before the program begins. Thus the probability for it to be behind any particular door is 1/3. It is assumed also that contestants in general have no particular preference for any one of the letters A, B, or C. This makes the initial selection of a particular door by a contestant as probable as the selection of any other door, each having probability 1/3. There are at this time nine possibilities, each one as probable as the others. The probability that the car is behind a given door combined (the "and" rule; recall that "ands" multiply) with the probability that the game contestant will select a particular door makes the probability of each possibility 1/9, as shown.

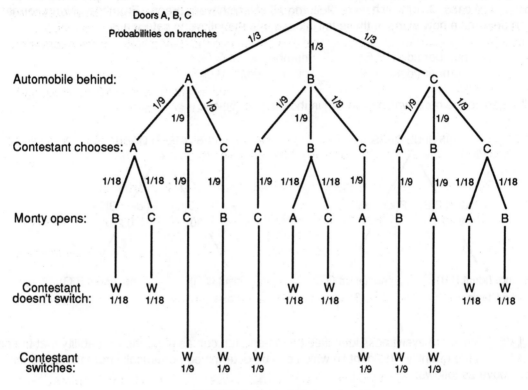

W signifies that contestant wins automobile

Conclusion: P(W | contestant doesn't switch) = 1/3

P(W | contestant switches) = 2/3

But now comes a deviation in the calculation of probabilities. After the contestant has selected one of the three doors it is now time for Monty to open one of the doors to show the contestant that the automobile isn't there, only a goat.

    <u>RECOGNIZE SITUATION</u>. What makes this situation different is that Monty *knows* where the automobile is. We know that he isn't going to open the door in front of the automobile. If the contestant has happened to select the door leading to the automobile Monty has two choices. He can open either of the other two doors to show the contestant that the automobile isn't there. But if the contestant has selected the wrong door, then Monty has only one choice. He isn't going to open the door the contestant has selected and he isn't going to open the door in front of the automobile. This leaves him with only one choice for the door he will open before the contestant must decide whether he is going to stick with his original door selection. When Monty has two choices we assume his selection of one of these two is

random and each possibility has an associated probability of 1/18. When Monty has but one choice the probability for arriving at this juncture is 1/9. This is the feature that makes the probability for the contestant to win the car greater if the contestant switches her choice. As can be seen from the decision tree, if she "sticks" her chances are 6/18 = 1/3 while if she "switches" her probability to win is 6/9 = 2/3.

BLUE AND GREEN TAXICABS. <u>IDENT PROB TYPE</u>. In this problem there are but two statements. First, the hit-and-run-cab is blue or it is not blue (green). Second, the eyewitness either correctly identifies this cab as blue or incorrectly as green. This assessment leads to two distinct methods for attacking this problem.

<u>IDENT FIRST METHOD</u>. Suppose the test of the reliability of the eyewitness consisted of her identification of 100 cabs, 85 of which were blue and 15 of which were green. From the given information one can then determine how many of these fell into each of the following categories:

number (ident B.B)	number (ident G.G)
number (ident G.B)	number (ident B.G)

A "tree" will organize the data which is shown in the diagram below:

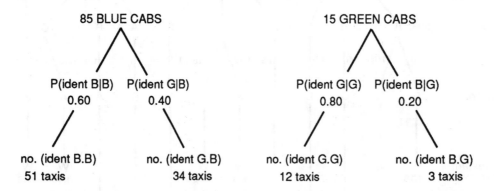

<u>SOLVE</u>. Since the eyewitness identified the hit-and-run cab as blue, the probability that the cab actually was blue is the quantity P(B|ident B) which can be determined numerically from the conjunctive probabilities above as follows:

$$P(B|\text{ident } B) = \frac{51}{51 + 3} = 0.94$$

Note that this method makes no explicit use of Bayes' Equation and could have been used to solve this introductory problem before the background information was known.

<u>IDENT ALTERNATIVE METHOD</u>. Bayes' Equation is ideally suited for the analysis of this problem. This method is more abstract than the method used above but is more generally applicable. We use it in the following form where the denominator is P(B).

$$P(B|\text{ident } B) = \frac{P(\text{ident } B|B)\, P(B)}{P(\text{ident } B|B)\, P(B) + P(\text{ident } B|G)\, P(G)}$$

Numerically,   P(B|ident B) = 0.94

MAMMALARY CANCER. <u>IDENT PROBLEM TYPE</u>. This problem seems to be similar to the problem of the BLUE AND GREEN TAXICABS because here, as there, there are two propositions: the individual either has cancer (C) or not (benign), and the mammogram is either positive (+) or negative (neg), i.e., is not positive. We expect there to be two methods for finding a solution, just as there were for the taxicabs, the first involving a tree structure and the second using Bayes' Equation.

      <u>IDENT GIVENS</u>. As with most problems, one of the first steps is to summarize the information that is given. In this case:

P(C) = prior probability that the patient has cancer = 0.10

then   P(benign) = prior probability that the breast mass is benign = 0.90

also   P(+|C) = probability for test to be + given that patient has cancer = 0.792

P(+|benign) = probability for + test if breast mass is benign = 1 - probability
for a correct negative test if breast mass is benign =
1 - P(neg|benign) = 1 - 0.904 = 0.096

The structure of the problem is clearly the same as that for the problem of the BLUE AND GREEN TAXIS. The two methods for attacking the problem will therefore be the same.

      <u>FIRST METHOD</u>. Suppose there are 100 individuals with the same diagnosis as that for the patient in this problem.

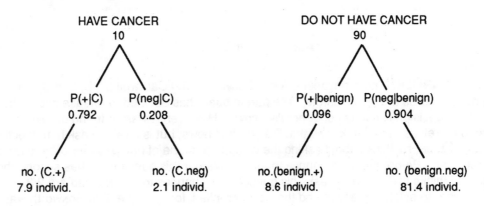

      <u>WANTED</u>: The desired quantity is P(C|+), the probability that the patient has cancer now that her mammogram is determined to be positive.

$$P(C|+) = \frac{7.9}{7.9 + 8.6} = 0.48$$

<u>ALTERNATIVE METHOD</u>. The second method involves the use of Bayes' Equation.

      <u>SOLVE</u>. The givens are the quantities that go into Bayes' Equation written as follows:

$$P(C|+) = \frac{P(+|C)\ P(C)}{P(+|C)\ P(C) + P(+|benign)\ P(benign)}$$

Numerically,   P(C|+) = 0.48

CASE OF THE RODEO GATECRASHERS. <u>RESTATE PROBLEM</u>. Recall that there were 1000 people in the stands at the rodeo but only 499 paid for admission. The obvious conclusion is that 501 individuals were "gatecrashers." It seems absurd that the rodeo management might select one of the thousand individuals in the stands and charge him with gatecrashing simply because the probability that he did not purchase a ticket is 501/1000. Since a person is guilty in a civil action by a "preponderance" of the evidence, the management might think it has a good case.

QUESTION. The following questions might help to clarify the situation. Appropriate responses to such questions are not difficult to find.

1. What if the ticket-takers at the rodeo let a number of people without tickets in free? Suppose for example, there were 51 such individuals. Then, of the 1000 people in the stands 550 either purchased tickets or were let in free. Presumably the remaining 450 individuals were gatecrashers. How would this affect a possible case the organizers of the rodeo might make against any one of the individuals in the stands?

2. What if the count of individuals in the stands is not 1000 precisely but only approximately 1000? Assume that the count is 1000 ± 50. It is also possible that the count of the number of tickets sold is, say, 499 ± 5. How would either or both of these assumptions influence a possible civil suit?

3. Suppose that 499 tickets to the rodeo were sold, but instead of the estimated 1000 people in the crowd there were approximately 2000, either in the grandstand or on the grounds. How would this affect any possible civil suit the management might bring?

Additional Problems

*CHANCES FOR PAROLE. Three prisoners, Allen, Bosworth, and Cardwell (A, B, and C), with apparently equally good records are up for parole. The parole board has decided to release two of the three prisoners, but their decision is not as yet generally known. However, a warder friend of Allen does know which two are to be released. Allen knows that the warder knows, but is afraid to ask him directly if he is to be released. Instead, he thinks about asking the warder the name of one prisoner *other than himself* who is to be released. Before he has a chance to ask the warder this question he has second thoughts on the matter. He thinks that before he asks his question his chances to be released are 2/3. However, he muses, if he were to ask the question and the warder replied, for example, that Bosworth was to be released, then his chances would go down to 1/2 because only he and Cardwell would be left to be the one remaining prisoner to be released. And so Allen decides not to ask the warder his question and thereby reduce his chances to be released. The problem here is to determine whether Allen is right or not in his conclusion not to ask. Explain.

THE TRUEL. Three men, A, B, and C (not Allen, Bosworth, and Cardwell) participated in a *truel* in accordance with the following rules. Each man was given a pistol and two bullets and positioned himself at the vertex of an equilateral triangle, 30 meters from each of the other two men. A was to fire one bullet first, next B, next C. They were to repeat this sequence until all bullets were fired or only one man survived. The probabilities for each man hitting his target 30 meters away were 2/3 for A, 3/4 for B, and 1 for C. This explains the reason for the sequence of firing. Assume that each man, when it is his turn to fire, always aims at that individual left standing who has the greatest shooting accuracy. The first part of the problem is to draw a tree that shows the sequence of firing until all shots are fired or only one of the three survives. Label all branches of this tree with the probabilities for hitting or missing one's target. It will be convenient with each firing to draw a branch downward and to the left to represent the hitting of one's target and downward and to the right for a miss. There will be 18 branches in all and 9 branch tips where the truel will terminate and where the final outcome can be shown. The second part of this problem is to determine the probability for A to survive this ordeal. There will be 5 outcomes that represent this occurrence. What is needed here is the application of both the "and" rule and the "or" rule. As an optional extension to this problem ask yourself whether Allen is better off or worse off if he misses C with his first shot than he is if his shot kills C.

PROBABILITY PARADOXES. So-called paradoxes involving the "and" rule are to be found both in medicine and in the law. The following example is related by E.A. Murphy in his book *Probability in Medicine*. A colleague of Murphy's is a physician who is intimately familiar with the probabilistic aspects of the diagnostic process. The following paradox is attributed to this colleague. Suppose that there are ten *independent* lab results that bear on a particular disease. To be definite, call this disease Murphy's anemia. Suppose further that each of these ten laboratory tests is positive for 90% of those who are afflicted. Each of the tests is therefore diagnostically important. If a patient takes only one of these tests, the probability of a positive result if the patient has the disease is 0.9. A second test is now made and it also turns out to be positive. The physician is naturally more convinced now that the diagnosis is correct than he was before when only a single test had been administered. However, the probability that both tests will be positive is, using the *and* rule:

$$0.9 \times 0.9 = 0.810$$

For three tests, all positive, the probability will be: $0.9 \times 0.9 \times 0.9 = 0.729$

and for four positive results: $(0.9)^4 = 0.656$

It appears that the greater the number of tests, all of which turn out to be positive, the lower the probability for this to occur and the harder it becomes to account for the result with a diagnosis of Murphy's anemia. How is this seemingly contradictory conclusion to be explained?

A similar paradox has also been described in the law. Civil cases are decided by a "preponderance of the evidence." This is generally construed to mean that when the evidence in support of the plaintiff has a probability value at any level greater than 0.50 the finding is then made in favor of the plaintiff. In *Probability and Inference in the Law of Evidence* Lempert discusses the following paradox. As we now know, the probability of two *independent* events A and B equals the probability of A times the probability of B. If there are two independent elements that a plaintiff must prove to make a case, each of which exists with a probability of 0.75, their conjoint probability [both true] is then 0.75 x 0.75 = 0.56. The plaintiff should recover in a civil suit since the preponderance of the evidence standard should mandate a verdict for the plaintiff. Suppose now that there is a third element in the plaintiff's case, independent of the other two, which has the same probability of existence. The plaintiff must prove the simultaneous existence of all three elements. But this probability is 0.75 x 0.75 x 0.75 = 0.42, and the defendant should now prevail. It would seem that with more and more evidence the plaintiff's case becomes more and more difficult to make. Lempert's conclusion is that Bayes' equation is wrong simply because it leads to wrong results. This conclusion, however, is totally unwarranted. What is your explanation?

*BLASTING A HYPOTHESIS. At one time a number of anthropologists accepted the following hypothesis concerning prehistoric agriculture in America: "The diet of people in Ecuador during the Valdivian Phase (3000 B.C.) was based on intensive maize agriculture." The hypothesis was a reasonable one because coastal Ecuador is quite similar to many other areas where there is evidence of early agricultural activity. While not all anthropologists accepted this hypothesis, it would be fair to assign the probability that it is correct at about 0.7. However, additional evidence relevant to this hypothesis was then obtained when 76 teeth were recovered from individuals buried in a Valdivian-period cemetery. Not a single cavity was found on any of these teeth. This was highly unusual in that it is well known that maize has a strong potential for producing cavities since it tends to cling to teeth. Let the hypothesis as stated above be represented by the letter *h* and the evidence regarding the 76 teeth be signified as evidence *e*. It was estimated that if the hypothesis were correct, there would only be one chance in a hundred of finding no cavities in 76 teeth. That is, $P(e|h) = 0.01$. Further, it is known that the incidence of cavities is much lower when the diet is not agriculturally based. The probability for finding no cavities in 76 teeth when the hypothesis concerning the maize is false can be set roughly at the value 0.10, ten times higher than if the diet included significant amounts of maize. To what level should one lower the probability that the maize hypothesis is true given the acquisition of the new evidence of cavity-free teeth from the Valdivian-period cemetery?

*DIAGNOSTIC VALUE OF ACNE. Medical researchers have found a relationship between severe acne and the presence of the XYY karyotype. The facts are as follows: Of all men, 1 in 500 have the XYY karyotype. Of those with the XYY karyotype, 44% have moderate or severe acne. Of those with the XY phenotype, 3% have moderate or severe acne. Assume that P(XYY) + P(XY) approximately equals one. What diagnostic value does the presence of acne have? That is, what is the probability for the XYY karyotype given that an individual has moderate or severe acne?

*THE ROBBERY AND THE TORN COAT LINING. Following Polya in *Patterns of Plausible Reasoning*, consider the businessman who, upon returning home late at night, was robbed by two masked individuals. When the police arrived and searched the premises they found a dark gray rag in the businessman's front yard. This rag might have been used by one of the bandits to serve as a mask. Next day the police questioned several suspects. One of the suspects was a vagrant with a record of petty theft. You decide to conduct a Bayesian analysis of the situation in an attempt to determine whether the suspect should be bound over for trial. At this point, take the probability that the suspect is guilty to be P(G) = 0.50.

Later, it was found that the suspect had a hole in his coat lining whose shape matched that of the rag found in the businessman's yard. In addition, the material in the coat lining seemed to match the material the rag was made of. Call this match hypothesis H. The police figured that if the vagrant actually was the robber it would then make sense that the rag actually came from the vagrant's coat. They took P(H|G) to be 0.95 and P(H|$\bar{G}$) to be 0.80. This last value is fairly high because the vagrant could very well have been passing nearby when he lost this rag which subsequently blew into the businessman's yard at almost any time before the robbery occurred. If the case were to come to trial the police wanted to know how strong their evidence would be in pointing toward the guilt of the vagrant. Consequently they calculated the quantity P(G|H). What is this value? Should the case go to trial?

X-LINKED LETHALS. Another Murphy example has to do with a woman about whose ancestry nothing is known. She has a son who is affected (A) with a form of muscular dystrophy which is in a class of X-linked lethals. Mutations that lead to this same affliction have a probability P(A|$\bar{C}$) = 0.00001 where $\bar{C}$ indicates that the mother is not a carrier. The carrier rate among women for such disorders is four times the mutation rate making P(C) = 0.00004. Furthermore, if the mother is a carrier a son is as likely to be affected (A) as not to be affected ($\bar{A}$). Thus P(A|C) = 0.5. If she is not a carrier and her son is afflicted, it must be due to a mutation. The mother now has an affected son. What is the probability that she is a carrier? not a carrier?

FAULTY SUSPENSION. An automobile manufacturer has learned that one model of the cars they produce has faulty suspensions (S) which have led to a number of accidents for their owners. They are, of course, worried that the government may order a massive recall that would cost them many millions of dollars. Consequently they undertake an analysis of the situation to better help them understand their problem. They have two plants that make this model, one in Xenia, Ohio (plant X), and another in Ypsilanti, Michigan (plant Y). Plant X produced 80 percent of this model and plant Y (not X) produced the other 20 percent. The production vice president determined that 50 percent of the cars produced by plant X have had faulty suspensions, i.e., P(S|X) = 0.50 and 90 percent of those coming from plant Y have had faulty suspensions, P(S|Y) = 0.90. Suppose you have purchased this make and model of automobile and learn that it has a faulty suspension. What is the probability it came from plant X?

30

HEMOPHILIA. Hemophilia, a disease of blood clotting, is a sex-linked defect that is passed along to sons of carrier mothers. It has occurred in a number of famous families including that of Queen Victoria of Great Britain. Since there was no known incidence of this disorder in the royal family before Victoria it is assumed that she became a carrier of hemophilia by a mutation in her germ line and this in turn was responsible for the disease in her offspring. The transmission of this defect is illustrated below. In this diagram the symbol X^S indicates the presence of a hemophilia gene on an X chromosome and X^A represents a normal gene on an X chromosome. In the first generation we have the union of a hemophiliac with a non-carrier female. This can produce in the second generation only normal males and carrier females. If one of these carrier females now marries a non-hemophiliac male, in the third generation all the genetic variations are possible: males that are hemophiliacs or normal and females that are carriers or non-carriers. Which of these occur is a matter of pure chance.

THREE GENERATIONS OF HEMOPHILIA

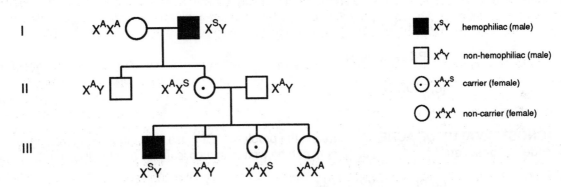

To illustrate the chance nature of the propagation of hemophilia consider the possible combination of chromosomes in the first generation (I) to produce offspring in the second (II). One X^A chromosome in the female can combine with the X^S chromosome in the hemophiliac father to form a carrier daughter $X^A X^S$. So too can the second X^A chromosome in the mother combine with the X^S chromosome in the father to produce a carrier daughter. In addition, each X^A chromosome of the mother can combine with the Y chromosome of the father to produce two more possibilities, both normal males which are $X^A Y$. Each of these four possibilities is equally probable. Probabilities for producing offspring in the third generation (III) from the union of a carrier mother in the 2nd generation with a normal male are determined according to the same kind of scheme.

Two questions that arise in this setting are the following. First, suppose that a known carrier mother, as in the 2nd generation above, has 10 normal sons. What is the probability that an eleventh son will also be normal? Second, suppose that the *daughter* of this known carrier mother has ten normal sons. It is not known whether the daughter is a carrier or not. What is the probability that an eleventh son of hers will also be normal?

*TESTING FOR THE HIV VIRUS. Testing for the presence of the HIV virus ordinarily consists of a battery of two tests. The first is the so-called EIA test, and if this test indicates the presence of the HIV virus, a second test called the Western Blot is then used to confirm the first result. According to the Center for Disease Control (CDC) in Atlanta, the chance that a person tests positive in both of these tests in spite of the fact that the individual actually doesn't have the HIV virus is seven per million in the general population giving a probability of $P = 0.000\ 007$. This figure is the rate for false positives. The corresponding rate for false negatives is thought to be very nearly zero. The final figure of interest is that in the general US population about 0.4 of one percent are afflicted with the HIV virus (with an estimated thirty to forty thousand new infections in the US population occurring annually). With these figures calculate, using Bayes' equation, the probability that a person who tests positive on both the EIA and the Western blot actually has the HIV virus.

Chapter II Self-Test — Selected Problems

1. THE TRUEL. What is the probability for the following sequence of events: A fires at C, killing him, and then B fires at A, killing him? _____

2. PROBABILITY PARADOXES. Let P(D) be the probability for an individual to have disease D and P(+|D) = 0.9 be the probability for a person with the disease to have a positive test. If a second *independent* test for the same disease is also positive, an expression for the probability that he has the disease is now (circle all correct):

(a) P(+|D) x P(+|D)

(b) P(D|+) x P(D|+)

(c) P(D|++)

3. DIAGNOSTIC VALUE OF ACNE. As stated in the problem: "Of those with the XYY karyotype, 44% have moderate or severe acne." This statement can be written symbolically as (circle all correct):

(a) P(acne|XYY) = 0.44

(b) P(acne|$\overline{XYY}$) = 0.56

(c) P(XYY|acne) = 0.44

(d) P($\overline{XYY}$|acne) = 0.56

4. FAULTY SUSPENSION. Since the probability for having a defective suspension produced in Ypsilanti is much higher (90%) than for the plant in Xenia (50%), it can be concluded that your car with its faulty suspension is more likely to have been assembled in Ypsilanti. True or False? _____

5. TESTING FOR THE HIV VIRUS. An individual learns that he has tested positive for both the EIA test and the Western Blot. What this individual wants to know is (circle all correct):

(a) P(++|$\overline{HIV}$)

(b) P(++|HIV)

(c) P(HIV|++)

Chapter II Self Test — THE POLLSTER

A prominent pollster once dreamed that he had conducted a poll of a thousand individuals and had gathered the results of that poll. Those polled were asked whether they favored a pro-life position or one that is pro-choice. They were also asked whether they favored capital punishment or were against it. Let two propositions be defined as follows:

A: favor pro-life position
B: favor capital punishment

Then, $\overline{A}$ represents individuals who favor the pro-choice position, i.e., not pro-life, and $\overline{B}$ those who are against capital punishment.

The results of this poll were as follows. 550 held the pro-life position making $P(A) = 0.55$. Of those who are pro-lifers 60% favored capital punishment and of those who were not pro-lifers 35% favored capital punishment. Find each of the following probabilities:

$P(B) = $ _____ = P(favor capital punishment)

$P(A|B) = $ _____ = P(pro-life among those favoring capital punishment)

$P(A|\overline{B}) = $ _____ = P(pro-life among those against capital punishment)

III. BEN FRANKLIN'S ADVICE AND OTHER DECISION STRATEGIES

Introductory Problems: BEN FRANKLIN'S ADVICE
                                          SIMPLIFIED POKER
                                          OIL DRILLING PROBLEM
                                          THE ROMAN SENATE

Background: DECISION MODELS
                                            AVERAGING OUT AND FOLDING BACK

Introductory Problem Solutions

Additional Problems   SAM PONDERS DIVORCE
                                          ADMISSION DECISIONS
                                          LOCATING A NEW DRUG COUNSELING CENTER
                                          KING CHARLES AND THE INDEPENDENTS
                                          SUSPECTED ACUTE APPENDICITIS
                                          PHYSICIAN PASSES AN ACCIDENT SCENE
                                            WHICH URN IS WHICH?
                                          THE OIL DRILLING PROBLEM REEXAMINED
                                          A CREDIT RATING SERVICE
                                          ACTIVITY — PLAY SIMPLIFIED POKER

Self Tests: SELECTED PROBLEMS
                                          SAM'S DECISION TREE

III. BEN FRANKLIN'S ADVICE AND OTHER DECISION STRATEGIES

People make decisions almost constantly. Some decisions are trivial, some habitual, many are made when we don't even realize we're making them. Some decisions, however, are extremely important— selection of a life's work, choosing a marriage partner, determining if one should stand up to one's boss, and selecting your candidates in the next election. Should one choose to participate in the war on poverty, fight discrimination in every form, and protest the pollution of our air and water? Just where should one drill in an attempt to find oil? How should a jury reach its findings in a murder trial? At what point should one take over the decision-making responsibilities for a terminally ill cancer patient?

A great many very important decisions are made in a qualitative and subjective manner—decisions of the Supreme Court, political decisions in both the legislative and executive branches of government, decisions made in the private sector that have a significant impact upon the economy and on the job market, and decisions made by parents in raising their children. Making decisions means making choices—making selections from among a variety of alternatives. For relatively simple problems decision-making strategies can be identified that will yield the best possible decision. When problems become more complex the identification of decision strategies becomes more difficult. As in most but not all of our work we will emphasize analysis of more straightforward problems, taking this as a good strategy before attempting more difficult and more challenging problems at a later time.

Introductory Problems

BEN FRANKLIN'S ADVICE. In 1772 Joseph Priestly, a well-known English clergyman, political theorist, educator, scientist, and the discoverer of oxygen, wrote his friend Ben Franklin concerning a problem that he had encountered. In his reply Franklin said he could not answer the particular problem that Priestly had described, but he could offer some advice on how to solve problems in a general way. Franklin advised him to divide a sheet of paper in two, labelling one side as *Pro* and the other side as *Con*, and then during several days of deliberation write down everything he could think of that fell in either of these two categories. As a next step, Franklin continued, write down to the best of your ability to do so the weight of each of these items, recognizing that there may be a fair amount of uncertainty in these estimates. Adding the weights of all items on the Pro side and doing the same on the Con side enables one to make a comparison of one to the other. Thus, according to Franklin, a better decision can be made than might otherwise be possible. Franklin's system is well-suited to answer the question of whether to buy or lease an automobile, or whether to buy or to rent a home.

Given this background, consider the following problem taken from Dawes in *Rational Choice in an Uncertain World*. Suppose you are assigned by the CIA to select a spy from two candidates to be trained as a mole in a Spanish-speaking terrorist organization. Each of the candidates is to be scored on each of four attributes. Multiplication of these scores by the weights you have assigned to each attribute and adding gives the weighted average for each candidate.

Candidate A: a native Spanish speaker
moderately intelligent
no evidence in the past of being particularly trusted or liked
is highly committed to your cause

Candidate B: speaks Spanish fluently, but not a native speaker
highly intelligent
evidence in his past of being trusted and liked
there are doubts about the strength of his commitment to your cause

Use Ben Franklin's advice to Priestly to make your decision regarding the two candidates.

SIMPLIFIED POKER. To make decisions one must know one's alternatives. This is particularly true in playing poker, a game that so intrigued von Neumann. He was a mathematician and physicist and co-author of the book *Theory of Games and Economic Behavior* which was to leave an indelible mark on the field of economics. Incidentally, the poker metaphor is often used in the field of international politics. Instead of playing regular poker, imagine a game of simplified poker in which the deck consists of but three cards, an Ace, a King, and a Queen, and a player's hand is but one card, not five or seven. There are two players, Tom and Nancy. Each antes some fixed amount, the same as the amount of a bet. Tom deals one card face down to Nancy and one to himself. Since Tom dealt it is now up to Nancy to either pass or bet. After she does so it is then Tom's turn to either pass or bet followed by Nancy's turn. The game terminates in any one of three ways: by two successive bets, two successive passes, or by a player who passes following an opponent's bet. In this game neither player can raise the other's bet.

There are six deals, i.e., six different combinations of hands that can be dealt to Tom and Nancy. For each deal the plays of the game can be diagrammed as shown below. As can be seen, for each deal there are five ways possible to play the game. This makes 30 possible plays altogether.

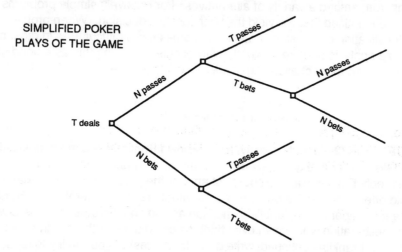

SIMPLIFIED POKER
PLAYS OF THE GAME

Suppose that you are a player, like Nancy, who is the first to bet because your opponent has dealt the cards. The central question concerns your strategy. Strategy is of course making decisions regarding passing or betting at each point in the game. You have but three possible strategies once you have your hand. You may pass then pass again assuming that you have a chance to do so. You may pass then bet, again assuming you have a chance to do so. And finally you simply may bet. What do you do assuming you were dealt a Queen? What if you were dealt a King? Finally, how would you play if you hold the Ace? Assume that your opponent is just as good a poker player as you are.

OIL DRILLING PROBLEM. The oil drilling problem is one described by Howard Raiffa in his book *Decision Analysis, Introductory Lectures on Choices under Uncertainty*. It concerns a wildcatter who has a lease to drill at a given site and must decide whether or not to drill before his lease expires. There is a good deal of information available to the wildcatter but most of it is uncertain. The records of previous drillings in the area, both successful and otherwise, are available, but he doesn't know how deep he might have to drill. Some uncertainties can be lessened by hiring a team to make seismic soundings. This is not done without cost and the value of the information the wildcatter might gain is uncertain.

Draw the wildcatter's decision tree. Start with his decision whether or not to obtain seismic soundings. Show the cost of obtaining the soundings. With no soundings he must decide to drill or not, and if he does drill he will or will not find oil. On the other hand, if he obtains soundings these will or will not indicate that the site is a favorable one for striking oil, and in either case he may or may not decide to proceed with drilling which then may or may not find oil.

THE ROMAN SENATE. Almost two thousand years ago an incident arose in the Roman Senate as to the action it should take in the case of the death of the consul Afranius Dexter. It was not clear to the senators whether Dexter committed suicide or whether he died at the hands of his freedmen. In the latter case it was also uncertain whether Dexter ordered his own death, or whether the deed was done with malice by the freedmen. If it was suicide then the action against the freedmen should be that of acquittal (represented by the letter "a"). If it was a mercy killing then the freedmen should be banished (letter "b"). If, however, it was murder the freedmen would be condemned to death (letter "c"). The decision tree describing the situation faced by the Senate is shown below.

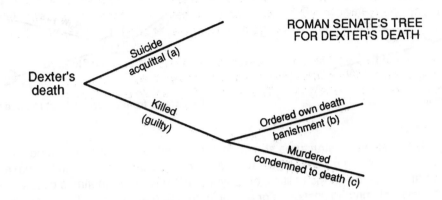

As it turned out there were, according to Pliny the Younger, three groups of senators: group A favoring action a, group B favoring action b, and group C favoring action c. The percentages of senators favoring the various actions are shown in the table.

	Group		
	A	B	C
Preferred action	a	b	c
Percent	40	35	25

The outcome of the trial not only depended on the information available to the senators but also upon the voting procedure that was used. Describe as many different decision (voting) procedures as you can that the Roman Senate might have used in this case. What would the decision be for each voting procedure?

Background

DECISION MODELS. As we have seen, a decision tree provides a useful model for a sequence of decisions. A fork in the branching is either a decision fork or a chance fork. At a decision fork the decision maker determines the number of alternatives he has at that point and therefore the number of continuing branches. He then decides which of these alternative paths he will follow. At a chance fork the branching is governed by the laws of probability. Labelling of the decision tree is done according to convention. The tips of the branches are labelled according to the outcome and the utility (value) of that outcome. A branch extending from a chance fork is labelled by the probability of going down that particular path. For example, in the tree at the left below an outcome A or $\bar{A}$ is followed by B or $\bar{B}$ to produce outcomes $A.B$, $A.\bar{B}$, $\bar{A}.B$, and $\bar{A}.B$. Application of this general scheme is illustrated in the second figure below where colored balls, either red or white, are drawn from an urn one after the other without replacement of a drawn ball. While the contents of the urn are also shown, the final outcomes of the draws are labelled at the right and the probabilities entered along the branches.

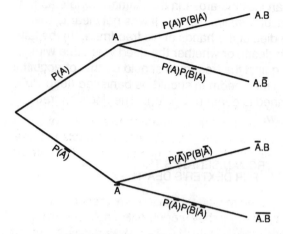

Tree for conjunctions of A and B

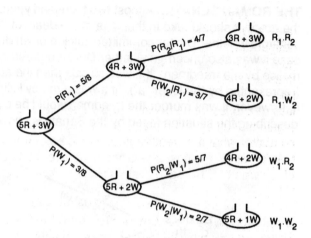

Two draws from an urn without replacement:

As an alternative to the tree structures above, matrices such as the one shown below can also be used to model the decision-making process. Both rows and columns are labelled. In the boxes at the intersections of rows and columns go the utilities, or "payoffs" as they are sometimes called, that go with the outcomes for the row-column conjunction. For example, in a 320 acre plot of land recently purchased by a giant agri-business corporation, the selection of crops to be planted next year is being made. It is felt that they should choose from among soybeans, alfalfa, and hothouse tomatoes. Their choice, however, is strongly influenced by what they think the weather will be next season. To make an extreme simplification of the weather possibilities, suppose that the weather can be classified as ideal, fair, or bad. They obtained the nine possible combinations of crop with state of the weather as shown in the matrix below.

WEATHER

	Ideal	Fair	Bad
Soybeans	10	1	- 2
Alfalfa	8	6	2
Hothouse Tomatoes	3	3	3

CROPS
PAYOFF
MATRIX

The numbers in the boxes represent "utiles." Let each utile represent an arbitrary unit of value, either in dollars or in some other kind of satisfaction. At this point the decision as to which crop to plant remains open. To be completely rational, the corporation should learn from the weather service what the probabilities are for ideal, fair, and bad weather. Suppose that P(ideal) = 0.20, P(fair) = 0.55, and P(bad) = 0.25. Then the following calculations were made for the expected value (EV) of each choice. The EV is simply the weighted average for each choice of crop.

$$EV \text{ (soybeans)} = (0.20)(10) + (0.55)(1) + (0.25)(- 2) = 2.05$$
$$EV \text{ (alfalfa)} = (0.20)(8) + (0.55)(6) + (0.25)(2) = 5.40$$
$$EV \text{ (tomatoes)} = (0.20)(3) + (0.55)(3) + (0.25)(3) = 3.00$$

The choice determined by strictly playing the probabilities is clearly alfalfa.

There is an alternative decision strategy that can be used here. Suppose the manager of this farm land is a young fellow very anxious to move up the corporate ladder. What he thinks he needs desperately is a modest first-year profit without taking any unnecessary risks. He can accomplish this goal by thinking of the weather god as an adversary out to minimize the manager's return from the land. In effect, the manager's stance is to assume the role of a "cautious pessimist" as regards the weather. He looks at the soybeans row in the matrix. The worst that can happen if he were to plant soybeans is a loss of 2 utiles. If he decides to plant alfalfa, the worst outcome again comes with bad weather, this time a gain of 2 utiles. If he plants a hothouse crop of tomatoes, however, he is guaranteed a return of 3 utiles no matter what the weather turns out to be. From among this list of worst outcomes, he selects the one that for him is the best, the outcome of 3 for hothouse tomatoes. His criterion has been to select "the best of the worst." This cautious pessimist strategy is perhaps the one most often used.

Jurors in a murder trial have the awesome task of determining the guilt or innocence of a defendant. When they render their verdict they must recognize that their judgements could be wrong. There are four possible outcomes represented in the matrix below in which utility values for each outcome have not as yet been assigned. The four outcomes are: Jury finds the defendant innocent and the defendant is actually innocent, jury finds the defendant innocent and he is actually guilty, jury finds the defendant guilty and he is actually innocent, and jury finds the defendant guilty and the defendant is actually guilty.

TRUE STATE

	Innocent I	Guilty G
Innocent I	I, I	I, G
Guilty G	G, I	G, G

JURY FINDS

OUTCOMES IN A JURY TRIAL

In each box, the first letter goes with the row (what the jury finds) and the second letter goes with the column (the true state of affairs). As a juror, or anyone else for that matter, it is a difficult task indeed to assign relative utility values to each outcome. Considerable satisfaction is obtained when the truly innocent are judged to be innocent and the truly guilty are found by the jury to be guilty. However when an innocent person is found to be guilty or when a guilty person is found to be innocent, we think that the criminal justice system has somehow failed us. Perhaps a more meaningful description of how society would like to see capital homicide cases handled would be to assign desired probability values to each of the four conjunctive outcomes in the matrix: P(I.I), P(I.G), P(G.I), and P(G.G). These values would then lead to the conditional probabilities P(judged I | actually I), P(judged I | actually G), P(judged G| actually I), and P(judged G | actually G). It is the first and fourth of these that society would like to see have high probabilities, and the second and third low probability values. Between these latter two it appears that one kind of individual worries more about letting some guilty defendants go free by setting a too-high value for P(judged I | actually G), and another type of person concerned more about incarcerating too many innocent individuals by permitting too high a value for P(judged G | actually I).

AVERAGING OUT AND FOLDING BACK. "Averaging out and folding back" is an expression Howard Raiffa uses to describe his technique for using outcome utilities in a decision tree to determine the single most desirable path through the tree. This technique is an important model for evaluating various decisions that might be made and determining which of these is the best. This process is perhaps best understood through the use of an example. Although the example is one taken from the field of medicine it will also serve to illustrate the decision-making process in other fields.

In an article entitled "Decision analysis in medicine" by J.G. Thornton, R.J. Lilford, and N. Johnson that appeared in the British Journal of Medicine, 1992; 304: 1099 -1103, the authors describe a case of cervical cancer. A 29 year old nurse was diagnosed by means of a biopsy as having occult cervical cancer. The tumor was excised, and the pathologist later reported a fairly wide margin of normal tissue around the area from which the tumor was removed. Now comes decision time. What program of treatment should be undertaken? A simple hysterectomy was immediately ruled out as an option since it would not remove possible metasteses (spreading of the cancer), was unlikely to improve the patient's chances for survival, and would automatically render her infertile. Remaining were but two treatment options. The first was to "undertake no further treatment" and the second to "perform an extended hysterectomy with lymphadenectomy" (radical hysterectomy). Four possible outcomes were identified, these being survival with fertility retained, survival with infertility with or without the spread of cancer, delayed death from cancer, and immediate death resulting from complications arising during surgery.

At this point the decision tree shown in Step 1 in the figure on the page following can be drawn. The square node at the left indicates a decision fork. The patient can elect either to undergo no further surgery of to have a radical hysterectomy. All further forks as shown by open circles are chance forks over which the patient has no control. All six final branches of the tree are labelled according to one of four possible outcomes.

In Step Two the utilities of the possible outcomes were placed at the ends of the branches. Utility values ranging from 0.00 to 1.00 (alternatively, from 0 to 100) were obtained as follows. Let a utility of 1.00 be assigned to the outcome of survival with fertility retained and 0.00 be assigned to imme-diate death resulting from surgical complications. The remaining two utility values will then lie between these two extremes. Now the patient was asked to imagine two doors through one of which she must pass. Behind the left hand door there was no risk of death but she would be rendered infertile. This is the outcome whose utility is in the process of being determined. Behind the right hand door she would encounter, for starters, a 50% chance of fertile survival (1.00 utility) and a 50% chance of immediate death (0.00 utility). The patient chose the left hand door indicating a preference to live but be rendered infertile over a 50% chance of fertile survival and a 50% chance of immediate death. The stated risks of immediate death through the right hand door were then gradually decreased but the patient maintained her preference for the left hand door. A point was reached where the patient became indifferent to the choice of one door over another. This occurred when the right hand door represented a 95% chance of fertile survival and a 5% chance of immediate death. This indicated that her utility level for infertile survival had been set at 0.95 compared to 1.00 for survival with fertility retained. A similar two-door test was then administered to determine the patient's utility value for delayed death represented by the left hand door. Again we start at the right hand door with a 50% chance for fertile survival and a 50% chance for immediate death. This time she of course preferred the right hand door. The risk of immediate death behind the right hand door was then gradually increased until this risk became 95% and the chance for fertile survival 5%. At this point the patient became indifferent to the choice of either door over the other. Thus her utility value for delayed death was set at 0.05. The patient's four utility values can now be entered at the extreme right as part of Step 2. The other part of this step is to enter the probabilities for each outcome. This of course was not for the patient to do but for the attending physicians. If the patient were to elect not to have further surgery, her attending physicians believed she had a 98% chance for fertile survival and consequently a 2% chance for delayed death. If the patient elects to have surgery, however, the physicians estimated the probability of surgical death as 0.005, the probability for no spread of the cancer beyond the biopsy region with a radical hysterectomy as 98%, and the chance for infertile survival following surgery, if in fact the cancer had spread, as 50% with the chance for delayed death at this point also 50%. These probabilities can now be entered along the appropriate branches of the decision tree and this has been done as the final part of Step 2.

The final step is the one of "averaging out and folding back." The purpose of this step is to assign utility values to each chance fork. This can be accomplished by starting at the right and moving toward the left (folding back). Consider the chance fork encountered near the upper right side of the tree. The weighted average for this fork equals the utility value of 0.05 times its probability of 2% and this result added to the utility value 1.00 multiplied by its probability of 98%. This gives an averaged out utility of .981 as shown in larger type in the figure. The utility values of the three chance forks appearing along the bottommost branch are, folding back from right to left, (.50)(.95) + (.50)(.05) = .500, (.98)(.95) + (.02)(.50) = .941, and (.005)(0) + (.995)(.941) = .936. Their entry completes Step Three.

AVERAGING OUT AND FOLDING BACK

Step 1. Create and label
decision tree.

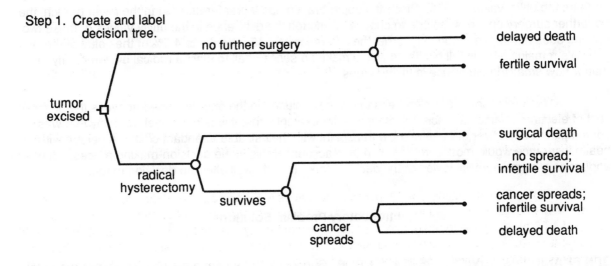

Step 2. Add outcome utilities
and probabilities.

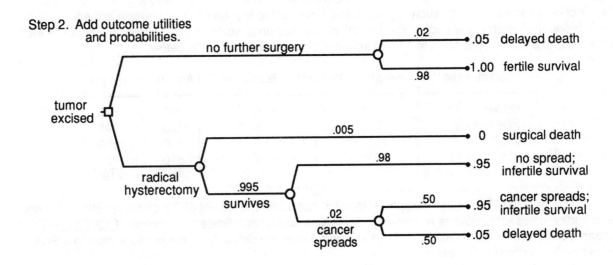

Step 3. Calculate utilities
at chance forks.

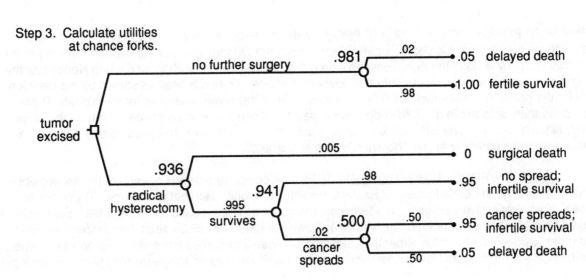

Having completed the tree diagram it remains only for the patient to choose her path at the decision fork at the extreme left. Looking up and to the right along the "no further surgery" branch she sees a utility value of .981. Looking down and to the right along the "radical hysterectomy" branch there appears the utility value of .936. Since the upper branch has a greater utility than the lower branch, the no further surgery option is the one to choose. Although the difference in the utility values of these two options does not appear to be very large, the difference of .045 represents 4.5% of the value of the patient's remaining life in full health. It would make no sense at all to elect a radical hysterectomy, no matter how small the difference in utility values.

A feature of some decision trees that is not included in the one described above is the possible cost of electing a particular decision. Suppose, for example, that it was not a hysterectomy that was contemplated but a liver or bone marrow transplant with their sizable attendant costs. A person without health insurance would most surely want to take account of this in the decision-making process. It would appear as a negative utility levied at the decision fork. It could well alter the decision made.

Introductory Problem Solutions

BEN FRANKLIN'S ADVICE. <u>RESTATE PROB</u>. Suppose that you are a member of a small group that has been assigned the task of selecting a spy from the two candidates presented to you. Perhaps a better choice can be made by such a group rather than trust to the advice of any single individual. In one such group the weighting of each of the four characteristics on a scale of 1 to 100 and the score of each candidate expressed on a scale of 1 to 10 turned out as shown in the table below.

characteristic	weight	A's score	B's score	A's pts.	B's pts.
native speech	100	10	6	1000	600
intelligence	60	7	9	420	540
inspire trust	75	4	8	300	600
commitment	90	9	5	810	450
				2530	2190

<u>CONSTRUCT TABLE</u>. Multiplying for each candidate the weight of the characteristic by his score and adding gives for candidate A a total of 2530 points and for candidate 2190 points. <u>CONCLUSION</u>. Clearly, Ben Franklin would have chosen candidate A over candidate B for the job as a mole in a Spanish-speaking terrorist organization.

SIMPLIFIED POKER. <u>RECAPITULATE PROB</u>. In the game of simplified poker played by Tom and Nancy there are six possible deals: when Nancy is dealt the Queen, Tom can hold either the King or the Ace; when Nancy is dealt the Ace, Tom can hold either the Queen or the King; and when Nancy has the King, Tom must have been dealt either the Queen or the Ace. For each deal, as shown by the decision tree for the game, there are five possible outcomes. Nancy has three strategies for each deal. These are: pass then pass again given the opportunity, pass first then bet, and simply bet. Tom on the other hand, since he has but one decision to make for each deal, has only two strategies: either pass or bet. These strategies combine to give the five possible outcomes.

<u>ANALYSE PROB</u> <u>DRAW DECISION TREES</u>. A complete analysis of each of the six possible deals is shown on the page following. Each player antes one unit; each bet is one unit. There are no raises. Two successive bets or passes terminate the game as does a pass following a bet. Each hand is played from Nancy's point of view; the winnings shown are hers. As will be seen, her strategy if quite straightforward when she holds either the Queen or the Ace. It becomes more involved, however, when she is dealt the King. Both Nancy and Tom are out to maximize their winnings (or minimize their losings).

The Six Deals of Simplified Poker

Both Tom and Nancy ante 1 unit and bet 1 unit. Tom deals. Winnings (or losings) are Nancy's.
Pass branches slope upward; bet branches slope downward.

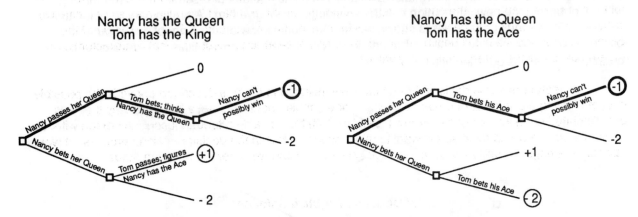

When Nancy is dealt the Queen, as in the top row of decision trees, her preferred strategy (shown by the heavier branches) is to pass at every opportunity. These upper tracks lead to a loss of 1 unit. Exceptions occur in the upper row when she attempts to bluff Tom by betting her Queen and succeeds at the left but fails at the right. When she has the Ace, however, as in the middle row of diagrams, she bets at every opportunity and these lower tracks lead to a gain of 1 unit. When she attempts to bluff Tom by passing initially even though she holds the Ace, she gains nothing at the left but wins 2 units when Tom falls for the gambit.

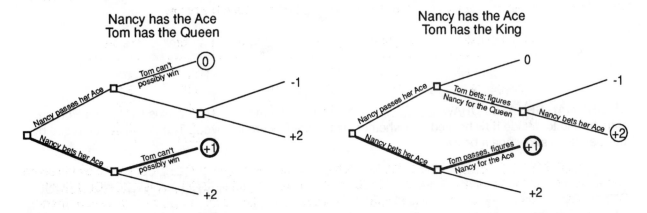

When Nancy is dealt the King, the middle card in the deck of three cards, the situation becomes somewhat more complicated. In this case, as shown in the lower row of decision trees, it makes no difference whether she initially passes or bets. If she passes initially she wins nothing when Tom fails to bet but loses one unit equally often when he does bet for an average loss of 1/2 unit. If, on the other hand, she initially bets she wins 1 unit just as often as she loses 2 units, again for an average loss of 1/2 unit.

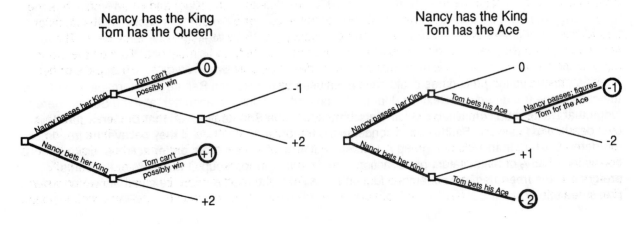

OIL DRILLING PROBLEM. <u>IDENT POSSIBLE DECISIONS</u>. Very little information is given in the statement of this problem. We are told only that the wildcatter has the option of paying a fairly large amount for seismic soundings to better evaluate his prospects for finding oil if he were to go ahead with drilling. On the basis of other information available to him he could of course go ahead with drilling without obtaining the new information that the soundings might give him. A preliminary decision tree that describes the various possibilities is shown below. Additional knowledge no doubt would put further branches on this tree by describing further options. Other outcome possibilities include finding various quantities as well as qualities of oil.

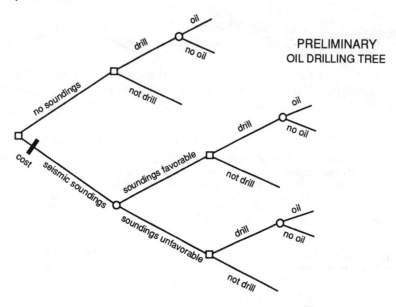

PRELIMINARY
OIL DRILLING TREE

THE ROMAN SENATE. <u>DRAW TREE</u>. In the case of the death of consul Afranius Dexter the Roman Senate had to decide how he died and whether his freedmen were involved. The decision tree faced by the Senate is show again below.

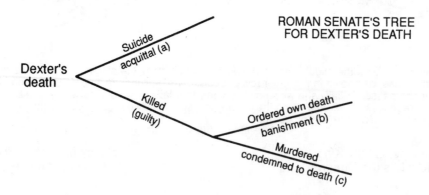

ROMAN SENATE'S TREE
FOR DEXTER'S DEATH

Various voting procedures could have been used by the Roman Senate to determine a verdict in the case of the freedmen and Dexter's death. The possible actions are acquittal "a" if the Senate were to judge that Dexter had committed suicide, banishment "b" if the Senate believed that Dexter ordered his own death, and finally the Senate could condemn the freedmen to death "c" if they believe the freedmen murdered Dexter. In the Senate, group A consisting of 40% of the senators prefer action a, group B consisting of 35% of the senators prefer action b, and a third group, group C with 25% of the votes, prefers that the freedmen be condemned to death c. All of these preferences are summarized in the table presented earlier.

<u>WRITE IT (DATA) DOWN</u>.

	Group		
	A	B	C
Preferred action	a	b	c
percent	40	35	25

<u>IDENT POSSIBILITIES</u>. Five different voting procedures that the Roman Senate might have used are as follows. In each case the decision that would be made is given.

1. Plurality. In this case the winning vote need not consist of a majority of the votes cast. Assuming that each senator votes his belief, the decision of the senate is for acquittal because 40% of the senators prefer this action, a greater percentage than for either of the other two possible decisions.

2. Sequential voting. In this case the first vote decides between guilt and innocence with a second vote to be taken as to the sentence should the freedmen be found guilty. A majority of the votes is required at each of these two steps. The first vote results in the judgment that the freedmen are guilty because 60% (groups B and C) vote this way while only 40% (group A) vote that the freedmen are innocent. In the second vote group A can be assumed to vote with group B (75% of the senators) for banishment as opposed to group C (25%) that favors the death penalty.

3. Sequential voting, but starting out by first deciding an appropriate punishment should the freedmen be judged guilty. This time group A quite naturally votes with group B making 75% who favor banishment as opposed to the death penalty. The second vote decides the question of guilt or innocence. In this case, as in the prior case, groups B and C with 60% of the vote determine that the action to be taken is banishment.

4. Rank and score. Each of the three groups of senators could have been asked to rank their preferences in order from the most desirable to the least desirable, awarding 3, 2, or 1 points accordingly. Suppose that for group A their ranking is actions *a*, *b*, then *c*. For group B their rankings, in order, are *b*, *a*, and lastly *c*. Finally, group C rankings are *c*, *b*, and *a*. Action *a* is therefore awarded 6 points, action *b* 7 points, and action *c* 5 points. The decision once again is for banishment.

5. Pairwise comparisons. Here we compare action *a* to action *b*, action *b* to action *c*, and action *a* to action *c*. When comparing *a* to *b*, those favoring action *c* naturally side with those favoring action *b* since both actions *b* and *c* are harsher than action *a*, i.e., *b* is preferred to *a*. When comparing actions *b* and *c*, those favoring action *a* side with *b* because both actions *b* and *a* are less harsh than action *c*, i.e., *b* is preferred to *c*. When comparing action *a* to action *c*, those favoring action *b* can either side with those favoring action *a* or they can vote with those voting for action *c*. If they side with *a* then their total of 75% overwhelms *c*. If on the other hand they side with *c*, the total of 60% outvotes *a*'s 40%. That is, those supporting action *b* win in all eventualities.

Additional Problems

SAM PONDERS DIVORCE. A young married couple, Sam and Josette, have two children, Samantha, age 14, and Joseph, age 8. Sam has not been happy in his marriage for some time. He questions his love for Josette. He and his wife don't seem to have much in common and communication between them is infrequent. He knows that his wife is loyal and a good mother for his children. He loves his children. However, he feels that his family responsibilities may be requiring so much time that he will not advance in his accounting firm as rapidly as he would like. In contemplating a possible divorce action he visualizes in his mind a number of scenarios.

Scenario 1. He decides to stay with his wife and family. He knows that they will continue to live happy and meaningful lives in spite of the negatives he sees for himself in a continuing marriage.

Scenario 2. Instead of divorce action he considers a trial separation. His wife will of course be hurt and the children may suffer some but it will give him the opportunity to collect his thoughts and also, to spend more time with his professional life.

Scenario 3. He decides to divorce his wife. He knows that his family will be seriously disrupted. It may scar his children for many years. Josette, in her late 30's, will not in all likelihood have an opportunity to remarry. It will clear the air for him professionally, and, who knows, he may yet find someone he would be interested in as a wife.

Put yourself in Sam's shoes. Weigh in numerical terms the value of the happiness Sam thinks he might have in each of the three scenarios. Sam also estimates happiness values he thinks Josette and the children might have in each situation. Make both evaluations on a scale of +10 to -10 thus indicating that Sam thinks he is no more important than his wife and children. From the net value for each scenario, what should Sam decide to do?

ADMISSION DECISIONS. In an anthology edited by Dowie and Elstein, Robyn M. Dawes describes the decision process for admitting students to a university There are two different decision making strategies used to determine which applicants are admitted to their schools and which are rejected. The first can be called a "clinical integration" method and the second a "statistical" one. In the clinical approach the members of an admissions committee examine each application and discuss such things as the applicant's college board score, his or her class rank, grade-point average, and whatever else is in the applicant's file. Also folded in to the decision is whether a parent of the applicant is an alum of the school, whether the applicant is white, brown, or black, whether the football coach is interested in the applicant, and whether the candidate's parents are likely to become benefactors to the institution. Letters of recommendation are also seriously considered as well as the geographical region from which the applicant comes. The statistical decision making process, by contrast, is one that could be given to a computer. All the same basic information used in the clinical process, basic test scores and biographical facts, is also used in the statistical process. The statistical approach employs a model that weighs the various factors by a scheme that is intended to maximize predictability. The existence of the two distinct decision making processes naturally poses a problem. Which of the two is superior? Before attempting to answer this question it might be helpful to ask yourself in what ways the nature of this problem is similar to those previously encountered and in what ways it is different. How is one expected to arrive at a "solution"?

*LOCATING A NEW DRUG COUNSELING CENTER. Edwards and Newman describe a relocation problem for a community service organization called "The Drug-Free Center." It lost its lease but now has identified a short list of six possible new locations. The Director of the Center has prepared what she calls a "value tree" for her staff to consider. It will serve to evaluate each of the sites. Suppose you have been provided with a copy of this new kind of tree and asked to evaluate it. Your first job is to understand it. What do the columns of numbers signify? What is the relationship of one column to the others? How might this value tree be used? What are its shortcomings?

48

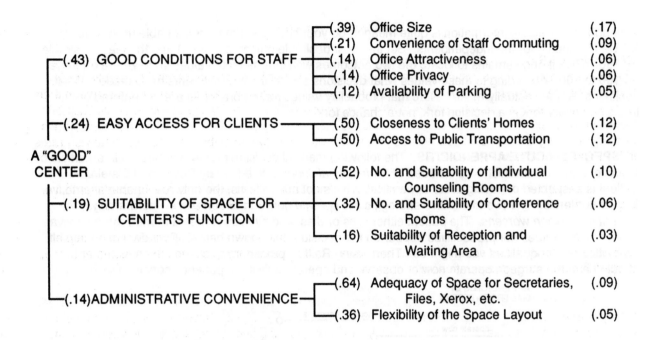

			(.39)	Office Size	(.17)
			(.21)	Convenience of Staff Commuting	(.09)
(.43)	GOOD CONDITIONS FOR STAFF		(.14)	Office Attractiveness	(.06)
			(.14)	Office Privacy	(.06)
			(.12)	Availability of Parking	(.05)
(.24)	EASY ACCESS FOR CLIENTS		(.50)	Closeness to Clients' Homes	(.12)
			(.50)	Access to Public Transportation	(.12)
			(.52)	No. and Suitability of Individual Counseling Rooms	(.10)
(.19)	SUITABILITY OF SPACE FOR CENTER'S FUNCTION		(.32)	No. and Suitability of Conference Rooms	(.06)
			(.16)	Suitability of Reception and Waiting Area	(.03)
(.14)	ADMINISTRATIVE CONVENIENCE		(.64)	Adequacy of Space for Secretaries, Files, Xerox, etc.	(.09)
			(.36)	Flexibility of the Space Layout	(.05)

A "GOOD" CENTER

KING CHARLES AND THE INDEPENDENTS. In spite of the fairly bloody history of the royalty of England, King Charles I was the only reigning monarch to be executed. By the winter of 1648-49 Charles had managed to alienate almost everyone in England, the independents led by Oliver Cromwell, the Presbyterians who held a parliamentary majority, and the Levellers who had considerable support from the army. The independents were really in control, so if the enormous simplification of ignoring both the Presbyterians and the Levellers is made, we are left with a two-party conflict with, as events unfold, decisions to be made on both sides. These events are described by Wedgewood in *A Coffin for King Charles*. The over-simplified decision tree below looks strikingly similar to that for the game of simplified poker. In the King Charles "game" the independents have an opportunity to make two decisions while the King has only one. In any event the King was executed and, if he had had any sense, he would have realized that just how he made his decision would matter little. He was to be executed no matter what. On the other hand, Cromwell and the independents were to remain in power, so they were very concerned with the appearances created by doing things in one way or another. The four possible outcomes for this simplified decision tree are shown below.

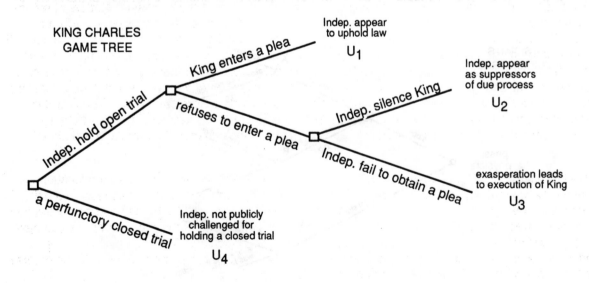

KING CHARLES GAME TREE

Indep. appear to uphold law U_1

King enters a plea

Indep. hold open trial

refuses to enter a plea

Indep. silence King

Indep. appear as suppressors of due process U_2

Indep. fail to obtain a plea

exasperation leads to execution of King U_3

a perfunctory closed trial

Indep. not publicly challenged for holding a closed trial U_4

Although the available information is quite meager, do your best to estimate reasonable utility values U_1, U_2, U_3, and U_4 for the independents. Set the most desirable outcome at +100 and the least desirable at -100. Thus it only remains to locate the two outcomes with intermediate values somewhere on a scale of -100 to 100. According to these values what decisions should the independents have made? What decisions did they actually make? Note that probability values for the branches are not entered on the tree since every fork is a decision fork, not a chance fork.

SUSPECTED ACUTE APPENDICITIS. The following medical decision problem appeared in an article by Doubilet and McNeil which was included in *Professional Judgment* edited by Dowie and Elstein. A patient is suspected of having acute appendicitis. If it's not appendicitis, the only reasonable alternative is gastroenteritis. The two alternative strategies are *operate now* and *observe and operate only if the patient's condition worsens.* The patient either lives or dies, and by *lives* is meant a one-month survival. Neither utility values nor probabilities appear on the decision tree shown below. Provide these yourself no matter how unqualified you might be. Then, using Raiffa's procedures, tell the patient whether he should have the surgeon operate now or observe and operate only if the patient's condition worsens.

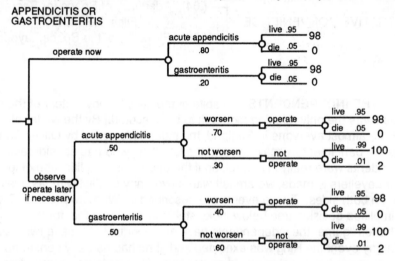

*PHYSICIAN PASSES AN ACCIDENT SCENE. Should a physician in a state without a Good Samaritan law stop at the scene of an automobile accident to render needed medical attention? His decision tree shows utility values at the right and probabilities along the branches. Find the utilities at the chance forks A, B, C, and D. What decision should the doctor make? Should he or should he not stop at the scene of the accident?

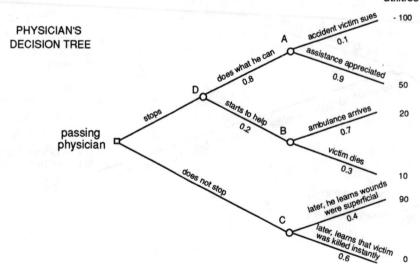

*WHICH URN IS WHICH? There are two urns, call them urn I and urn I I. Urn I contains 4 red balls and 6 white balls. Urn I I contains 8 red balls and 2 white balls. Since the urns are unmarked and appear to be identical, when one is presented you have no idea which urn it is nor can you see inside the urn to examine its contents. You are then asked to reach into the urn presented and withdraw a ball. It is a red ball. What is the probability that it was taken from urn I? This is the posterior probability $P(I|R_1)$ having started with the prior value $P(I) = 0.5$. Without replacing the red ball now draw a second ball from this same urn. This time it is a white ball. Find the updated probability $P(I|W_2)$ using as priors the results from the first draw, i.e., the values of $P(I|R_1)$ and $P(I I|R_1)$.

THE OIL DRILLING PROBLEM REEXAMINED. Recall that the oil wildcatter was trying to make a decision whether or not to drill on a property for which he held a temporary lease. Since he had no information about the underlying geologic structure at this site, he was contemplating whether or not to pay for seismic soundings to be made which would reveal whether there was no structure, open structure, or closed structure. No structure would be a bad sign, open structure would be a so-so indicator, and a closed structure would be a very hopeful sign. In addition there could be three results if he were to drill on this site. The hole could be dry (no oil), wet (some oil), or soaking (large amounts of oil). At no charge to the wildcatter, a consulting geologist provided the wildcatter with the following 3X3 probability matrix. Each of the nine elements in this matrix is a conjunctive probability. For example, the probability in the upper left corner is $P(Dry.No\ S) = 0.300$.

Seismic Outcome

	No S	Open S	Closed S	
Dry	.300	.150	.050	.500
Wet	.090	.120	.090	.300
Soaking	.020	.080	.100	.200
	.410	.350	.240	

GEOLOGIST'S PROBABILITY MATRIX

Also shown outside the 3x3 conjunctive probability matrix above is a column of so-called marginal probabilities at the right and a row of marginal probabilities below. For example, at the top of the column at the right we have $P(Dry) = P(Dry.No\ S) + P(Dry.Open\ S) + P(Dry.Closed\ S) = 0.500$. The marginal probabilities at the right, reading down from the top, are $P(Dry)$, $P(Wet)$, and $P(Soaking)$. Those at the bottom are $P(No\ S)$, $P(Open\ S)$ and $P(Closed\ S)$. The figures in the column at the right add to 1 since $P(Dry) + P(Wet) + P(Soaking) = 1$ and those in the row at the bottom are $P(No\ S) + P(Open\ S) + P(Closed\ S) = 1$.

The geologist also provided the wildcatter with the decision tree below. At the "gate" shown at the lower left there is the $50,000 charge for making the seismic soundings. The utilities in dollars are shown on the decision tree for each of the three possible outcomes. The $350,000 cost of drilling has already been deducted from these figures. Your job is to enter the fifteen probabilities that belong on the branches of the tree using data from the above matrix and then decide whether the wildcatter should or should not have seismic tests made.

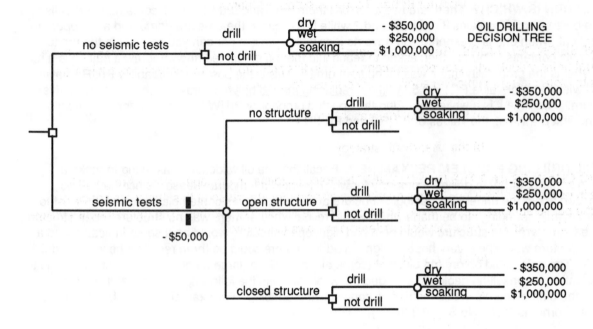

OIL DRILLING
DECISION TREE

*A CREDIT RATING SERVICE. A credit rating service (CRS) is in the business of providing bank clients with the service of evaluating loan applicants as to whether they are "safe" or "risky." CRS can inform a bank that is considering hiring their services as to the track record of banks already using those services. This information consists of the following. For a thousand new loan applicants who desired loans of $1000 at 18% simple interest, 160 were considered by CRS to be too risky. The remaining 840 were considered "safe." Of course the loan officers at these banks may not always follow the CRS recommendation. Of those who ultimately paid off their loans, 85% were given a safe rating by CRS. On the other hand, 35% of those who had defaulted had also been given a safe rating by CRS. The overall default rate was 8%. From this information find the percentage of those awarded loans who were given a "safe" rating by CRS. In addition, find the percentage of those given a safe rating by CRS who defaulted on their loans. (Note that the banks are somewhat more stringent in their loan policies than is CRS). Note: In this problem we are not concerned with the *applicants* for loans, but with those who actually received loans whether they received a safe rating by CRS or not. Therefore the percentage of *applicants* given a safe rating by CRS need not concern us. All of the remaining quantities refer to those who were awarded loans.

ACTIVITY— PLAY SIMPLIFIED POKER. Find an opponent who doesn't know what you know about the game of simplified poker. Alternating being the dealer, play 100 games with him/her. Use your knowledge of the game to see if you can beat his strategy for playing the game, whatever that turns out to be. Record the amounts you win or lose in each game and calculate a total won or lost. You surely should be the overall winner using the strategies graphed in the manual. What are your net winnings, whether these be regarded simply as points, as pop bottle caps, or as pennies?

Chapter III Self Test—Selected Problems

1. **ADMISSION DECISIONS.** Subjective information, like subjective probability, is dependent on the individual or individuals who provide the information. In this problem which strategy does subjectivity enter into more strongly in making admission decisions: (circle one)

(a) the "clinical integration" strategy

(b) the "statistical" strategy

2. **KING CHARLES AND THE INDEPENDENTS.** Recognize that the Independents were going to remain in power after the King Charles matter was disposed of. Because of this they were concerned about the public appearance for having taken one course of action or another. The Independent's utility values U_1, U_2, U_3, and U_4 were therefore ordered as follows (circle one):

(a) $U_1 > U_4 > U_2 > U_3$

(b) $U_4 > U_1 > U_2 > U_3$

(c) $U_1 > U_4 > U_3 > U_2$

(d) $U_2 > U_3 > U_4 > U_1$

3. **PHYSICIAN PASSES AN ACCIDENT SCENE.** Referring to the decision tree that accompanies this problem determine the utility of:

(a) branch point A _____

(b) branch point B _____

(c) branch point D _____

4. **WHICH URN IS WHICH?** To analyse this problem one can use Bayes' Equation. Suppose a red ball has been drawn from the urn you are trying to identify. We want to know whether this urn is urn I :

$$P(I|R_1) = [P(R_1|I)\,P(I)] / P(R_1)$$

In this equation what are the numerical values of the following:

(a) $P(I)$ _____

(b) $P(R_1)$ _____ . . . make an educated guess

(c) $P(R_1|I)$ _____

5. **OIL DRILLING PROBLEM REEXAMINED.** From the probability matrix given in this problem, determine the following:

(a) P(dry|no S) _____

(b) P(wet|open S) _____

(c) P(soaking|closed S) _____

Chapter III Self Test—Sam Ponders Divorce Decision Tree

Already encountered is the problem entitled SAM PONDERS DIVORCE. Here, in contrast to the prior problem, Sam does a more sophisticated analysis. He anticipates how Josette might react to his actions in each of the three scenarios. This leads to seven possible outcomes as shown on the decision tree below. Sam has already put on this tree his values for each of the outcomes together with his estimates of the probabilities for Josette to react one way or another. These probabilities label all branches stemming from chance forks.

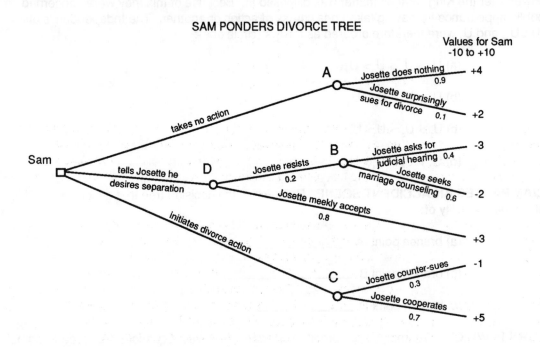

SAM PONDERS DIVORCE TREE

Values for Sam
-10 to +10

Calculate the utility values for each of the following branch points.

A: _____

B: _____

C: _____

D: _____

What should Sam decide to do? _____

IV. PRISONER'S DILEMMA AND OTHER GAMES

Introductory Problems: PRISONER'S DILEMMA
THE PBS DILEMMA
CALLING HEADS OR TAILS
BATTLE OF THE BISMARCK SEA

Background: GAME THEORY - THE CAMPERS
COOPERATION OR DEFECTION

Introductory Problem Solutions

Additional Problems: NUCLEAR CHICKEN
VOLUNTEER'S DILEMMA
THE HUCKSTER
MUTUAL POLLUTION
THREAT GAMES
THIRD DOWN AND SHORT
FAST BALL OR CURVE
ENVIRONMENTAL LOBBYISTS
ACTIVITY - SHUBIK'S DOLLAR AUCTION
ACTIVITY - ITERATIVE PRISONER'S DILEMMA

Self Tests: SELECTED PROBLEMS
EARLY OR LATE

IV. PRISONER'S DILEMMA AND OTHER GAMES

By the term "game theory" is meant something far more important than a friendly game of tennis, golf, basketball, or tiddly-winks. Game theory was the brainchild of John von Neumann who, along with Oskar Morganstern, published the theory in 1943 in their book *Theory of Games and Economic Behavior*. While this book dealt with economic theory, the principles presented have, since then, been applied to war "games," social behavior, international politics, problems of society, and theories of biological evolution. Game theory also has application to our personal lives. Shall we contribute to public television, take the bus to work rather than drive a car, and pitch the next batter high and inside? As a dog owner should I take my poop scoop along when I exercise my dog or is it too much trouble? How long should I stay on hold when I'm trying to complete an important phone call?

Games of this kind are competitive and adversarial. Players are out to maximize their payoffs. Many individuals can play or only two. Groups can play. There can be zero-sum games in which the winnings of one player are taken from the resources of the other. In non-zero sum games all players can win or all can lose. Some games are fair in that each player's chances to "win" are the same while other games are by no means fair. All players are presumed to be equally good game players. No one wins because of the stupidity of an opponent. All players are "cautiously pessimistic," that is, they realize that an opponent is out to maximize his own gain and take advantage of you if that should be possible. There are of course many other strategies that might be employed. This "best of the worst" strategy is just the one the cautiously pessimistic player will normally adopt. It is the one that was used by the young agribusiness executive when he decided to plant hothouse tomatoes rather than soybeans or alfalfa.

In what follows we will concentrate upon two-player games. A *player* may be an individual or a group of individuals. Moreover, just to keep things simple and as straightforward as possible, we will consider that each player has only two game strategies. More complicated games with three or more strategies add to game situations just that, extra complications.

Introductory Problems

PRISONER'S DILEMMA. Prisoner's Dilemma is an old and venerable game. It is as fresh a problem as ever since new applications of the basic idea keep cropping up in unexpected places. The original story goes like this. Two members of a criminal gang are arrested and imprisoned. They are placed in solitary confinement to prevent them from communicating with each other. The district attorney would like to charge them with a recent major crime but at present has insufficient evidence to convict either of them. He does, however, have the evidence to convict each prisoner of a lesser charge. It would seem that his only chance to convict either or both on the major charge is to obtain a confession from one or both of the prisoners. To do this he offers each prisoner a chance to turn state's evidence. If only one prisoner turns state's evidence and testifies against his partner he will go free while the other will receive a sentence of three years. Each prisoner knows that the other has been offered the same proposition. Neither knows, however, what the other decides. The catch is that if both decide to turn state's evidence, they each receive two-year sentences. If both refuse the deal each is imprisoned for one year on the lesser charge. The resulting game matrix is shown below where the first entry in each box is the number of years for A and the second, those for B. What would you do if you were in prisoner A's shoes?

	Prisoner B refuses deal	B turns state's evidence
Prisoner A refuses deal	1 year, 1 year	3 years, 0 years
A turns state's evidence	0 years, 3 years	2 years, 2 years

PRISONER'S
DILEMMA

THE PBS DILEMMA. Member stations in the Public Broadcasting System regularly hold fund drives to support their television programming. Some of their financing comes from other sources of course, but without public support of any kind a station would probably go off the air. During these drives they appeal to individuals to contribute amounts that range upwards from a few dollars. Contributions of $50 or so are strongly suggested. They point out how little this is compared to the costs over a year's time of other forms of entertainment. The station offers a variety of gifts to the potential subscriber, gifts whose value depends upon the size of the donation. Mailing in a pledge means becoming a "member," and this makes for a good feeling for those who do. While some dutifully send in their contributions year after year many do not. Those who do not contribute enjoy the same programming as those who do. For the individual listening to the appeal he or she must decide whether or not to respond. For the PBS station, depending upon the success of the fund drive, their immediate future is cloudy or bright. It is easy for an individual to conclude that the success or failure of the fund drive most certainly will not depend on one person's contribution, or lack of it. Put yourself in the place of a person trying to decide what to do. What would you do, and why? Are you in a game situation? Explain.

CALLING HEADS OR TAILS. J.D. Williams, in his book *The Compleat Strategyst*, describes the experience of a young man named Steve steaming down river on a Mississippi paddle boat of the kind made famous by Mark Twain. Such boats were well known to carry individuals known as riverboat gamblers. One such gambler approached Steve with the following proposition. "Let's match coins," the stranger said. "But I've done a lot of that as a youngster," responded Steve. "But I've got a different version of coin matching that you might find interesting." "Allright, what is it?" The stranger continued "We'll just lie here and speak the words 'heads' or 'tails' rather than actually flipping coins. I'll give you $30 whenever I call 'tails' and you call 'heads' and I'll give you $10 when it's the other way around. Just to make things fair, you give me $20 whenever we match, either with 'heads' or with 'tails'."

Steve ponders the proposition. "Surely something is wrong, but what?" he muses. Steve knows that this is a game situation in the von Neumann sense. Both Steve and the stranger have two strategies, *calling heads* or *calling tails*. The payoffs are shown in the 2X2 matrix below.

		Stranger	
		Calls heads	Calls tails
Steve	Calls heads	- $20	$30
	Calls tails	$10	- $20

CALLING
HEADS OR TAILS

Steve has entered in the matrix the payoffs to him, recognizing that the payoffs to the stranger are just the negatives of the dollar amounts he has entered. In a zero-sum game, which this is, it is always the row players payoffs that are entered. Steve gazes at the game matrix intensely. He still can't see why the game isn't perfectly fair. Can you help Steve to decide whether to play or not, and give him reasons?

BATTLE OF THE BISMARCK SEA. In his book *Game Theory and Politics* Steven J. Brams recounts a famous World War II battle in the Pacific. In February of 1943 the Allies and the Japanese were fighting for control of the island of New Guinea, shown on the accompanying map. At this time the Allies controlled the southern half of the island and the Japanese the northern half. Allied intelligence reports indicated that the Japanese were preparing a troop and supply convoy to reinforce their troops on New Guinea. General Kenney, commander of the Allied Air Forces in the Southwest Pacific Area, knew that in order to get to New Guinea the Japanese convoy would have to sail either to the north or to the south of the island of New Britain (just east of New Guinea). Along the northern route rain and poor visibility (for Allied planes) were expected while along the south coast of New Britain the weather was expected to be

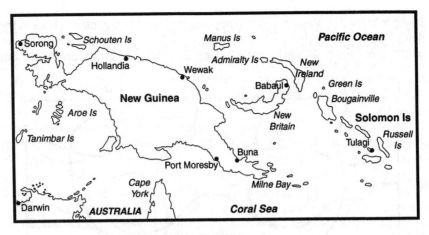

NEW GUINEA

clear and bright. The trip for the Japanese convoy was presumed to take three days no matter if they sailed north or south of New Britain. What Kenney wants, of course, is a maximum number of days of bombing runs for his bombers as the Japanese convoy heads to New Guinea. His orders from General Douglas MacArthur said that he was to inflict maximum damage to the convoy. Kenney, however, had a problem. He had insufficient aircraft to search both to the north and to the south of New Britain. He had to choose whether to search in one direction or the other. He was prepared to invest either half a day in a search to the south or a full day in a search to the north but he couldn't do both. If his aircraft first searched north and the Japanese convoy sailed that way, his planes, after a day's delay because of bad weather in the north, would have 2 days of bombing runs. If, however, the planes first searched north and the convoy had sailed south, there would still be a day's delay in the futile search to the north and with very little further delay would find the convoy in the south and so could inflict nearly two days of bombing. If Kenney's first search was to the south and the convoy had gone north, there would first be a 1/2 day delay in the exhaustive search to the south followed by a 1 day delay in the north giving 1 1/2 days of bombing. Finally, if the first search was to the south and the Japanese had chosen to go south, with little or no delay nearly a full 3 days of bombing would ensue. These figures were then inserted in the payoff matrix as show below.

		Japanese strategies	
		Sail North	Sail South
Kenney's strategies	First search north	2 days	2 days
	First search south	1 1/2 days	3 days

Can you advise both Kenney and the Japanese commander what each should have done and why?

Background

You already have learned something about the construction and use of payoff matrices in 2-person 2-strategy games from the examples that were given above. These ideas will be elaborated in what follows. We once again will use a series of examples with commentary to provide background knowledge that will be useful in finding solutions for the introductory problems and many others as well. You may be surprised to learn that we are all game players of one kind or another. You may be even more surprised to learn that the world's political powers, both large and small, play games whenever they threaten other countries, are engaged in warfare, accept financial and other kinds of aid, incarcerate political prisoners, boycott other countries, impose trade barriers, negotiate trade agreements, form alliances, and engage in international political activity of almost any kind.

THE CAMPERS. As told by J.D. Williams, two campers, Ray and Dotty, plan a hike in the mountains. Ray likes high elevations but Dotty prefers low elevations. Crisscrossing the area they wish to hike are four trails that run more or less in an east-west direction and four more that run mostly north and south.

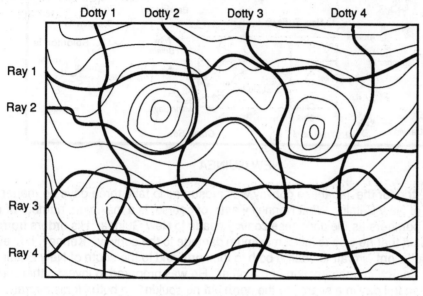

RAY AND DOTTY'S TOPO

As can be seen from the topographic map above Ray's east-west trails intersect Dotty's north-south trails at sixteen locations. The elevations in thousands of feet of the points of intersection are given in the 4X4 matrix below. These numbers are, in essence, payoff utiles to Ray since he prefers high elevations.

	Dotty 1	Dotty 2	Dotty 3	Dotty 4
Ray 1	7	5	2	1
Ray 2	2	3	2	4
Ray 3	5	4	3	4
Ray 4	3	1	2	6

RAY AND DOTTY'S
4X4 MATRIX

Ray is to take one of the E-W trails and Dotty one of the N-S trails. They agree in advance to set up camp wherever the two trails selected cross. They agree further to let game theory decide for them which two trails to take. The answer both seek is the elevation of the place where the two trails they will take intersect, for that will be the elevation of their campsite.

Dotty notices that one of her N-S trails is of no use to her whatsoever. She learns this by comparing the elevations she will encounter at every point of intersection with Ray's trails to the elevations along each of her other trails. This involves six comparisons altogether. In comparing the two trails labelled Dotty 1 and Dotty 3 she finds that the elevations along Dotty 1 are, for every intersection with E-W trails, higher or the same as those along Dotty 3. Since she prefers lower elevations she discards Dotty 1. It is said that strategy Dotty 3 "dominates" Dotty 1 and therefore Dotty 1 is discarded. Ray now does the same in comparing each of his E-W trails with one another. After making all six comparisons he learns that the trail Ray 2 is at every point of intersection with Dotty's N-S trails lower than or the same as the elevations along Ray 3. Since Ray prefers the higher elevations he immediately discards Ray 2 as a possible trail for him. We say that Ray 3 *dominates* Ray 2 and therefore the strategy Ray 2 is discarded. There are no other trails, either Dotty's or Ray's, that dominate any other trail.

Having started with a 4X4 matrix it has now been simplified to one that is 3X3. Checking for dominance is always the first step in the analysis of a game matrix. The simplified camper's matrix now appears as shown below.

	Dotty 2	Dotty 3	Dotty 4	worst:	
Ray 1	5	2	1	1	
Ray 3	4	3	4	3*	best of the worst
Ray 4	1	2	6	1	
worst:	5	3*	6		
		best of the worst			

The payoff matrix in this case is similar to the one encountered by the young executive of the agri-business corporation. Each "player" there, and both Ray and Dotty here, will employ the cautious pessimist strategy, that is, identify the "best of the worst." Ray identifies for each one of his strategies the worst that can happen to him. For him, the worst is the lowest elevation. He enters these elevations to the right of the matrix. Next he identifies the best of all these worst outcomes, and as can be seen to the right of the matrix, this is an outcome of 3000 feet, marked with an asterisk. This occurs for Ray 3.

Dotty does the same. At the bottom of each of her columns she writes down the worst outcome for that column and by "worst" in this case she means the highest elevation in that column. Having done this for all three columns she sees that the best of the worst for her is the elevation of 3 thousand feet. This occurs for her strategy Dotty 3. The best of the worst for Ray gives the same outcome as the best of the worst for Dotty, viz., 3000 feet. Each will settle for this figure and the game is now over. It is the pair of strategies Ray 3 and Dotty 3 that make the elevation of their planned campsite 3000 feet. It isn't always true that the best strategy is a single strategy for each player as it is in this case. We say that the strategies Ray 3 and Dotty 3 are "pure" strategies, strategies for which there is equilibrium. "Equilibrium" means that if Ray were to change strategy in an attempt to get a higher elevation for the campsite, Dotty could immediately change her strategy to take advantage of Ray's change in strategy. Likewise, if Dotty were to change her strategy in order to get a lower elevation for the campsite, Ray could immediately take advantage of Dotty's change to thwart her attempt.

The day before the intended camping trip Ray and Dotty learn that there have been heavy rains in the mountains. Both trails Ray 1 and Dotty 4 have been washed out and closed by the forest service as being too dangerous for hikers. Dotty and Ray are in no mood to scrap their camping plans. Instead they decide to reassess their game situation. What was originally a 4X4 game matrix was reduced to a 3X3 matrix upon identification of two dominance situations. Now the 3X3 matrix has been reduced to a 2X2 matrix because of the rains. The matrix under consideration now is as follows.

	Dotty 2	Dotty 3	worst:	
Ray 3	4	3	3*	
Ray 4	1	2	1	
worst:	4	3*		

Ray notes, having identified the worst outcomes both for himself and for Dotty, that the "best of the worst" strategy for each of them leads to an equilibrium situation with pure strategies Ray 3 and Dotty 3, the same as before. Dotty remarks that the technique used to identify the solution to the problem with the

2X2 matrix is the same as that used when they had a 3X3 matrix. Ray noticed one more thing. His Ray 3 strategy dominated his Ray 2 strategy pointing toward the same result for him as when he looked at the "best of the worst" criterion. For Dotty, however, neither of her strategies dominated the other.

Upon returning from their camping trip Dotty noted that for both the 3X3 and 2X2 matrices with which they had been working before leaving for their camping weekend they had found a pure strategy, a strategy that was stable and therefore resistant to any changes either player might want to impose. Dotty now was playing a game of "what if" when she came upon the following. "What if," she said," it had been the trails Ray 3 and Dotty 3 that had been closed by the storm instead of the ones that were. What then?" The resulting 2X2 game matrix would then be as shown.

		Dotty 2	Dotty 4
		q	1 - q
Ray 1	p	5	1
Ray 4	1 - p	1	6

DOTTY'S
"WHAT IF" MATRIX

Ignoring the p's and the q's in the above for the time being, examine the four payoffs that form the 2X2 matrix. It is not difficult to determine that a pure strategy doesn't exist. The "best of the worst" strategy simply doesn't work. If Dotty uses Dotty 2, a column which gives the best of the worst for her, Ray will immediately adopt Ray 1 to give a payoff of 5000 feet. Seeing this Dotty will immediately shift to Dotty 4 changing the result to 1000 feet. This will be followed by Ray changing strategies to Ray 4 giving a payoff of 6000 feet. It should now be clear that there is no equilibrium solution. The players will continually shift strategies with no end in sight. The above matrix presents Ray and Dotty with something entirely new not previously encountered. One thing seems quite clear. The final agreed upon solution will most likely lie somewhere between 1000 feet and 5000 feet.

What is called for in this case is a *mixed* strategy, i.e., one in which two strategies are played in a certain mix. This means that one strategy is used part of the time and the other another part of the time. More explicitly, Ray plays Ray 1 with a probability of p as indicated in the Ray 1 row, and he plays Ray 4 the rest of the time with a probability 1 - p. Likewise Dotty plays Dotty 2 with a probability q and employs the strategy Dotty 4 with a probability 1 - q. All this of course assumes that this game is to be played over and over again. Ray can't know when Dotty will play one of her strategies for if there were any pattern in her choice of one strategy or another, Ray would be able to pick up on that and use that knowledge against her. Likewise Dotty mustn't be able to detect any pattern in Ray's choice of strategies. The only way to guarantee the avoidance of any pattern is to make the choices totally random while sticking to some particular probability value for each choice. Randomness can be achieved, for example, by selecting a ball from an urn whose color has a probability that is the same as that for the strategy. But what should be the probability values for both p and q? The cautious pessimist strategy dictates that a player should lose (or win) no more when an opponent uses one strategy than when he uses another. This is the key. Ray can do this as follows. If Dotty were to use her strategy Dotty 2, Ray will then use Ray 1 "p" of the time and Ray 4 "1 - p" of the time. The expected value (EV) for Ray becomes

$$5p + 1(1 - p)$$

If on the other hand, Dotty were to use Dotty 4 the expected value for Ray would be

$$1p + 6(1 - p)$$

As a cautious pessimist Ray now sets these two values equal to one another <u>so that he will become indifferent</u> to Dotty's choice of strategies. This gives

$$5p + 1(1 - p) = 1p + 6(1 - p) \quad . \quad . \quad . \quad \text{principle of indifference}$$

so that, after a little algebra, we find that

$$p = 5/9 \quad \text{making} \quad 1 - p = 4/9$$

Dotty makes a similar calculation to determine the best mix of her two strategies. She desires to lose (or win) no more when Ray uses one strategy than when he uses the other. Setting this amount when Ray uses Ray 1 equal to the amount when Ray uses Ray 4 gives

$$5q + 1(1 - q) = 1q + 6(1 - q) \quad . \ . \ . \quad \text{principle of indifference}$$

so that

$$q = 5/9 \quad \text{making} \quad 1 - q = 4/9$$

It is simply an accident that in this case p = q.

As a final step we calculate the EV of the strategy mix for both Ray and Dotty. Plugging the values of p and q back into each of the indifference equations for Ray and Dotty we obtain:

$$EV (Ray) = 29/9 \quad \text{that is} \quad 3{,}222 \text{ feet}$$

and

$$EV (Dotty) = 29/9$$

Both EV's must be the same since both settle for the same elevation. This time the equality is no accident. If this "game" is to be played just once the result of 3,222 feet is of course absurd because the only elevations possible are 1000, 5000, and 6000 feet.

COOPERATION OR DEFECTION. Cooperation or Defection is a label that Poundstone gives to all symmetric 2x2 games. "Symmetric" means that each player has exactly the same preferences as the other. Although there are 24 such games altogether, the more interesting and more important ones are the four games illustrated below. The magnitudes of the payoffs are not meant to represent utiles of each outcome. Their *relative* magnitudes, however, properly indicate the rank-order of the preferences.

Prisoner's Dilemma

	COOPERATE refuse deal	DEFECT state's evidence
COOPERATE refuse deal	^{2}1,1^2	^{4}3,0^1
DEFECT state's evidence	^{1}0,3^4	^{3}2,2^3

payoffs are years in prison

Nuclear Chicken

	COOPERATE accommodating	DEFECT aggressive
COOPERATE accommodating	^{2}2,2^2	^{3}1,3^1
DEFECT aggressive	^{1}3,1^3	^{4}0,0^4

Defection Preferred

	COOPERATE	DEFECT
COOPERATE	^{3}1,1^3	^{4}0,3^1
DEFECT	^{1}3,0^4	^{2}2,2^2

Defection Suspected

	COOPERATE	DEFECT
COOPERATE	^{1}3,3^1	^{4}0,2^2
DEFECT	^{2}2,0^4	^{3}1,1^3

What distinguishes each of these games from the others is the rank-order of the preferred outcomes as indicated for each player by the superscripts. For example, in the Prisoner's Dilemma game, where the payoffs are years in prison, each player prefers to defect when the other player cooperates. Next in order are that both cooperate, both defect, and finally the worst outcome for each player, he cooperates while his opponent defects. These preferences are in the same order for both players.

Although it may be labelled differently, any symmetric game with the same rank-order of preferences as the "Prisoner's Dilemma" game is a Prisoner's Dilemma game. Nuclear Chicken, a game to be encountered as an Additional Problem, is different. The numbers in the boxes for Nuclear Chicken there are not the same as those in the Nuclear Chicken boxes above. Their rank-order, however, is the same. The game called Defection Preferred above (also known as Deadlock) is so named because the Defect strategy for each player dominates the Cooperate strategy. Each player wants to defect. This distinguishes it from the Prisoner's Dilemma game where each player would prefer to Cooperate (refuse the deal) if they could only be assured that the other player would do likewise. The game called Defection Suspected above is more commonly known as Stag. In this game it would seem obvious that each player should Cooperate, but each player, suspecting that the other player will Defect, also defects.

Introductory Problem Solutions

PRISONER'S DILEMMA. <u>RESTATE PROB</u>. What would I do if I were in prisoner A's shoes? As the row player the number of years I would spend in prison for each of the four outcomes of the game are given first and those of prisoner B are given second.

    <u>IDENT STRATEGY</u>. I am concerned only with my own situation. As a cautious player I expect the other prisoner to feel the same way about his situation as I feel about mine. I see that if the other prisoner, whom I know only professionally, refuses the district attorney's deal then I am better off to turn state's evidence because then I will serve no prison time compared to the 1 year in prison if I too refuse the deal. If on the other hand B turns state's evidence, then it is apparent that turning state's evidence is again my best option because in this eventuality I will receive 2 years in prison rather than the 3 years I would get if I refuse the deal. Of course I expect B to be thinking along the same lines and he too will elect to turn state's evidence. The conclusion is that we will both get 2 years of jail time.

    <u>EVAL SOL'N</u>. It would be great to get only a single year, but neither of us trusts the other to a sufficient degree to expect the other to refuse the deal. I therefore turn state's evidence rather than risk 3 years in prison. The "best of the worst" analysis also leads prisoner B to the decision to turn state's evidence.

THE PBS DILEMMA. This is a very real dilemma for every adult who enjoys watching public television. At least once a year a PBS station spends a considerable amount of on-the-air time to conduct a fund raiser.

    <u>CONSIDER EXAMPLE</u>. If 20,000 viewers pledge an average of $50 each the amount raised is $1,000,000. If on the other hand there are 10,000 pledges which average only $25 each, the amount raised is but $250,000. Perhaps not in a single year, but in the long run, the successful fund drive will support excellent programming while the drive with lesser success will lead to mediocre programming. Excellent programming is worth, say, $500 per year for a family of two. Mediocre programming, let us say, is worth only half this amount.

    <u>CREATE GAME MATRIX</u>. Game matrix entries below are payoffs to a single viewing family.

	Few contribute raise $250,000 mediocre programming	Many contribute raise $1,000,000 excellent programming	THE PBS DILEMMA
You contribute $50	$200	$450 [*]	
You do not contribute	$250	$500	

In the top row of this matrix, when you contribute $50 the net value to you for mediocre programming is the $250 it is worth minus the $50 you contributed and for excellent programming the net value is the $500 it is worth minus your contribution of $50. A potential contributor does not know how successful a fund drive will be. Will it raise $1,000,000 or only $250,000 just to mention some concrete figures?

ASSESS STRATEGY. In either case his contribution will hardly matter to the PBS station. If the potential contributor does not send in a $50 contribution he is $50 better off no matter how much money is raised. It would seem that this is his better strategy. However, notice the asterisk in the upper right hand box in the matrix. This represents the personal satisfaction (difficult to put in terms of dollars and cents) the contributor might have in making a contribution to excellent programming. This factor makes the contribution option the preferable one for many individuals willing to take the risk that many others will also wish to make the same or a similar contribution.

CONCLUSION. For an even greater number of viewers, however, the asterisk means little or nothing. Hence these individuals choose to view but not to contribute. The dilemma is resolved only by noting the presence or absence of a little asterisk.

CALLING HEADS OR TAILS. IDENT RELATED GAME. The game of Calling Heads or Tails is quite different than the game of matching or not matching when each of two players flips a coin. Betting on a *match* means betting on both players flipping heads or both flipping tails. Betting on *no match* means betting that one player will flip a head while the other player tosses a tail. As is well known, for a single toss of the two players, each has a 50 percent chance of winning.

RECAP PROB. In Calling Heads or Tails, by contrast, each player can call whatever result he wants to, either heads or tails, without actually having to flip a coin. He could call heads always, at least for a time before the other player catches on to what he is doing, or he could call tails always. He might even call heads half the time and tails half the time. A final possibility is to call heads and tails in some proportion other than 1:1.

ANALYSE GAME. Steve should definitely not play this game with the Stranger. To understand the reasons for this, consider once again the game matrix as proposed by the stranger.

		Stranger	
		Calls heads	Calls tails
Steve	Calls heads	- $20	$30
	Calls tails	$10	- $20

Recall that the entries in the matrix are payoffs to Steve. Negatives of these entries are payoffs to the Stranger. What makes the Stranger's proposition sound somewhat reasonable is the fact that if both Steve and the Stranger were to call heads and call tails just half the time on average, then the game is quite fair with each player winning half the time in the long run. Since Steve is worried that the Stranger might somehow take advantage of him, suppose, just to play it safe, that Steve plays a 50:50 strategy just to see what the Stranger might do. If the Stranger learns what Steve is doing he is sure to call heads all the time, at least until Steve changes his strategy. In this way the stranger will win $20 just as often as loses $10. Yes, the Stranger can take advantage. Because of this Steve abandons (in his mind) the 50:50 strategy in favor of a strategy in which he calls tails somewhat more often than he calls heads. In this way he will lose $20 to the stranger less often than he wins $10. Steve presumes that if he can find the right mix for calling heads and calling tails he may be able to hold his own with the Stranger *provided* the stranger sticks to his "all heads" strategy. Steve is quite sure that the Stranger will find some other strategy to play that gives him an advantage. At this point Steve's head begins to spin. Since he is not sure whether he has an even chance in this game, he says no to the Stranger, he would rather not play. He is quite sure that he has no chance of winning in the long run, otherwise the Stranger would never have suggested the game in the first place.

IDENT STRATEGY. When Steve learned the lesson from Dotty's "what if" matrix he was able to determine that he should use a mixed strategy when playing the Stranger. He should play the strategy *call heads* 3/8 of the time and the strategy *call tails* 5/8 of the time. He also learns that the stranger should play *call heads* 5/8 of the time and *call tails* 3/8 of the time. Steve's expected value turns out to be - 5/4 and that for the Stranger +5/4. No wonder the Stranger was so anxious to play.

BATTLE OF THE BISMARCK SEA. <u>RESTATE PROB</u>. Here we are to advise each side in the Battle of the Bismarck Sea how they should have deployed their forces, not only to take maximum advantage of the other, but at the same time permit the other side to gain the least possible advantage. Waging war by hindsight is undoubtedly the best way to wage war because countries would then only be refighting old wars and not any new ones. To give such advice another look at the game matrix is needed.

	Japanese strategies		worst for the Allies:
	sail north	sail south	
first search north	2 days	2 days	2*
first search south	1 1/2 days	3 days	1 1/2
worst for the Japanese:	2*	3	

Kenney's strategies (label at left of rows)

IDENT STRATEGY. Suppose each game player adopts a conservative strategy which aims only to minimize the damage your opponent can inflict upon your forces. You assume that the other side is your equal when it comes to identifying the best possible strategy to accomplish their purpose. Upon inspection of the payoff matrix Kenney sees at once that he can inflict a greater number of days of bombing upon the Japanese fleet if he decides to search first in the north. His reason: His planes are able to make approximately 2 days of bombing runs no matter which way the Japanese have sailed. On the other hand, if his planes were to search first in the south, there would be only 1 1/2 days of bombing if the Japanese convoy sailed north and nearly 3 days of bombing if the Japanese sailed south. The Japanese commander knows all this and consequently is sure not to sail south. He settles for 2 days of bombing runs which is the best he can do. His strategy therefore is for his convoy to sail north knowing that the bombers would first attempt to find the convoy there.

RECAPITULATION. The stratetgies for both the Allies and the Japanese can be described in more general terms as "best of the worst" strategies. Alongside the payoff matrix to the right of each row are the worst payoffs for the Allies, a tie at 2 days should they decide to first search north and 1 1/2 days should they decide to first search south. The best of these two values for the Allies is 2 days of bombing, marked with an asterisk. Making a similar calculation the Japanese commander figures his own best of the worst outcomes. These figures are at the bottom of each column. They indicate that 2 days of bombing is also the best of the worst for him. This leads to the strategies of *first search north* for Kenney and *sail north* for the Japanese giving 2 days of bombing. This is the best each side can do. This was by no means a "fair" game.

66

Additional Problems

*NUCLEAR CHICKEN. The original game of chicken involved two teen-age drivers speeding their cars directly toward one another. The "game" was to see who would swerve his car thus avoiding a head-on collision. The driver who swerved his car to avoid a head-on collision was "chicken." Each driver had two strategies, to swerve or not to swerve. This provides us with a two-person dilemma game. If both swerved simultaneously then both are chicken but both survive. If one decides to swerve and the other does not, again they both survive but only one is "chicken." Disaster strikes when both drivers, fearing to be called chicken, decide not to swerve. This game, as idiotic as it seems, has its counterpart in the field of international relations. Suppose two countries are in conflict and each chooses either to use nuclear weapons or to not use such weapons. Call a country choosing to use nuclear weaponry the aggressor, and the country that chooses not to do so the country that accommodates. If both countries choose to accommodate (the status quo), let the payoff have utilities 0,0. If one country is aggressive and the other accommodates, that is, becomes a "nuclear chicken," let the aggressor be awarded 1 utile and the country that backs down a utility of - 2 due to possible strategic, diplomatic, and trade losses. If neither backs down and both become aggressors, there is nuclear disaster giving a joint score of -10, -10. Create the payoff matrix for the game of nuclear chicken involving countries A and B. Then play the game and state your reasons for choosing one strategy over another. Your matrix should be a symmetric 2x2 in the Cooperate/Defect family.

VOLUNTEER'S DILEMMA. In 1964 one of the more dreadful murders in New York City history occurred. Kitty Genovese was being attacked as she screamed for help within earshot of 38 neighbors who stood idly by. Kitty died while none of those neighbors ran to her aid, none called the police — nobody did anything. To be or not to be a sole volunteer in some relatively dangerous situation is a fairly frequent occurrence, thus the name "volunteer's dilemma," a label used by Poundstone to apply to this kind of game. In a volunteer's dilemma the game is played by an individual against a group of individuals. In fact, the game is the multi-person version of the game of chicken. This analogy should help you to identify utiles to enter into the game matrix shown below. Having done so, then determine, as an individual, what strategy you might have selected in the rape and murder situation alluded to above.

	At least one person volunteers	Everyone says let someone else do it
You volunteer		
You say, let someone else do it		

VOLUNTEER'S DILEMMA

*THE HUCKSTER. This is the story of Merrill, as he was called by J.D. Williams in *The Compleat Strategyst.* In Rubinstein's *Patterns of Problem Solving* he was referred to simply as a "student."
In any case, he had the concession for selling sunglasses and umbrellas at all of Michigan's home football games at Ann Arbor. This was a good business opportunity since the stadium seats more than 100,000 people. Because of last year's experience Merrill has learned that he can sell about 500 umbrellas when it rains. When the weather is sunny he can sell about 100 umbrellas and, in addition, about 1000 pair of sunglasses. Umbrellas that cost him $1.00 he sells for $2.00. Sunglasses that cost him 40 cents he sells for $1.00. He has $500 to invest prior to each game. Thus, if Merrill thinks it will rain he invests his $500 in 500 umbrellas and, if it does rain, he sells them all at $2 each for a profit of $500.

On the other hand if he thinks it will be sunny he invests $100 in 100 umbrellas and $400 in 1000 pair of sunglasses. If the day turns out to be sunny he sells all of the umbrellas and all of the sunglasses for a profit of $100 for the umbrellas and $600 for the sunglasses. However, if he buys for rain and it shines instead, he will sell only 100 of the 500 umbrellas he has purchased taking in only $200 for his $500 investment. If he buys for shine and it rains he will sell all the umbrellas and none of the sunglasses, again taking in only $200. A condition imposed by his supplier is that he must return all unsold merchandise with no refund. Treating the weather as a game player and making the gross assumption that it can only rain or shine on Saturday, Merrill's opponent (the weather) has the two strategies, Rain and Shine. Likewise, Merrill has two strategies and these are to Buy for Rain and Buy for Shine. Merrill creates for himself the following game matrix where the entries are profits.

		States of Nature		
		Rain	Shine	
	Rain	$500	- $300	RAIN OR SHINE
Merrill buys for				
	Shine	- $300	$700	

After inspecting the game matrix Merrill learns that there is no pure strategy he can use. He proceeds to determine the probability with which he should buy for rain and the probability with which he should buy for shine. Determine these probabilities for yourself and then determine, using these figures, how much Merrill can expect to profit, on average, during each home football game.

Merrill realizes that he can't buy for rain or for shine with mixed strategies for a single game. He therefore decides to invest in rainy day goods that fraction of his $500 investment which is the probability for buying for rain, and he invests in sunny-day goods that fraction of the $500 which is the probability found for buying for shine. If he does this, what is his expected profit no matter what the weather.

*MUTUAL POLLUTION. Henry Hamburger in *Games as Models of Social Phenomena* describes the game of mutual pollution. Two cities border a lake. Each city has been dumping its garbage into the lake for many years as this was the cheapest method of disposing of it. The manager of one of the cities estimated that it would cost his town $30,000 per year to create a landfill for its garbage. The manager of the other city agreed that this amount would also be required to create a landfill for his city. The parks department supervisor of one of the towns estimated that his town could create about $20,000 per year in recreational value (swimming and boating) if his city stopped polluting the lake with its garbage and double this figure if the other city were to stop polluting the lake as well. Both city managers agreed with these figures. Letting each utile represent $10,000 the payoffs in the game matrix become:

		City B		
		uses landfill	dumps into lake	
City A	uses landfill	1,1	-1,2	MUTUAL POLLUTION
	dumps into lake	2,-1	0,0	

Is there a pure strategy for playing this game and if so what is it? As an environmentalist would you like to see a change in the way this game is played? If so, how would you change it?

It is of interest to compare the preference order for mutual pollution with the preference orders for the Cooperate/Defect games described in the Background section. You will find that it is in fact a Prisoner's Dilemma game.

THREAT GAMES. Threat games arise whenever one country threatens another, for example, with an embargo on goods, with the use of biological warfare, with the killing or keeping of political prisoners from the other country, with not returning prisoners of war either dead or alive, or with bombing the oil fields of the other country. A professor can also threaten his students with the possibility of a pop quiz. The possible use of threat is illustrated starting with the game matrix below.

Country S

		S_1	S_2
Country R	R_1	4, 1	2, 3
	R_2	2, - 2	0, 0

THREAT GAME

As can be observed, there are dominant strategies for this game which are R_1 and S_2 with payoffs 2,3. Country R now begins to threaten S with a possible shift from R_1 to strategy R_2. For country S this would mean loss of 3 utiles. But this of course is not what country R really wants. What do you suppose this is and how can country R manage to get it? As another example of a threat game consider a kidnapping situation. So long as the kidnappers do not kill their hostage and the demanded ransom goes unpaid, the situation is in equilibrium — there is a stalemate. But now the kidnappers threaten to kill their hostage, an outcome that nobody wants. What do the kidnappers hope to achieve with this threat?

*THIRD DOWN AND SHORT. In National Football League (NFL) action the Redskins are playing the Niners and the Skins have the football on the Niner's 40 yard line. It is third down and short. Many in the stands know it is somewhat more likely for the Redskins to run the ball than to pass in the hope of getting a first down. Of course San Francisco knows this also. In this kind of situation the Redskins can't always run and they can't always pass for to do either would mean that their strategy would be predictable. The Niners could then better defend against whatever this consistent strategy might be. What the Skins will do, and this will depend not only on the talents of their own players but upon those of the San Francisco defenders as well, is to run the ball part of the time and pass it part of the time. With payoffs expressed as probabilities for the Skins to make first down, let the game matrix for Third Down and Short be as shown below.

San Francisco

		defend the run	defend the pass
Washington	run	0.5	0.8
	pass	0.7	0.2

RUN OR PASS

What is the probability that Washington will run the ball? pass the ball? What is the probability that Washington will make first down?

FAST BALL OR CURVE. Abner Smith is on the mound facing the number four batter in the opponent's lineup, Jose Gonzales. Abner has to decide with each pitch whether to throw a fast ball (F) or a curve (C). These are his only two pitches. When Jose is expecting a fast ball (EF) his batting percentage is .500 but against a curve ball is only .100. When Jose is expecting a curve (EC) and he gets a curve his batting percentage is .400, while if a fast ball is thrown instead his percentage drops to .200. Of course Abner knows that he must mix up his pitches. With what probability should he throw a fast ball and with what probability should he throw his curve ball? All season long Abner faces Jose and each time he uses the same mix of his two pitches. What batting average should Jose have against Abner by season's end?

ENVIRONMENTAL LOBBYISTS. In Washington there are lobbyists promoting almost every conceivable cause and on occasion an equal number opposing those same causes. Environmental legislation is just one such issue of many. Environmentalists are sponsoring two pieces of legislation. One would protect old growth forest watershed, the other the habitat of wildlife in riverside riparian areas. Anti-environmentalists are vehemently opposed to both these pieces of legislation. The payoffs in the "game" between the two sides depends on many factors such as the effectiveness of arguments, both pro and con, and the resources assigned to the causes on both sides. A fraction of the resources of the environmentalists will go to support one of these pieces of legislation and the balance will support the other. Similarly, for the anti-environmentalists, they must divide their resources in fighting both pieces of legislation. Suppose the payoffs for each side are the utiles listed in the game matrix below.

		Anti-environmentalists	
ENVIRONMENTAL LOBBYISTS		against protection of old growth forest watershed q	against protection or riverside riparian areas $1 - q$
Environmentalists	protect old growth forest watershed p	4,2	8,5
	protect riverside riparian areas $1 - p$	6,7	3,3

It is apparent from the matrix that no pure strategy is available to either side indicating that an allocation of resources must be made. Determine the mix for the environmentalists and also for the anti-environmentalists. Also calculate the expected value (EV) of the game for the environmentalists and for the anti-environmentalists.

ACTIVITY — SHUBIK'S DOLLAR AUCTION. Martin Shubik of the Rand Corporation spent a certain amount of his time devising new and unusual games. One of the questions he asked himself was whether addiction could be incorporated in a game. This was the question that led to the dollar auction. The dollar auction game is advertised as a simple but amusing parlor game in which a dollar bill is auctioned off subject to the following two rules.

1. As in any auction the dollar bill goes to the highest bidder who pays whatever his high bid is. Each new bid has to be some minimum amount higher than the last (10 cents for example). The bidding stops after there is no new bid within a specified time limit.

2. Unlike any other kind of auction, however, the second highest bidder also has to pay the amount of his last bid and he gets nothing in return. Yes, nothing! No one wants to be the second highest bidder.

This is a game that really has to be played to appreciate how wild things can get. Dollar bills have been known to be auctioned for amounts in the $3 to $5 dollar range. Play the game at least once to see what kind of bidding takes place. Then analyse the game to determine what persuades people to get involved. Games can not only be analysed through the use of payoff matrices, they can also be played and analysed using an appropriate tree structure. Limit your analysis to the behavior at some point in the bidding of the second-high bidder, the one who at the moment has the amount of his bid to lose and nothing to gain. Suppose he bids, say, 10¢ more than the present high bid and 20¢ more than his own second-high bid. How much does he stand to lose and how much might he win? Recognize that his situation changes and becomes more interesting as bidding proceeds from less than a dollar to more than a dollar. How does such a player become attracted to the game? What might induce him to bid again? How can he extricate himself once in the position of being the second-high bidder?

70

ACTIVITY — ITERATIVE PRISONERS' DILEMMA. To "iterate" a Prisoner's Dilemma game means to play it over and over. Rather than use the Prisoner's Dilemma game itself, where the payoffs are years in prison, use a Cooperate/Defect game with positive rather than negative payoffs, and with the same rank-ordering of preferences. To play the game each player selects one of his two strategies without the other player knowing what that is. They then reveal their selections simultaneously and each player is then credited with the payoffs in the appropriate box.

COOPERATE OR DEFECT	B cooperates	B defects
A cooperates	2,2	0,3
A defects	3,0	1,1

In 1980 Robert Axlerod, professor of political science at the University of Michigan, conducted a competition to determine who could devise the best strategy for playing this game in an iterative way, i.e., over and over. The winner was Anatol Rapoport, who had submitted the simplest and most effective strategy. The winning strategy was: Cooperate on the first round, then do whatever the other player did on the previous round.

Find a column player willing to play 100 consecutive games with you. Without telling your friend anything about your strategy, play Rapoport's TIT FOR TAT strategy. Suggest to your friend strategies he might use. For example, he could always defect or he could always cooperate. Then again he might mix these two strategies randomly according to the toss of a coin. A final possibility for him is to analyse your strategy as play develops and try to devise a strategy of his own to counter it. Keep a record of both your scores and those of your friend to determine the effectiveness of the TIT FOR TAT strategy compared to whatever strategy your friend has come up with. For scoring, use the points shown above in the Cooperate or Defect matrix.

Chapter IV Self Test—Selected Problems

1. NUCLEAR CHICKEN. Four payoff matrices are shown below. Circle the one that is described in the statement of the problem.

(a)

	swerve	drive straight
swerve	0, 0	1,-2
drive straight	-2, 1	-10,-10

(b)

	swerve	drive straight
swerve	0, 0	1,-2
drive straight	-10,-10	-2, 1

(c)

	swerve	drive straight
swerve	0, 0	-2, 1
drive straight	1,-2	-10,-10

(d)

	swerve	drive straight
swerve	0, 0	-10,-10
drive straight	1,-2	-2, 1

2. MUTUAL POLLUTION. In this game

(a) "uses landfill" dominates "dumps into lake."

(b) "dumps into lake" dominates "uses landfill."

(c) neither strategy dominates the other.

Circle the best response.

3. THREAT GAMES. In this game there is a pure strategy for each country which points to the outcome R_1,S_2.

(a) R's threat is to shift to R_2 producing the outcome R_2,S_2.

(b) R really wants outcome R_1,S_1.

(c) Both of the above are true.

Circle the best response.

4. THIRD DOWN AND SHORT. In this game the Skins should run 5/8 of the time and pass 3/8 of the time. Assuming San Francisco defends the way it should, the probability that Washington will make first down is ______________________

5. ENVIRONMENTAL LOBBYISTS. In this problem p = 3/7 and q = 2/7. For which side is the value of the game greater? ______________________ or are the EV's the same? ______________

Chapter IV Self Test — EARLY OR LATE

Henry is a house-husband, temporarily out of work, married to Angela who, as an attorney in a large firm, is paid quite well. Today is Angela's birthday and Henry has agreed to pick her up in his car at the entrance to her office building at 6:00 pm. They have planned a dinner out and a show afterward. It is a stormy day, and rain mixed with snow is falling. If Henry arrives early and Angela is late he will have to drive around the block one or more times since there is no place to park. He rates this circumstance for himself as a -2. If, on the other hand, Angela arrives early and he is late, she will get cold and wet waiting. Henry estimates this as a utility for him of -3. If they are both early its worth +1 for Henry because he would like a little extra time for dinner before the show. If they are both late Henry rates it at -1.

Angela

		early	late
early p		+1	- 2
late 1 - p		- 3	- 1

Henry

Note: Angela's values
are not presumed to
to be known.

With what probability should Henry arrive early? _____

With what probability should he arrive late? _____

What is the value of the game for Henry? _____

V. THE KNIGHT'S TOUR AND OTHER GRAPHS

Introductory Problems: KÖNIGSBERG BRIDGES PROBLEM
                             THE SWISS POSTMAN
                             TRAFFIC SIGNAL MAINTENANCE
                             ARCHITECTURAL PROBLEM

Background: EULER CIRCUITS
                             HAMILTONIAN CIRCUITS
                             CRITICAL PATH ANALYSIS
                             BRACING SUBGRAPHS

Introductory Problem Solutions

Additional Problems: THE CHINESE POSTMAN PROBLEM
                             RECTANGULAR STREET NETWORKS
                             THE TRAVELING SALESMAN PROBLEM
                             MODEL HOME BUILDING
                             WINE BOTTLES PROBLEM
                             THE KNIGHT'S TOUR
                             CANNIBALS AND MISSIONARIES
                             BRACING A 3X3 GRID
                             ACTIVITY—CONSTRUCT A CROSSBRACING MODEL
                             ACTIVITY—FIND ALL THE HAMILTONIAN CIRCUITS

Self Tests: SELECTED PROBLEMS
                             EULERIZING THE TOWN

V. THE KNIGHT'S TOUR AND OTHER GRAPHS

In our work in problem solving up to this point there have been a number of opportunities to employ visual representations to aid in problem analysis. In Chapter III, for example, decision trees were used to clarify decision alternatives. Chapter IV included the use of square or rectangular arrangements of outcomes called *matrices*. Matrix elements are due both to actions and circumstances. In the present chapter the use of pictures and diagrams is extended, becoming a more important tool in problem analysis. In the chapter to follow the present one visual aids and visual thinking are presented as important if not crucial parts of the analysis of a wide variety of problems.

"Graphs," as the term is used in this chapter, are geometric arrangements of points called *vertices* and connecting lines referred to as *edges*. A decision tree is simply a special kind of graph. Other kinds of graphs are useful in the analysis of social relationships, in the description of molecular structures, and in the analysis of traffic problems. Graphs serve to organize our thinking, to impose structure on a problem in a way that will help us find a problem solution.

Introductory Problems

KÖNIGSBERG BRIDGES PROBLEM. Graph theory was born when a Swiss mathematician named Leonhard Euler (pronounced "oiler") solved the problem of the Königsberg Bridges. It is said that the people of Königsberg amused themselves by trying to devise a walking path around their city which would cross each of their seven bridges once and only once and return them to their starting point. As it happened no one ever found such a path and so people naturally suspected that no such path existed. This problem came to the attention of Euler and he subsequently published his solution in *Commentarii Academiae Scientiarum Imperialis Petropolitanae*. In short, he was able to prove that it was impossible to devise a path that crossed each of the bridges only once. First, he drew a sketch of the town labelling the four land masses as A, B, C, and D and the seven bridges a, b, c, d, e, f, and g. This is shown below.

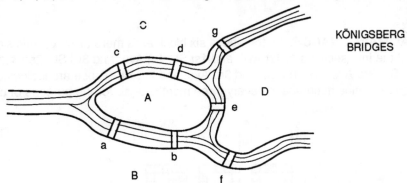

KÖNIGSBERG
BRIDGES

Euler than simplified this picture by drawing a graph with the four land masses represented by vertices and the seven bridges by edges which connect the land masses. This produced the following graph.

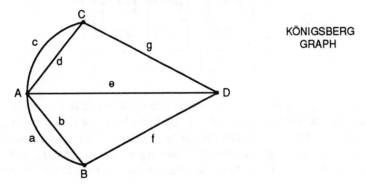

KÖNIGSBERG
GRAPH

At this point the Königsberg Bridges Problem is "set up" and ready for analysis. Euler started by representing the walking trip as a sequence of the land mass letters A, B, C, and D. Between adjacent letters, of course, a bridge is crossed. He then noted that land mass A has 5 bridges crossing into it or out of it and the other land masses 3 such bridges. The final question he asked himself was how many appearances of each land mass letter did there have to be in the sequence of letters. With this beginning you may now be able to complete a proof that the Konigsberg Bridges problem has no solution.

THE SWISS POSTMAN. This problem is called the "Swiss" postman problem in honor of Euler, who was a native of Switzerland. The Swiss postman desires perfection in his route as he delivers mail. For him "perfection" means that as he delivers mail to every address in his territory he never has to backtrack. He finds a route which will carry him past all the houses on his route once and only once. He starts at a certain point and completes his route at the same point. Consider the six square block area of row houses shown below. The shading indicates houses which receive mail. Ignore the steps taken in crossing the street at intersections. Can you find a route for the postman that will take him past every row of houses once and only once and end up, if not where he started, then at some other location? To begin with let each street intersection be a vertex of a graph and each row of houses an edge.

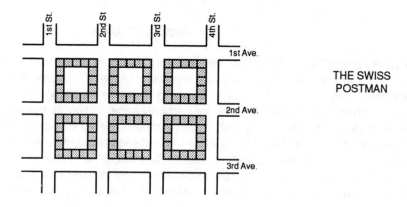

THE SWISS
POSTMAN

TRAFFIC SIGNAL MAINTENANCE. In the above six block area there are six traffic signals that hang over the middle of the intersections at 1st Ave. and 1st St., 1st Ave. and 3rd St., 2nd Ave. and 2nd St., 2nd Ave. and 4th St., 3rd Ave. and 1st St., and 3rd Ave. and 3rd St. These are indicated by a ¤. The traffic signals require routine maintenance every three months or so for the purpose of cleaning and

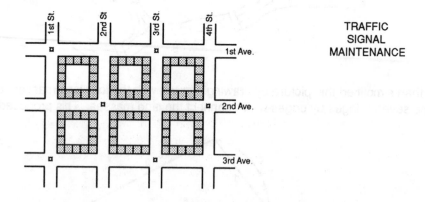

TRAFFIC
SIGNAL
MAINTENANCE

replacement of broken glass lenses. A maintenance truck would like to move from light to light along a path that encounters each of the traffic lights once and only once and without traversing any street more than once. Can you sketch a satisfactory route for the driver? Suppose now that the town council decides there should be a flashing yellow light over a pedestrian crossing at the half block on 2nd Ave. between 1st and 2nd Streets. How does this change the situation for the maintenance truck?

ARCHITECTURAL PROBLEM. An architectural problem is presented by Kappraff that has been adapted from the work of Baglivo, Graver, Bolker, and Crapo. It is this. An architect wishes to use a rectangular grid of squares as part of an overall design project. Each side of a square consists of a steel beam which is pin-jointed at each end to the other beams. A pin-joint permits rotation about it. The problem is to make the entire grid completely rigid with each square lying in a single plane. To make things relatively simple consider a set of six squares in three rows and two columns. This requires seventeen beams and twelve pins.

As you can well imagine, with each beam free to rotate about the pins at both ends, this arrangement is easily distorted. To make the grid rigid the architect must include in his design a number of crossbraces that extend diagonally from one corner of a square to the opposite corner. This crossbrace is also pinned at each end. A crossbrace makes the square that it spans completely rigid. The reason for this is that it forms two triangles each of which is a figure that cannot be deformed by rotation about any of the vertices. The basic design problem is simply this. With no crossbracing the arrangement of beams distorts easily in many different ways. With a crossbrace across each of the six squares it seems quite clear that a rigid plane structure results. But can *fewer* than six crossbraces be used and if so, what is the least number that will do the job and where must these be placed? How many different arrangements are there for their placement in the six squares?

This is a problem in graph theory. Each of the seventeen beams that form the six squares can be thought of as edges which connect the twelve pins which are the vertices. Each crossbrace adds another edge between vertices. The one constraint present in all figures below as they are being distorted is that each of the four beams that started as a square must remain a rhombus, i.e., an equal-sided parallelogram of which a square is a special case. As noted earlier, a crossbrace makes the square whose diagonal it spans perfectly rigid. These squares are indicated by bolder lines in the figures below. As can be seen, even with three crossbraces placed as shown these are insufficient to make the entire grid a rigid rectangle.

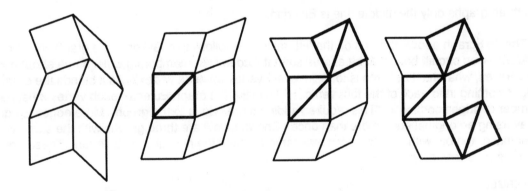

Inspection of the four distorted figures reveals that all have one thing in common. All of the more vertical edges in a row are parallel to one another. This goes for row 1, row 2, and row 3, and is equally true for each of the four figures. In addition, all of the more horizontal edges in each column are parallel to one another. This is true for both the first column and the second in each of the four distorted figures. The next step is to draw a 2x3 grid (two columns by three rows) with four crossbraces located somewhere in the six squares. Can such bracing make the entire grid a rigid plane? Or are five crossbraces required, or even six? Can you convince yourself that for your solution all squares must form a rigid rectangular network? Use the observation about the parallelism of the more vertical edges in each row and the parallelism of the more horizontal edges in each column to persuade yourself that your proposed solution is in fact a solution to the architect's problem.

Background

A graph is simply a collection of points and lines. These lines, or edges, always terminate in a point called a vertex. Vertices may have any number of edges coming in including zero. In a so-called digraph (short for "directed graph") the edges have a direction indicated by an arrowhead. Trees are graphs that contain no loops. There are also "signed" graphs meaning that edges are assigned either a + sign or a - sign. Properties of graphs are selected to model the particular situation being analyzed.

Eulerian graphs. Eulerian graphs are those for which it is possible to find a path along the edges of a graph such that every edge is traversed once <u>and the path ends at the vertex from which it started.</u> Euler was the first to identify a foolproof way to determine for a graph whether or not this is possible. The test involves the concept of the *degree* of a vertex. The degree is simply the number of edges coming into the vertex. A degree one vertex is one that has but one edge, degree two vertices have two edges, etc. Euler was able to prove that if all vertices of a graph are of even-numbered degree, then the graph is Eulerian. If one or more vertices are of odd degree then it is not possible to find a path that traces all edges once and returns to the vertex where it started. Using this simple rule it is possible to predict without resorting to trial and error whether the following graphs are or are not Eulerian.

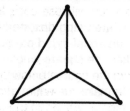 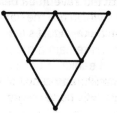 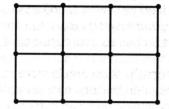

Of these three graphs only the middle one is Eulerian.

The first graph above, the one on the left, raises the following question. The graph does not contain an Eulerian circuit, but can it be altered so that it does? Remembering Euler's rule about even and odd vertices, what must be done is to make every vertex an even vertex? As it stands the graph has three edges coming in to each of the four vertices. To make the graph Eulerian each vertex must have an even number of edges coming in. This requires adding more edges to the graph. More edges is equivalent to traversing an original edge more than once. Shown below are three graphs with the same vertices as the original graph but with reused edges that serve to make the new graphs Eulerian. These are referred to as *Eulerized* graphs.

EULERIZED
GRAPHS

 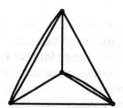 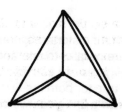

Hamiltonian Graphs. The Irish mathematician Hamilton took a different tack. Instead of asking whether one could traverse all the edges of a graph to make a circuit without repeating any edge, he asked whether one could identify a path that would <u>visit each vertex</u> of a graph once and only once *and* <u>wind up back where one started.</u> Hamilton's problem may seem like a minor variation of Euler's problem, but the change has significant consequences. Most importantly, Hamiltonian circuits (we could have referred to Eulerian graphs as having Eulerian *circuits*) have far more applications than Eulerian circuits. Although Hamiltonian circuits are confined to the edges of a graph, not all edges need to be traversed.

For example, consider the three graphs shown previously to illustrate Eulerian circuits. All edges of these graphs are not shown below. What is shown is a Hamiltonian circuit that each of these graphs contains.

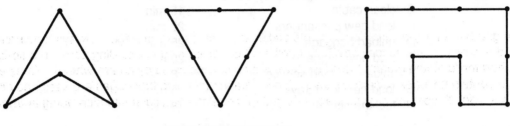

HAMILTONIAN CIRCUITS

Identification of the Hamiltonian circuits in the above was made by trial and error. For the graph at the left there are similar Hamiltonian circuits that are not shown. How many are there altogether? For the graph at the right there is at least one more Hamiltonian circuit not shown. How many are there altogether?

The determination in advance whether a given graph contains a Hamiltonian circuit or not cannot be made by the application of some rule as was the case for Eulerian circuits. If such a rule exists that applies to every conceivable graph no one has as yet found it. For certain special classes of Hamiltonian graphs, however, there are such rules. If a Hamiltonian circuit cannot be found for a particular graph, no matter how hard or how long one has tried, it may still be possible that one exists. For quite complicated graphs computer methods can often find Hamiltonian circuits if there are any. Such methods, however, do not prove that all such circuits can be found.

For graphs that contain more than one Hamiltonian circuit there remains a most interesting question. Which Hamiltonian circuit is the shortest? Consider a graph with four vertices where each pair of vertices is connected by an edge (6 edges in all). This graph is an asymmetrical version of the one at the left above. Each of the three Hamiltonian circuits for such a graph are shown below. As before, two of the edges are not shown. The total path length of the four edges that make up the circuit is different for each of the three circuits. To determine the circuit of shortest length one needs only to measure the four distances in each case, add the results, and then compare this to the totals for the other circuits.

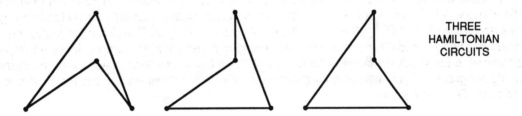

THREE HAMILTONIAN CIRCUITS

In the above it is a simple matter to identify which Hamiltonian circuit of the three is the shortest. For a circuit with a great many vertices, however, the problem becomes entirely different, one that can't be solved exactly even with computer techniques. Thus Hamiltonian circuits are not only impossible to identify in general, but once identified, the shortest of the Hamiltonian circuits cannot always be found.

Critical Path Analysis. Think of a situation in which a number of operations must be performed to complete a certain job. For example, a passenger plane flies from Los Angeles into Logan Airport at Boston. It is to turn around and as quickly as possible take off for Chicago. To accomplish this the Boston bound passengers must be unloaded, their baggage must be unloaded, the cabin must be cleaned, the aircraft must be fueled, the old food trays must be taken off the plane, new food brought on board, the Chicago bound passengers loaded, and the Chicago bound luggage loaded. Altogether this is eight operations, call them operations A through H. Four different groups handle these responsibilities: the baggage handlers, the cleaning personnel, the flight attendants, and the personnel who fuel the plane. Suppose that the times required for each of the eight operations are as follows:

Operation	Time
A: unload passengers	13 min
B: clean cabin	15 min
C: load new passengers	27 min
D: unload baggage	25 min
E: load new baggage	22 min
F: unload old food service	8 min
G: load new food trays	5 min
H: fuel the aircraft	18 min

Certain operations must be completed before the next can be started whether it's the same crew doing the work or not. From this we can draw a flow diagram for all the operations and label the required times as well.

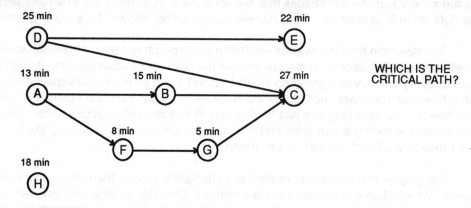

In this case we have a digraph whose arrows indicate the operations to be completed before another can be begun. Recall that what is desired is the least time for all these operations to be completed. The *least time* comes from that path of *greatest time* and then, only if this path is executed without any time gap between operations. (Think about this statement). Adding the time figures on the graph we see that each of the paths through the digraph requires the following total times:

$$D \rightarrow E \ldots \ldots \ldots \ldots \ldots 47 \text{ min}$$
$$D \rightarrow C \ldots \ldots \ldots \ldots \ldots 52 \text{ min}$$
$$A \rightarrow B \rightarrow C \ldots \ldots \ldots \ldots 55 \text{ min}$$
$$A \rightarrow F \rightarrow G \rightarrow C \ldots \ldots \ldots 53 \text{ min}$$
$$H \ldots \ldots \ldots \ldots \ldots \ldots 18 \text{ min}$$

These total times assume that there is no time interval between any of the tasks. From the above it seems clear that 55 minutes is the best that can be done given the times assumed for each of the separate operations. The path A → B → C is the path of least time and is called the *critical path*. This is the path requiring the unloading of the passengers followed by cleaning the cabin followed finally by the loading of passengers for the flight to Chicago. Critical path analysis such as this has a great many applications.

CROSSBRACING. In the Introductory ARCHITECTURAL PROBLEM students are left to their own devices to count the number of 4-brace solutions for a 2x3 grid of steel beams. There is an alternative method for identifying solutions that provide rigidity to the entire grid. This method is as applicable to a grid with *any number* of rows and *any number* of columns as it is to our 2x3 grid. The first thing to do is to create what is called a "bracing subgraph." In this graph each row and each column of a grid is represented by a vertex. For our 2x3 grid there are five vertices since there are two columns and three rows. An edge that connects a row vertex and a column vertex represents a single square in the grid. We then invoke the following two-part theorem.

A bracing of an n by m grid (n and m are integers) is rigid if and only if the corresponding subgraph is connected. Also, a bracing of an n by m grid is a minimum rigid bracing if and only if the bracing subgraph is a tree.

By "connected" is meant that for any pair of vertices it is possible to find a path that connects one vertex to the other. Thus a connected graph is "all in one piece." By "tree" is meant a connected graph that contains no circuits (loops).

The three rows of figures at the top on the following page show twelve subgraphs for the 2x3 grid. Each edge of a subgraph indicates a square that is crossbraced. Our task is to identify all the possible sub-bracings that will make the entire 2x3 grid rigid and to do this using four crossbraces (if this is possible). Since there are more row vertices than column vertices we know that one of the row vertices must have two edges coming in while the other two row vertices must have only one edge connected to it. In the top row of four subgraphs this row vertex is r_1, in the second row of subgraphs it is r_2, and in the third row of subgraphs it is r_3. In the first two subgraphs in the top row an edge also connects r_2 and c_1. Since r_3 must be connected somewhere there are two choices, c_1 and c_2. In the third and fourth graphs in the top row r_2 is connected to c_2. This leaves us with two choices for connecting r_3. A similar examination of all possible connections in the second row is made starting with r_2 already connected to both c_1 and to c_2. A similar procedure for the third row of subgraphs completes the total of twelve possible connected graphs with four braced squares.

Beneath the subgraphs are the twelve crossbracings that correspond to the twelve subgraphs shown above them. The braced squares are shaded so as to better identify the pattern of braced squares in each case. Note that there are four L-shaped patterns, one at each corner of the grouping. We know that all twelve are rigid bracings because their subgraphs are connected and contain no circuits. Among these twelve there are but four basic shapes as shown in the solution to the Introductory Problem on crossbracing. Recall that there are also three arrangements for four crossbraces that permit distortion of the grid. For these three cases (illustrated there but not here) one of the row vertices in the subgraph is not connected to any edge. Since there are three row vertices there are three vertices that can remain unconnected and therefore there are three arrangements of the four crossbraces that do not provide rigidity for the entire grid.

The above procedure is one in which we start with the twelve subgraphs and from these determine the location of the bracings. We know that the bracings will make the entire grid rigid because the subgraphs are connected and form a tree. Alternatively, one could begin with the bracings and from these determine their subgraphs. Once again, the bracings provide complete rigidity if the subgraphs are connected and form a tree.

Twelve Bracing Subgraphs for a 2x3 Grid

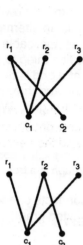

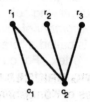
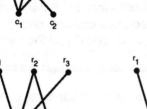
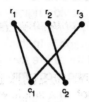

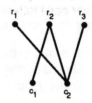
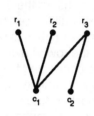
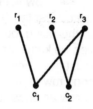
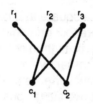
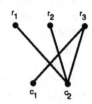

Corresponding Crossbracing Patterns

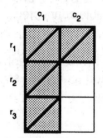
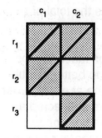
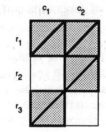
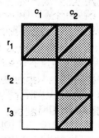

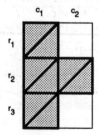
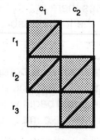
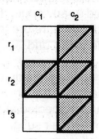
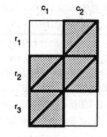

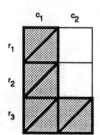
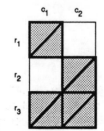
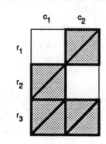
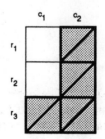

KÖNIGSBERG BRIDGES PROBLEM. <u>RESTATE PROBLEM</u>. To recount Euler's proof that each of the seven bridges of Königsberg could not, in a single walking trip, be crossed once and only once, we start with Euler's simplified graph that shows land masses in capital letters A, B, C, and D and the seven bridges in lower case letters a, b, c, d, e, f, and g.

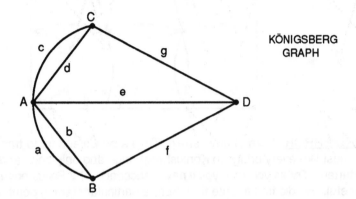

KÖNIGSBERG
GRAPH

<u>CONSIDER EXAMPLE</u>. Euler represented the crossing of a bridge from A to B, for example, either by way of bridge a or bridge b, by writing the letters AB, with the first letter representing the land mass from which a person comes and the second letter the land mass one crosses into. If a person then crosses bridge f to land mass D, the trip to this point is represented by the letters ABD. If now the traveller crosses bridge g to C, the trip to this point is represented by the letters ABDC. As can be seen each space between letters represents the crossing of one of the seven bridges. Thus, when the trip is done, assuming it is possible, there must be a sequence of exactly eight letters selected from the four letters representing the land masses.

<u>IDENT PATTERN</u>. Notice now that there are five bridges to and from land mass A and three bridges to and from each of the land masses B, C, and D. Suppose that there is a land mass X with only one bridge connected to it. (Such a bridge is not to be found in Königsberg). Then, Euler argues, a lettering scheme of the kind adopted would contain the letter X but once no matter whether the walking trip started in land mass X or led into X. If three bridges lead to X, the same lettering scheme would require the appearance of X twice whether the journey is started in X or not. Finally, with five bridges leading to X there must be three appearances of the letter X in the letter sequence. Think hard about these last three statements. To summarize the situation for the four land masses in the city of Königsberg we construct the following table.

land mass	no. of bridges	no. of appearances of the land mass letter
A	5	3
B	3	2
C	3	2
D	3	2

<u>CONCLUSION</u>. From the last column it can be seen that the required total number of appearances of the four letters must be nine. Nine land mass letters means eight connecting bridges. Since Königsberg had but seven bridges we can conclude, as did Euler, that the proposed trip was impossible.

THE SWISS POSTMAN. Does a perfect postman's path exist for the six square block area shown? That is, can the postman deliver his mail by walking past every house just once without ever having to back-track, and terminate his route at the point from which he started?

DRAW GRAPH. The first step in attempting to answer this question is to draw a graph of the six square block area with each street intersection represented by a vertex of the graph and each row of houses by an edge of the graph. The desired graph is shown below.

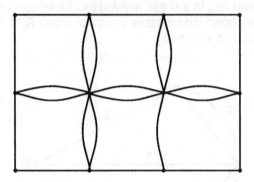

TRIAL AND ERROR. Start at any vertex. Take a pencil and try to trace a path that takes you along every edge (just like every bridge in Königsberg) once and only once and finally, back to the vertex from which you started. Try as you may you'll never succeed. The Swiss postman however, if not perfect, is resourceful. He did find a route that, from a particular starting point, carried him past every one of the houses for which there might be mail, and ended at a different location. You can find it too.

APPLY RULE. A "trial and error" method isn't necessary to identify an Eulerian circuit because the Background section of the manual gives Euler's solution to this problem. Since two of the vertices in the above graph are odd, for this graph an Euler circuit simply does not exist. An *Eulerian path*, however, does exist. The postman can start at one odd vertex, say at the corner of 3rd St. and 2nd Ave., then pass every house once and only once, but end up at the corner of 3rd St. and 3rd Ave.

TRAFFIC SIGNAL MAINTENANCE. RESTATE PROB. In the six square block region there are six traffic signals. A maintenance truck must service these lights every three months or so. The problem is to sketch a route for this truck to visit each of these signals once and only once and return to its starting point.

CREATE GRAPH. The six block area and the traffic signal locations are shown below.

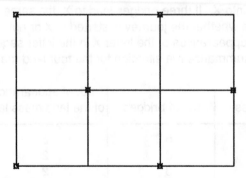

EXHAUST POSSIBILITIES. As shown below there are four paths that the maintenance truck can use to visit each of the six traffic signals. In this case it is the signals that are the vertices of the graph in which we are interested, not the street intersections.

86

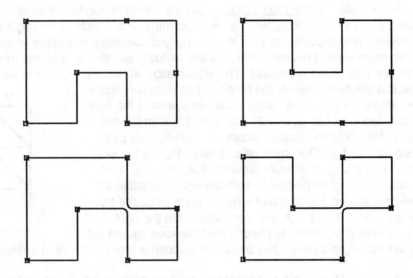

Notice that in each of the lower two truck route graphs there is a *street intersection* that the truck visits twice, but not a *vertex* where a signal light is located. The maintenance truck could just as well go straight through this intersection rather than turn as shown. Each of the four routes shown requires a total of twelve blocks travel from a starting intersection back to that same intersection.

STATE NEW PROB. Now a signal light is to be installed over a pedestrian crossing at the half block on 2nd Ave. between 1st and 2nd Streets. The maintenance truck is now faced with the problem of visiting all seven lights for a maintenance checkup, hopefully without retracing any part of its route, and end up back where it started. In the diagrams below the new light is shown at its mid-block location on each of the four truck routes that visited the old set of six lights.

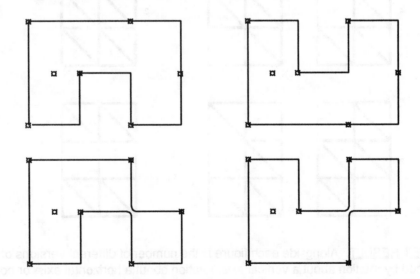

If the new signal light were to be located on any of the edges in any one of the graphs the maintenance truck could then use the old route, 12 blocks in length, to service the new light as well as the six lights it had previously been assigned without ever retracing its route.

STATE CONCLUSION. However, that is not the case. Because of its location at mid-block the traffic signal maintenance truck must now travel an extra block to service the new light.

ARCHITECTURAL PROBLEM. <u>THINK OUT LOUD.</u> Given a sufficient number of steel beams and crossbraces to make a 2x3 grid of squares, what is the least number of crossbraces required to make the entire grid rigid? It is extremely important to note that in any grid consisting of beams of uniform length, distorted or not, all the more vertical beams in any row are mutually parallel, and all the more horizontal beams in any column are also mutually parallel. This observation will tell us, given that we have pro-

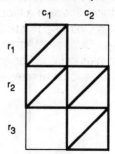

duced what we hope is a solution, whether the proposed solution is in fact a solution. Take for example the proposed bracing pattern shown at the right. Let the squares be labelled 1,1 1,2 2,1 2,2 3,1 and 3,2 with the row number coming first and the column number second in each number pair. Think of the unbraced square 1,2. Our observation tells us that its top side is parallel to both the top and bottom sides of squares 2,2 and 3,2. Also, the right side of square 1,2 must be parallel to both the right and left sides of square 1,1. Therefore square 1,2 is in fact a rigid square since the top and bottom sides of squares 2,2 and 3,2 are perpendicular to the right and left sides of 1,1. A similar argument applied to the unbraced square 3,1 tells us that it too is in fact a rigid square. The proposed solution is therefore a valid solution.

    <u>IDENT STRATEGY.</u> All possible arrangements for crossbracing a 2x3 grid can be identified most easily by looking at the location, *not* of the crossbraces, but of the squares that are not braced, in this case only two. These two unbraced squares can be located vertically at any one of the four corners of the grid, at opposite ends of either column, at opposite corners of the grid, at one corner and at the middle of the other column, or the two can be side-by-side, either at one end of the grid or in the middle. The method of identifying these arrangements through use of bracing subgraphs could have been used in this problem but will instead be employed in an additional problem involving a 3x3 square grid.

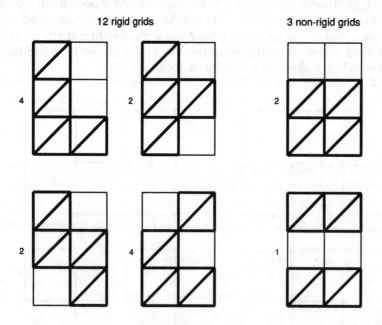

12 rigid grids   3 non-rigid grids

    <u>INTERPRET RESULT.</u> Alongside each figure is the number of different versions of the pattern that can be produced by rotation about a vertical axis, rotation about a horizontal axis, or both. For example, the upper left figure has four versions obtained by flipping over the figure shown about a vertical axis and also about a horizontal axis. The two unbraced squares consequently can appear at the upper right (as shown), at the upper left, and at both the lower right and lower left. All four of these figures are simply four views of the same physical grid consisting of steel beams, pins, and crossbraces. All figures add to 12 for the rigid grid and to 3 for the ones that can be distorted. By analysis such as that given previously, one can be persuaded that all those patterns claimed to make a rigid grid do in fact do so. It is easy to see that the crossbracings at the right side of the figure allow the grid to distort easily.

Additional Problems

THE CHINESE POSTMAN PROBLEM. As you will recall, the "Swiss postman" was an individual who insisted on walking his route and ending up where he started without ever having to go along the same row of houses twice. By contrast, the "Chinese postman" is not so particular, but far more practical. He is willing to walk down a block a second time if he must in order to complete his deliveries. The problem is called the Chinese Postman Problem simply because the mathematician who first investigated it was Chinese. Consider the same six block area we had before, but now some changes are contemplated by the Redevelopment Agency. As shown below the west side of 3rd St. between 2nd and 3rd Ave. is to be filled in with town houses and 2nd Ave. between 1st and 4th St. is to become a pedestrian walkway.

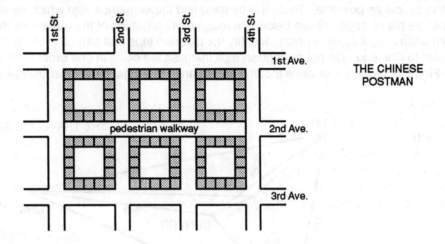

THE CHINESE POSTMAN

The postman counts the walkway as a single edge on his mail delivery graph since now it is so easy to cross back and forth across the walkway to deliver mail. As before, street intersections locate a single vertex on the graph. Is there an Eulerian circuit for him to follow? Definitely not! But what is the least number of blocks he must walk in order to deliver all his mail recognizing that he may have to backtrack to complete his deliveries?

*RECTANGULAR STREET NETWORKS. A truck is to pick up old newspapers to be recycled from an area that is five blocks east-to-west and three blocks north-to-south. It does this simply by driving down the middle of the street while helpers bring the bound newspapers to the truck from both sides of the street. To model this situation we use a graph whose vertices are street intersections and whose edges are the streets.

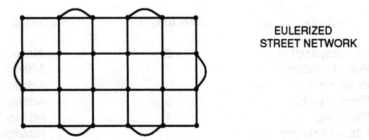

EULERIZED
STREET NETWORK

The graph of the streets and intersections as shown has already been "Eulerized" by directing the truck to repeat its path along two separate blocks on the north, two more on the south, and by a single block both on the east and on the west. Thus the truck must go six extra blocks in addition to those blocks travelled when picking up newspapers. All vertices are now even having either 2 or 4 edges coming in. Can you convince yourself that the extra six blocks is the least number of extra blocks necessary?

Now consider two additional situations. First, Eulerize the graph for an area that is six by four blocks in area. Second, repeat the exercise for an area that is four by five blocks in area. When you are finished you will have Eulerized examples for rectangular street networks whose height and width in blocks are two odd numbers, two even numbers, and one odd and one even number.

*THE TRAVELING SALESMAN PROBLEM. A traveling salesman working out of his Chicago office plans to visit retailers in four cities throughout the west. These are at Denver, Los Angeles, Salt Lake City, and Seattle. His wife wants to go along so they plan to drive their van and make the trip a combined business and vacation trip for the two of them. His desire is to make the total mileage required to visit all four cities as low as possible. To do this he must find the sequence with which he visits these cities that will minimize his mileage. Given below is a rough representation of the trip where the highway mileage between each pair of cities is given. Identify the different trips that can be made that visit all four cities and return to Chicago. Do not distinguish trips that visit the cities in one order from those taken in reverse order. Find the sequence of cities that the salesman learned gave the least overall mileage.

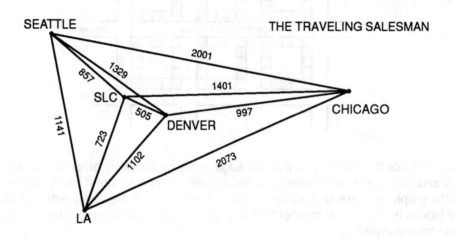

THE TRAVELING SALESMAN

*MODEL HOME BUILDING. A developer plans to have a model home built in order to advertise a new development. He hires a contractor to do the job and instructs him to complete the work at the earliest possible date. Malkevitch and Meyer in *Graphs, Models, & Finite Mathematics* describe the contractor's problem. He first divides the work into nine component activities each of which must be preceded by the completion of certain other activities (all except site preparation). The contractor then prepares the following table.

Activity	Time (days)	Immediate Predecessor
(1) Site preparation	2	None
(2) Build foundation	3	Activity 1
(3) Build main structure	14	Activity 2
(4) Electric wiring	5	Activity 3
(5) Plumbing	4	Activity 3
(6) Interior finishing	7	Activities 4 and 5
(7) Exterior finishing	11	Activity 3
(8) Furnishing	2	Activities 6 and 7
(9) Landscaping	4	Activity 7
(10) End	0	Activities 8 and 9

What is the minimum number of days required to complete the whole job?

*WINE BOTTLES PROBLEM. There are a great many problems involving unmarked vessels. One of these is described by Chartrand in his book *Introductory Graph Theory.*

> Three wine bottles have capacities of 8, 5, and 3 liters, respectively. The 8-liter bottle is filled with wine and the other two bottles are empty. We want to divide the wine into two equal portions using these bottles (which are not graduated), and no others, by pouring successively from one bottle to another. The problem, then, is: How can we obtain 4 liters of wine in the largest bottle and 4 liters in the medium-size bottle, using the fewest possible number of pourings?

Motivating this problem are two individuals who want to make sure that each gets his fair share of the wine. It will be helpful to focus on the 5 and 3 liter bottles and consider the 8-liter bottle as if it were both a "faucet" and a "drain" for the wine. In this way you can graph the number of liters in both the smaller bottles and keep track of their contents after each pouring. At any point one knows how much wine is in the larger bottle because the total, barring any spillage, is always 8 liters. To start the problem draw a graph such as the one below. The horizontal scale runs from 0 to 5 to represent the contents of the 5-liter bottle. The vertical scale runs from 0 to 3 to represent the contents of the 3-liter bottle. The contents of the 8-liter bottle from which and into which wine can be poured from the other bottles need not be represented on the graph.

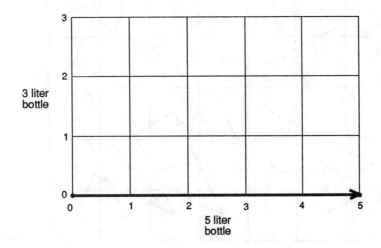

One starts at the 0,0 point at the lower left corner of this graph with the 8-liter bottle full and the other two bottles empty. To divide this wine into two equal portions without any markings on any of the three bottles one can start either by pouring wine into the 3-liter bottle until it is brimful or by pouring wine from the 8-liter bottle into the empty 5-liter bottle until it is brimful. The heavy line with the arrowhead on the graph above indicates that the latter option has been taken. It is of course our objective, by means of a series of pourings, to wind up with exactly 4 liters of wine in the 5-liter bottle with the remaining 4 liters of wine in the 8-liter bottle. Each pouring will be represented by a new edge of the graph continuing from the lower right-hand corner. There are a number of possibilities for the next pouring, but only one makes good sense. For example, one surely doesn't want to immediately pour the 5 liters of wine back into the 8-liter bottle at this point. It is the problem solver's task to identify new edges and new vertices for the graph that will carry him to the point on the bottom edge of the graph that indicates that the 5-liter bottle contains 4 liters of wine and the 3-liter bottle is empty. Count the number of required pourings. Is this the least number that will do the job? Can one achieve this same objective by starting out by first filling the 3-liter bottle brimful? How many pourings would be required in that case?

THE KNIGHT'S TOUR. Following the rule for the moves of a knight on a chessboard, is it possible for a knight to tour a chessboard, visiting every square once and only once, and return to the square where it began? (A knight's move is two squares in one direction and one square at right angles.) Put in more formal terms, taking every one of the 64 squares on a chessboard as a vertex of a graph and all possible knight's jumps as edges, can a Hamiltonian circuit be found for this graph? It is known that there are at least three Hamiltonian circuits for this graph. One is Chartrand's solution (shown below), one is Bob's, and one is that of a student. Find a different Hamiltonian circuit, that is, a different knight's tour.

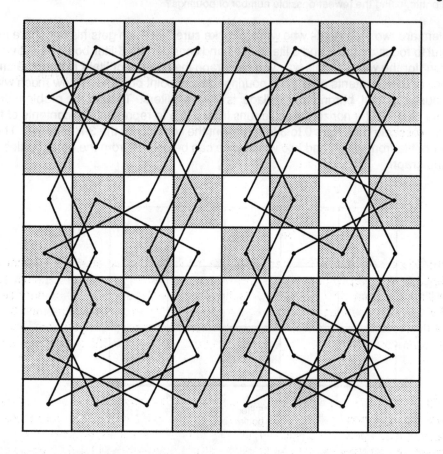

CHARTRAND'S
KNIGHT'S TOUR

As an alternative to the above exercise for a full 8 X 8 chessboard, investigate the Knight's Tour problem for a 4 X 5 chessboard in two ways. Will two Knight's tours fill the board? Also, is there a *path*, not a *circuit* that starts at one corner of the 4 X 5 chessboard and ends at the corner diagonally opposite?

CANNIBALS AND MISSIONARIES. The problem of the Missionaries and Cannibals (so named before the advent of political correctness) is a famous puzzle that you may have struggled with sometime in the past. It doesn't need graph theory to solve it, but graphical analysis does provide a marvelously simple method for finding its solution. As the story goes three Cannibals and three Missionaries arrive at the bank of a river which they must cross. There is available but a single boat, luckily on the near side of the river, a boat that holds at most two people. There are two restrictions, the first being that at no time on either bank of the river can there ever be more cannibals than missionaries. In such a case the Missionaries would be in grave danger. The second restriction is that when a boatload crosses the river its occupants <u>must go on shore</u> before turning around for the next trip across the river. How does this group of six individuals manage to cross the river?

On an ordinary graph with x and y axes, where we replace x and y with C and M respectively, we plot the number of C's and M's on the near side of the river at any one time. At the beginning we place a vertex at the point 3,3 meaning 3 Cannibals (written 1st) and 3 Missionaries (written 2nd).

We wish to somehow use the boat to lower this pair of numbers to 0,0 in which case all six are now on the far side of the river. Next we identify those pairs of numbers that are prohibited by the rule that C's can't outnumber the M's on either side of the river. First we rule out the pairs 3,2 and 3,1 and 2,1 because these represent cases where C's outnumber M's on the near side of the river. Second, we also rule out the combinations 0,2 and 0,1 and 1,2 because these numbers for the near side of the river represent more C's than M's on the far side of the river. We begin by plotting, in addition to the starting and ending points, the eight additional allowed combinations as vertices for a graph yet to be drawn.

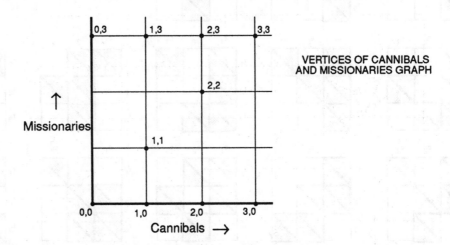

VERTICES OF CANNIBALS
AND MISSIONARIES GRAPH

The graph desired should be a digraph with edges starting at the vertex 3,3 directed in a manner than will terminate at the vertex 0,0. A digraph consists of edges with arrowheads to show their directions. It is your job to draw these edges, each of which represents the change in C's and M's on the near side of the river brought about by a certain boatload crossing. You may wish to try an alternative method by starting out with a sketch of a river and the boat crossings needed to solve the problem. If you approach the problem this way, translate your solution to a digraph so that you can compare the two representations of the problem solution.

BRACING A 3X3 GRID. The objective in this problem is to identify the least number of crossbraces that will make a 3x3 square grid rigid and to determine their arrangement in the grid. Since four crossbraces are required in the case of a 2x3 grid, there is little doubt that at least five will be required for a 3x3 grid. To determine the location of crossbraces one can start with all possible locations for the five crossbraces and then, from the corresponding bracing subgraphs, determine whether these locations do or do not make the entire grid rigid. Alternatively, one can start with the bracing subgraphs and from these determine the locations of the crossbraces. For this problem choose the first course of action. On the page following are shown eighteen arrangements of five crossbraces in a 3x3 grid. The braced squares are shaded as before so that the patterns made by the crossbraces are more easily seen. These eighteen patterns represent far more patterns than are shown. There are in fact four versions of each pattern except for the third in the top row of three and the fifth in the bottom row of five. The bracing pattern at the upper left, for example, looks something like a boomerang. The center of the boomerang can lie in the upper left corner of the grid, as shown, but also in any of the three remaining corners of the grid. Likewise, there are four versions for most of the remaining crossbracing patterns.

Given the crossbracing patterns at the top of the page, it should now be an easy task to draw the eighteen corresponding subgraphs at the bottom of the page and from these determine which crossbracings make the entire grid rigid and which do not.

3x3 Cross-Bracing Patterns

3x3 Bracing Subgraphs

94

ACTIVITY — CONSTRUCT A CROSSBRACING MODEL. Make a model of a 2x3 square grid complete with a supply of crossbraces. Observing the behavior of the physical model makes less demand on one's abilities in spatial visualization than attempting to visualize the behavior of the grid and crossbraces entirely in one's head. A model is relatively easy to construct using cardboard strips in place of steel beams and crossbraces, and roofing nails in place of steel pins. Cut light cardboard into one-half inch wide strips. Cut these into 3-inch lengths for the beams and 4-inch lengths for the crossbraces. A quarter inch in from the ends of each strip make a hole through which a roofing nail will extend vertically upward. Thus the hole-to-hole separation is 2 1/2 inches for the strips representing the beams (17 needed) and 3 1/2 inches for the crossbraces (up to six needed). The use of roofing nails serves to prevent the cardboard strips from slipping off.

The figure below illustrates the model with none, with one, with two, and with three crossbraces in place. Flex your model with one, two, and three cross-braces located as shown. Verify that the distorted figures appear precisely the same as the distorted figures shown in the Introductory Problem. Now add a fourth crossbrace to form patterns of crossbraces like those shown in the solution to the Introductory Problem. Do the four arrangements of four crossbraces that claim to make the grid rigid actually do so? Does your model permit distortions for the same arrangements of four crossbraces as those described in the Introductory Problem solution?

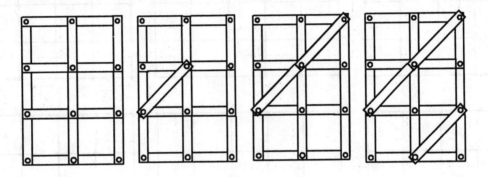

ACTIVITY—FIND ALL THE HAMILTONIAN CIRCUITS. Consider a 3x5 square block area of a downtown. Such an area is shown by each of the 15 copies on the page following. The problem here is to identify all the Hamiltonian circuits possible, circuits which visit each of the 24 street intersections (vertices) by following the edges of the graph which are the streets surrounding and within this 15 square block area. Count not only a particular circuit, but also its rotation about either a vertical or a horizontal axis or both if these produce different circuits from the original. Thus a particular circuit can have one version, two, or four. The fifteen graphs on the following page (or a xerox copy of this page) will be sufficient to draw all the circuits possible provided that reflected circuits are not duplicated. The greatest number that anyone so far has identified is thirty-seven. Make sure you use a heavier line when drawing a circuit so that it can easily be distinguished from the edges of the graph.

FIND ALL THE HAMILTONIAN CIRCUITS

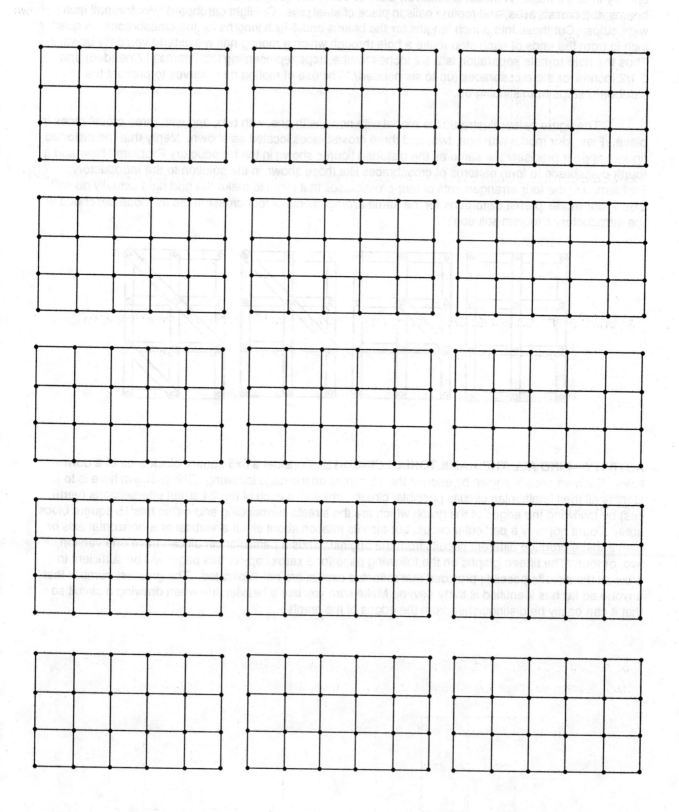

1. RECTANGULAR STREET NETWORKS. Different attempts to Eulerize a 2x3 street network are shown below. Which attempts result in an Eulerian graph? (circle all Eulerian graphs.)

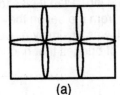
(a)

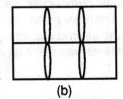
(b)

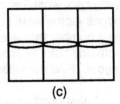
(c)

2. MODEL HOME BUILDING. The *critical path* is a path that in some sense is a path (circle all that apply):

(a) of greatest time.

(b) of least time.

(c) that connects activities which must be done in sequence.

3. WINE BOTTLES PROBLEM. In the graph of a solution for this problem (circle all that apply):

(a) one never finds both the 3 and 5-liter bottles completely full at the same time.

(b) except for the first pouring, one always transfers wine from either the 3 or 5-liter bottle to the other.

(c) considering only the 3 and 5-liter bottles, if one is partly full the other must be either empty or full, i.e., both are never partly full at any one time.

4. THE KNIGHT'S TOUR. Methods for solving this problem include (circle all that apply):

(a) trial and error.

(b) using a computer program that tries every possible path.

(c) the use of specialized procedures that solve all Hamiltonian circuit problems.

5. ARCHITECTURAL PROBLEM. Draw on the 2x3 square grids of pin-jointed beams shown below two different ways that four cross-braces can be placed that do *not* make the grid rigid.

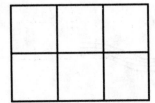

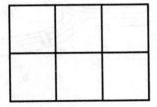

The citizens of Königsberg, despairing of being able to take a walk which would take them across each of their seven bridges just once and return them to their starting point, decided to fix things so they could accomplish just such a Sunday walk. Plan I was to build one or more new bridges to add to the seven they already had, whatever was the least number that would do the job. Plan II was to demolish one or more bridges (some were in need of extensive repair) to subtract from the seven they had, whatever was the least number that would yield the desired outcome. Plan III was to simply move one or more bridges from one point to another, whatever was the least number of bridges that had to be moved to achieve their goal. Find the following :

Plan I   Least number of bridges to be added _____ .

Plan II   Least number of bridges to be demolished _____ .

Plan III   Least number of bridges to be moved _____ .

In the figures below for each of the plans X out all bridges to be demolished or moved to another location. Draw in their proper locations all bridges to be built or those newly located.

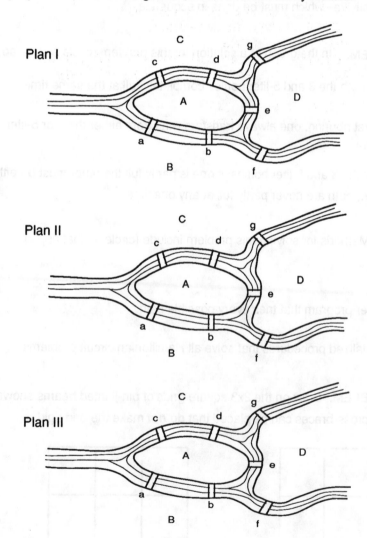

VI. VISUAL THINKING - SYMMETRY AND PATTERNS

Introductory Problems: FIBONACCI NUMBERS
                                FLIPPING AND ROTATING A BOOK
                                INVERSE ORIGAMI (constructing a cube)
                                THE EXISTENTIAL "THERE"

Background: SYMMETRY
                                PATTERNS
                                THE GOLDEN RATIO

Introductory Problem Solutions

Additional Problems: FIBONACCI'S PUZZLE
                                THE CHAMBERED NAUTILUS
                                DISTINGUISHING A "Z" FROM A "2"
                                PATTERNS IN BRICK
                                INVERSE ORIGAMI (constructing a tetrahedron)
                                PATTERNS OF THE ANCIENT MEXICANS
                                AGREEMENT RULES IN SPANISH
                                MUSICAL PATTERNS
                                ACTIVITY—DESIGN YOUR OWN STRIP PATTERNS
                                ACTIVITY—COMPUTER GENERATED PATTERNS

Self Tests: SELECTED PROBLEMS
                                BOB'S STRIP PATTERNS

VI. VISUAL THINKING - SYMMETRY AND PATTERNS

Visual thinking is that kind of thinking about which the least is known, and yet there is little question but what it plays a crucial role in the analysis of many kinds of problems. We employ pictures, graphs, and diagrams so often and so naturally that we hardly realize the extent to which we are dependent upon them. Thomas G. West, in *In the Mind's Eye*, defines visual thinking as follows:

> We may consider "visual thinking" as that form of thought in which images are generated or recalled in the mind and are manipulated, overlaid, translated, associated with other similar forms (as with a metaphor), rotated, increased or reduced in size, distorted or otherwise transformed gradually from one . . . image into another. These images may be visual representations of material things or they may be nonphysical, abstract concepts manipulated in the same way as visual forms.

Visual forms in art can evoke a variety of emotions. They can also communicate, but in a different way than with ordinary language. Who is to say which is the more powerful channel of communication? One of these is presumably governed by the "right brain" and the other by the "left brain." Which is which hardly matters. Religious, mythological, or ritual significance is attributed to the geometrical art of the natives in New Hebrides. Their figure, "The Wild Cabbage," is shown below as redrawn. As can be seen, it is an Eulerian circuit drawn in an interesting and appealing way.

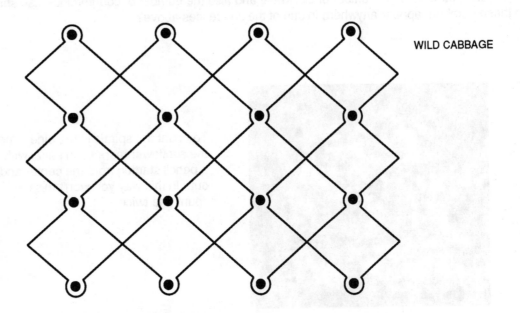

WILD CABBAGE

In the preceding chapter we saw how useful graphs can be in the analysis of a variety of problems ranging from those of the Swiss and Chinese postmen to vacationers to builders to architects wishing to create rigid structures. The visual strategy of graph construction was added to pictorial techniques encountered earlier that involve decision trees and ordinary graphs.

In the present chapter the progression toward greater use of visual representations continues. It is recognized that each picture or diagram is a complex "word" to be used in conjunction with other such words to provide food for visual thought. Decorative patterns are analysed by anthropologists seeking to better understand native cultures. Science has created visual representations that have had enormous impact. These include the periodic table of the elements, drawings of electronic circuits, representations of electric and magnetic fields, Feynman diagrams, and models for the structure of DNA, the hydrogen atom, and weather charts.

Introductory Problems

FIBONACCI NUMBERS. Numbers arrayed in sequence often exhibit a regular structure. As examples, inspect the six sequences below. Extend each sequence to include the three numbers that come next.

$$1 \quad 3 \quad 5 \quad 7 \quad 9 \quad 11 \quad 13 \quad . \; . \; . \; .$$

$$1 \quad 4 \quad 9 \quad 16 \quad 25 \quad 36 \quad 49 \quad . \; . \; . \; .$$

$$1 \quad 2 \quad 4 \quad 8 \quad 16 \quad 32 \quad 64 \quad . \; . \; . \; .$$

$$1 \quad 3 \quad 2 \quad 4 \quad 3 \quad 5 \quad 4 \quad . \; . \; . \; .$$

$$1 \quad 3 \quad 2 \quad 5 \quad 4 \quad 8 \quad 7 \quad . \; . \; . \; .$$

$$1 \quad 1 \quad 2 \quad 3 \quad 5 \quad 8 \quad 13 \quad . \; . \; . \; .$$

Now look at the scales on the end of the pine cone shown below. Count the number of spirals that turn in a clockwise direction. Count also the number of counterclockwise spirals. Do you find these two numbers anywhere in one of the sequences above? Conduct the same counting exercise for the sunflower. Count both the number of clockwise and also the number of counterclockwise spirals. Do these numbers appear anywhere in one of the sequences above?

To count the spirals in the pine cone and in the sunflower mark each spiral with a pen or a pencil starting from the center and working out. In this way you won't miss a spiral or count one twice.

Of course there are many other patterns in nature that have nothing to do with those in the pine cone and sunflower. How many petals are there on daisy-like flowers? How many rows on an ear of corn? Are these even or odd numbers?

FLIPPING AND ROTATING A BOOK. Here is an opportunity to practice using your powers of visualization in three dimensions. Take a book, any book, and place it on a table in front of you as you would if you were about to start to read it. There are eight "operations" of flipping and rotating that can be applied to this book. These are defined below and identified as operations I, A, B, C, D, E, F, and G. The four possible axes for flipping are shown on the diagram.

I   Identity operation, don't move book
A   Rotate book 90° counterclockwise
B   Rotate book 180° counterclockwise
C   Rotate book 270° counterclockwise
D   Flip book over around axis K - K
E   Flip book over around axis L - L
F   Flip book over around axis P - M
G   Flip book over around axis N - Q

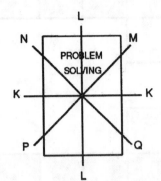

Now perform the following pairs of operations on the book. First, and this is a more difficult level of spatial visualization, try performing these operations in your head. Second, and this is clearly easier, do the operations on an actual book in front of you. Either way, the operations are visual, not verbal. First do operation D followed by operation B. Next, perform these same two operations, but in reverse order. The book ends up in the same orientation either way. We say that these two operations "commute," just as 3 x 4 gives the same result as 4 x 3. No surprise here. Now perform operation D followed by operation A. Note the resulting position for the book. However, this time, performing these same two operations in reverse order gives a different result. We say that the operations D and A do not commute. Find another pair of operations that commute and another pair that don't commute.

INVERSE ORIGAMI (constructing a cube). In origami one folds a standard size piece of paper to form a variety of three-dimensional figures. In "Inverse Origami" it is just the opposite. One begins with a variety of different plane figures each of which folds into a single three-dimensional shape, in this case a cube. Each plane figure used as a starting point consists of six squares, one for each face of the completed cube. These six squares must be attached to one another by at least one edge and not by a single corner. In addition, for plane figures that are mirror images of one another, count each as a separate figure. Counting in this way there are 20 different plane figures that can be folded to form a cube. Eighteen of the twenty consist of nine mirror-image pairs. On the following two pages 20 six-square plane figures are shown. However, four of these figures (two mirror image pairs) will not fold to form a cube. These are the so-called "imposter" pairs. Your first task is to identify these four figures.

The identification of figures that either will or will not fold to form a cube is an exercise in three-dimensional spatial visualization. This ability is part of a pictorial "language" that is one of the three basic language tools that are available to help in solving problems: ordinary language, mathematical language, and pictorial language. Try first to perform the operations of folding by visualizing these in your mind's eye. For a check, make cutouts of the figures and see if you can manually form a cube. Either way, you have applied visual thinking to the problem. Imagine, if you can, trying to solve this problem without use either of mental "pictures" or those directly perceived.

The second part of the problem is this: Having identified the two pairs of given figures that are not a part of the 20 that will fold to form cubes, now find the missing figures that belong in the complement of 20 that will fold in the required way. To accomplish this objective it will be best to devise some strategy so that you can avoid thrashing around endlessly. One strategy is to think of each of the six plane figures as consisting of a number of groups of pieces, each group being made up of three squares in a row, three squares forming a V-shape, two squares, or a single square. Manipulate these in all the ways you can think of. Having found as many six-square figures as you can, the ones that do and the ones that do not fold into a cube must be distinguished.

Inverse Origami
(with imposter pairs)

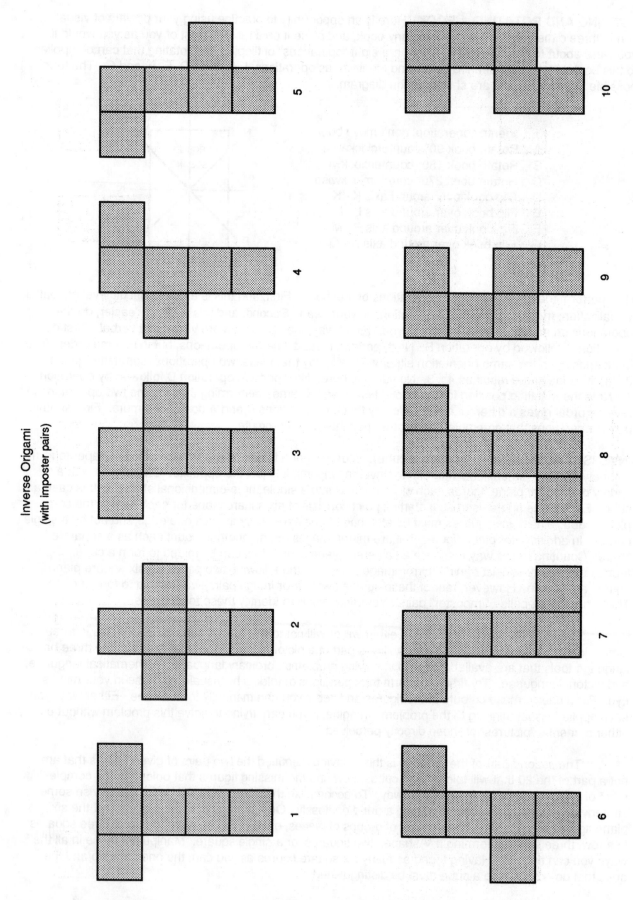

Inverse Origami
(with imposter pairs)

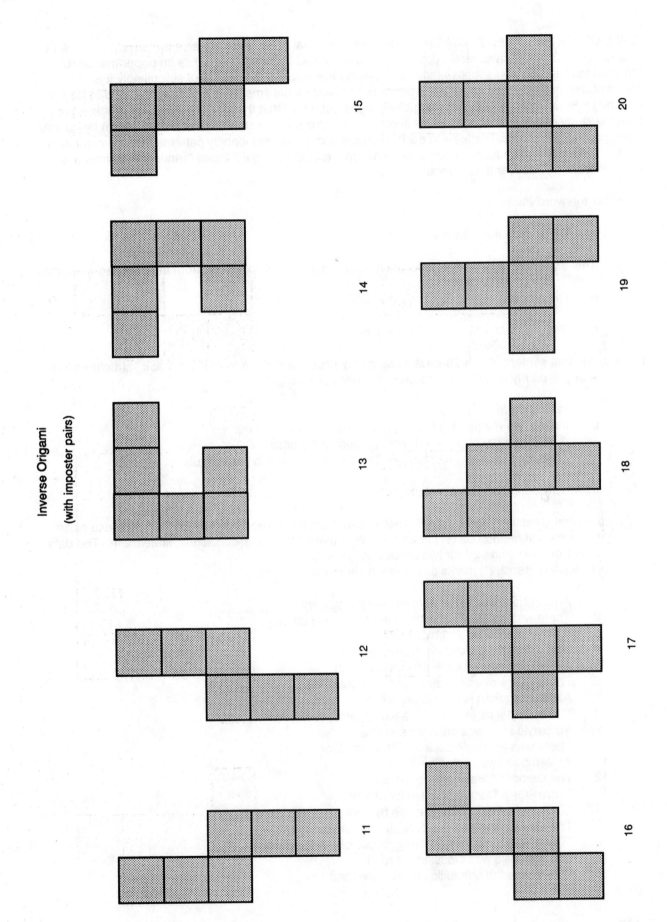

11

12

13

14

15

16

17

18

19

20

105

THE EXISTENTIAL *THERE*. While many patterns are visual ones, there are also patterns in music and in language. There are also tactile patterns in Braille formed by small raised dots on paper that enable the blind to read. Do you suppose there are patterns in smell and in taste? Not surprisingly it is the shape of the molecules we smell and taste that distinguishes the smell of a rose from that of diesel fumes and the taste of butter from that of margarine. It has been said that the study of language is little more than the study of patterns of one kind or another. Individuals with a command of two (or more) languages have learned grammatical patterns in each language and are able to identify patterns that are common to the two languages. The following linguistics problem created by linguist David Iannucci illustrates the point concerning patterns in language.

Consider the word *there*, as in:

a)   There is an amoeba in the bathtub.

This *there*, which can never take heavy stress, must be distinguished from the stressed *there* that occurs in sentences like

b)   The amoeba is over there near the drain.

c)   There is the aardvark that infected me.

I.   Assume that sentences like *There is a bug on my nose* are derived from more "basic" structures like *A bug is on my nose* by an operation that does two things:

a)   inserts *there*
b)   inverts two elements (phrases) of the more basic structure, e.g.,
      A bug is on my nose" —> *There is a bug* on my nose
      An amoeba is in the bathtub —> *There is an amoeba* in the bathtub

Informally state how this operation works.

II.   Under what conditions can it apply? That is, can *there* be inserted into any English sentence or are there special restrictions on this operation? If there are special conditions, state them. The data below provide evidence for two conditions. Give both.
Note: An asterisk (*) marks an ill-formed sentence.

1.   An elephant was in the garden near the parsley.
2.   There was an elephant in the garden near the parsley.
3.   A policeman killed a demonstrator.
4.   *There killed a policemen a demonstrator.
5.   A demonstrator was killed by a policeman.
6.   There was a demonstrator killed by a policeman.
7.   A mountain man had a big appetite.
8.   *There had a mountain man a big appetite.
9.   An argyle sock was on Tim's shoulder.
10.   There was an argyle sock on Tim's shoulder.
11.   A Democrat was eaten by Alfred.
12.   The Democrat was eaten by Alfred.
13.   There was a Democrat eaten by Alfred.
14.   *There was the Democrat eaten by Alfred.
15.   The parsley was growing peacefully in the garden.
16.   *There was the parsley growing peacefully in the garden.
17.   The armadillo was crossing the road.
18.   *There was the armadillo crossing the road.

Background

SYMMETRY. The essential ideas behind the notion of symmetry are similarity, repetition, and the arrangement of the repeated parts of an object, sentence, or musical phrase. A large five petal flower is similar to a smaller five petal flower. If a single petal could create a new petal, then a single rotating petal could replicate itself four times to create the entire five-petal bloom. A bouquet of roses with the power of replication could create a very long line of bouquets simply by the process of translation. A long-stemmed rose, when seen in a mirror, is similar to but not the same as the rose in front of the mirror. Together they form a symmetric pattern. The possible patterns that can be obtained by a single bloom or by a whole bouquet through the process of replication seem to be limitless. Simply establish a small scale arrangement of some sort followed by your choice of replication operations: rotation, translation, and imaging in a mirror. These operations assume that the replicating object itself does not change. In addition to these three familiar operations there is the operation of glide reflection. This motion combines a translation (glide) and a reflection with the two thought of as occurring at the same time. Footprints in the sand and certain decorative patterns exemplify glide reflections as illustrated below. In both cases the glide reflection axis runs horizontally through the center of the strips.

GLIDE REFLECTIONS

Thus there are four operations in a plane that can be performed on a rigid object or pattern: rotation, translation, imaging in a mirror, and glide reflection. In three-dimensional space there are many more operations. Operations in the plane taken either singly or in combination generate patterns that we think of as "symmetric." A useful way of thinking about the symmetry of objects is to perform an operation in a way that leaves the pattern indistinguishable from its appearance before the operation was performed. For example, the five-petal flower rotated through 72° (or any multiple of 72°) leaves the flower looking the same as it did initially. A border planting of petunias spaced a foot apart and planted in a long row, when shifted by 1 foot (or any number of whole feet) in either direction along the line of the planting, is indistinguishable from its original appearance (neglecting variations in the plants themselves and the ends of the rows). Many leaves of plants and trees are mirror symmetric about a line passing from the tip of the leaf to its stem. This means that every point on the leaf has a twin point on the opposite side of this line and at an equal perpendicular distance from it. There is also mirror symmetry in the lower of the two glide patterns above. Can you find the locations of the mirror surface? Finally, for glide reflection patterns, a forward shift of this pattern accompanied by a mirror reflection leaves the pattern indistinguishable from its appearance before the operation was performed. Note, however, that mirror reflection axes are not glide axes. Patterns can, of course, exhibit combinations of these four symmetries, and such cases are not difficult to identify.

PATTERNS. Patterns in a plane can be grouped according to the direction or directions used to generate repetitions of some sub-pattern, or motif. A sub-pattern may be rotated by some angle, it may be translated along a line in either direction, or it may be moved in two different directions by any amount:

- rotation through an angle - forming **rosette patterns**
- translation in exactly one direction (and its reverse) - **strip patterns**
- translation in two directions - **wallpaper patterns**

107

Rosette patterns are illustrated below by ancient Mexican stamps used to decorate pottery and other kinds of earthenware. These designs appear in *design motifs of ancient mexico* by Jorge Enciso.

ROSETTE PATTERNS

  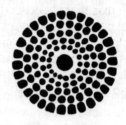

Strip Patterns. Surprisingly, there are only seven possible one-color strip pattern symmetries. The flowchart shown below can be used to identify which pattern of the seven a particular design exhibits. The chart is from Dorothy K. Washburn and Donald W. Crowe, *Symmetries of Culture: Theory and Practice of Plane Pattern Analysis.*

Flow chart for the seven
one-dimensional patterns

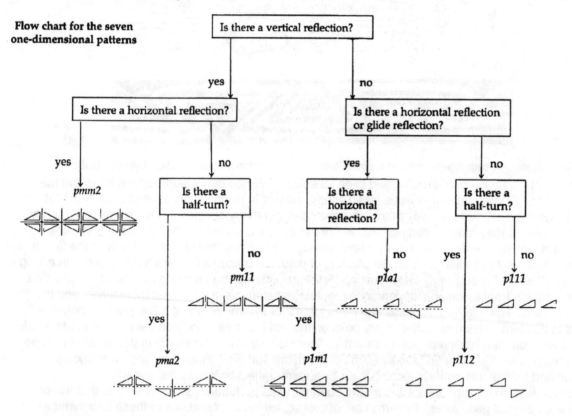

Note: Mirror axes in the above arrangements of asymmetrical triangles are shown by solid lines and glide reflection axes by dashed lines.

In the flow chart above a four-symbol notation in the form *pxyz* is used where each begins with a *p*.
    If there is a vertical reflection *x* is *m* (for "mirror"); otherwise *x* is *1*.
    If there is a horizontal reflection *y* is *m*, if there is a glide reflection but no horizontal reflection,
        y is *a*; otherwise *y* is *1*.
    If there is a half-turn, *z* is *2*; otherwise *z* is *1*.

108

Strip Pattern Examples. The Bakuba people of Zaire are well known for their use of patterns with symmetry of various kinds. All of the patterns shown below exhibit translation symmetry in the horizontal direction. All seven of the strip pattern symmetries are exhibited. These can be classified using the flow chart. Pattern (a), for example, shows no symmetry other than that of translation. Strip pattern (b) is mirror symmetric about a horizontal line running through the center of the strip. Pattern (c) also shows mirror symmetry, but about two different kinds of vertical axes. Rotation of pattern (d) by 180° about an axis that is perpendicular to the page (half-turn) produces a new pattern indistinguishable from the initial pattern. One rotation axis runs through the center of one of the small diamond shaped regions and another lies midway between two of these diamond-shaped regions. Strip pattern (e) exhibits glide reflection. The pattern of (f) shows a reflection about a vertical axis and in addition has a glide reflection axis. Also, a half turn can rotate the pattern into itself. Finally, pattern (g) shows reflection symmetry about two different vertical axes and another about a horizontal axis.

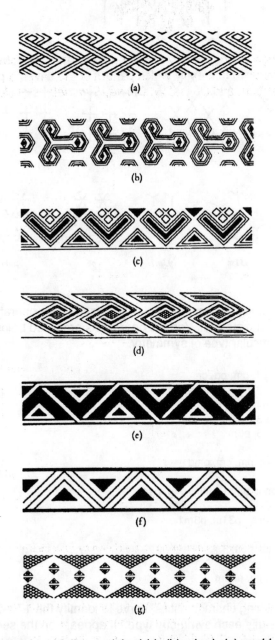

BAKUBA
STRIP
PATTERNS

(a)

(b)

(c)

(d)

(e)

(f)

(g)

The identification of the strips is as follows: (a) p111, (b) p1m1, (c) pm11, (d) p112, (e) p1a1, (f) pma2, (g) pmm2.

Wallpaper Patterns. Wallpaper patterns show repetitions in two directions, often but not always at right angles to one another. We generally think of such patterns as being important in design, not only in art, but also on pottery, in fabrics, in decorations of all kinds, and in two-dimensional crystals. However, as pointed out earlier, the whole idea of symmetry, and the patterns that display one kind of symmetry or another, is of vital importance in anthropology, biology, chemistry, physics, geophysics, materials science, and engineering. There are exactly 17 one-color wallpaper patterns possible. These are illustrated schematically below.

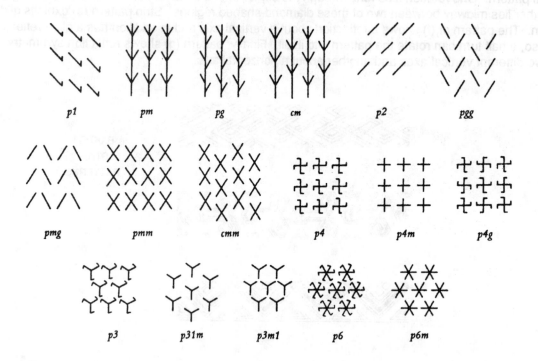

Recall that symmetry of one kind or another is characterized by an operation that leaves the pattern identical to that with which one started. Various operations are listed below together with the patterns above that exhibit that particular type of symmetry.

        Smallest rotation   360°: p1, pm, pg, cm
                            180°: p2, pgg, pmg, pmm, cmm
                             90°: p4, p4m, p4g
                            120°: p3, p31m, p3m1
                             60°: p6, p6m

    Reflections in one direction: pm, cm, pmg

    Reflections in two directions: pmm, cmm, p4g, p4m

    Reflections in three directions: p31m, p3m1

    Reflections in six directions: p6m

    Glide reflections: pg, cm, pgg, p31m

These, plus several more distinguishing characteristics, serve to identify the 17 1-D 1-color patterns. The flow chart for such patterns will identify each symmetry type. It appears on the second page following.

The seventeen wallpaper patterns can be illustrated by designs that originate in a variety of cultures worldwide. The patterns below exemplify each of the seventeen possible one-color two-dimensional patterns.

THE SEVENTEEN WALLPAPER PATTERNS FROM VARIOUS CULTURES

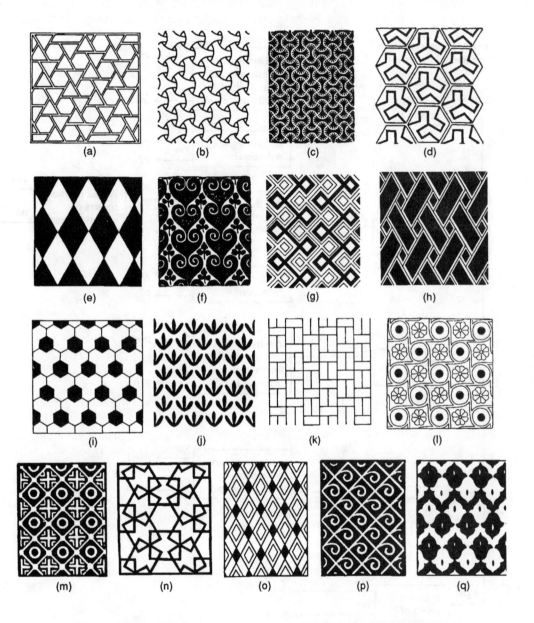

(a) Chinese window design. (p6)

(b) Japanese design. (p31m)

(c) Indian printer's block. (p4g)

(d) Persian drawing of tiles. (p3)

(e) Diamond-shaped 2-color design. (pmm)

(f) Egypto-Roman tapestry. (pm)

(g) Arabian design. (pg)

(h) Congo pattern. (pgg)

(i) Persian border pattern. (p3m1)

(j) Prehistoric New Mexican design. (cm)

(k) Brickwork pat tern. (p2)

(l) Egyptian painted ceiling. (p4)

(m) Greek ornamental design. (p4m)

(n) Mogul design. (p6m)

(o) Archibald Christie design. (cmm)

(p) Greek drapery pattern. (p1)

(q) Egyptian inlaid design. (pmg)

Flow chart for the seventeen two-dimensional patterns

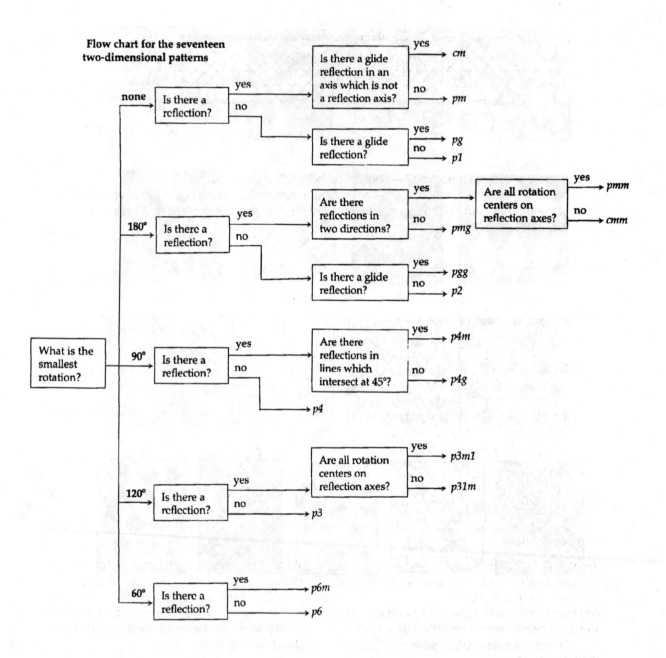

Using the Flow Charts — Hard to Find Rotation Axes. Axes of rotation are often quite easy to find. This is not the case, however, for the three patterns shown below where crosshairs show the location of rotation axes that are easy to miss. For the two wallpaper patterns all intersections of reflection axes mark rotation axes making these particular axes easy to locate.

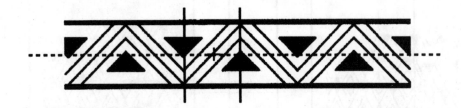

Is there a vertical reflection? — yes, about both of the axes shown.
Is there a horizontal reflection? — no, but there is a horiz. glide reflection axis (dashed).
Is there a half turn (180°)? yes, about a point such as the one marked with crosshairs.
IDENTIFICATION: pma2

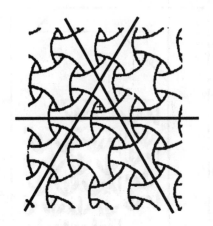

What is the smallest rotation? — 180°.
Is there a reflection? — yes, about axes
    such as those shown.
Are there reflections in two directions? — yes.
Are all rotation centers on reflection axes? —
    no, not the one marked with crosshairs.
IDENTIFICATION: cmm

What is the smallest rotation? — 120°.
Is there a reflection? — yes, about all
    of the axes of the type shown.
Are all rotation centers on reflection axes? —
    no, e.g., not the one marked with x-hairs.
IDENTIFICATION: p31m

On the page following there is presented a method for the identification of reflection and glide reflection axes. Although the presence of certain symmetry properties can sometimes be ascertained using only the "mind's eye," the superposition method provides an alternative way that makes a lesser demand on one's abilities in spatial visualization.

Superposition Method for the Identification of Symmetries

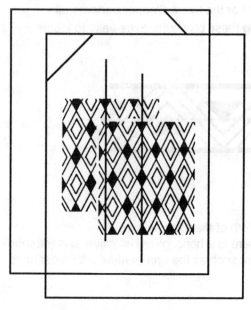

vertical reflection axes (cmm)

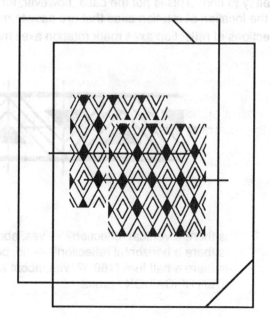

horizontal reflection axes (cmm)

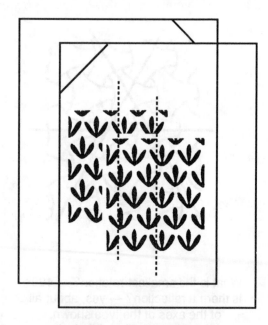

vertical glide reflection axis (cm)

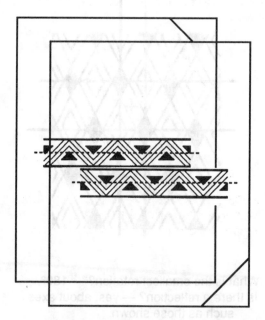

horizontal glide reflection axis (pma2)

It is not difficult to determine the smallest angle of rotation for wallpaper patterns. To check other symmetries use the procedure illustrated above. Make two xerox copies of patterns you wish to test. Draw on each copy and in the same place what you think is a vertical or horizontal reflection axis or glide axis. Take the front copy of the two and flip it over right-to-left to test for vertical axes. This is indicated by the shift in the upper right hand corner for each of the two figures at the left. Flip it top to bottom to test for horizontal axes as shown by the two figures on the right. Then, by looking through the two copies against sky light, superimpose the axes that you have drawn on the two sheets of paper. If the two patterns now coincide, the symmetry you're looking for has been established. For glide patterns such as those in the two bottom figures above there must also be a shift along the glide axis.

THE GOLDEN RATIO. It seems that man has always had a fascination with numbers. If you have mystical inclinations you might take a special interest in prime numbers, the astrological significance of your birth date, or numbers that appear on a lottery ticket. The ancient Greeks were intrigued by the properties of a number called the "geometric mean" of two other numbers. As we shall see, they thought that the geometric mean of two numbers played a crucial role in the design of a "perfect" rectangle. The *arithmetic mean* of two numbers is the result one obtains by adding the two numbers and dividing by the number of numbers added, in this case two. For example the arithmetic mean of the numbers 2 and 8 is $(2 + 8)/2 = 5$. The *geometric mean* of two numbers, however, is defined differently. It is the square root of the product of the two numbers. Thus the geometric mean of 2 and 8 is the square root of 2 x 8, and this is the number 4. Expressed symbolically, the geometric mean *s* of two numbers *a* and *b* is given by

$$s^2 = ab$$

which is the same relationship as

$$s / b = a / s$$

where it can readily be seen that the geometric mean *s* occupies some sort of middle position between the two numbers *a* and *b* just as the arithmetic mean does. Note that $4 / 8 = 2 / 4$. A geometric mean needn't be a whole number as it is in this special case.

Now think of rectangles of height h and width w as shown below. For a rectangle to be pleasing to the eye the ancient Greeks thought the ratio of height to width had to have a certain value. Put differently, the rectangle couldn't be too squarish with the ratio of height to width too large nor could it be too squat with the ratio of height to width too small. Which of the rectangles shown below do you find most pleasing?

WHICH IS MOST PLEASING TO THE EYE?

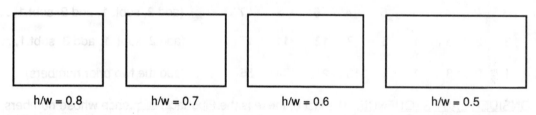

h/w = 0.8   h/w = 0.7   h/w = 0.6   h/w = 0.5

To make the ratio of height to width for a rectangle just right, the Greek numerologists (for that's what they were) felt that this ratio, h/w, had to be the same as the ratio of the width of the rectangle to the total length, height + width. Expressing this mathematically,

$$h / w = w / (h + w)$$

multiplying out $\qquad\qquad$ $h^2 + hw = w^2$

dividing through by w^2 $\qquad$ $(h^2 / w^2) + (h / w) = 1$

but h/w is a ratio "r," so that $\quad$ $r^2 + r = 1$ $\qquad\qquad$ and, if you remember the quadratic formula

one finally obtains $\qquad\qquad$ $r = 0.618 = h/w$ $\qquad$ for the most pleasing rectangle.

How does this value compare to the ratio for the rectangle you thought most pleasing? A classic example of this rectangle is provided by the front of the Parthenon on the Acropolis in Athens. Parts of the front, at a time when the Turks were in control of Athens, were sold to Lord Elgin (a hard "g") and later placed in the British Museum where they are today. The front of the Parthenon fits almost exactly into a "golden" rectangle, the name given to the esthetically pleasing rectangle. Golden rectangles appear in many architectural forms and paintings.

Shown below are four different Parthenons where the height to width ratios h/w given are the same as the four values for the rectangles on the previous page. When trying to answer the question as to which is most pleasing, you may now select a different h/w ratio. If that is the case, does the second figure from the right appear most pleasing simply because it is the image with which we're most familiar?

WHICH PARTHENON IS MOST PLEASING TO THE EYE?

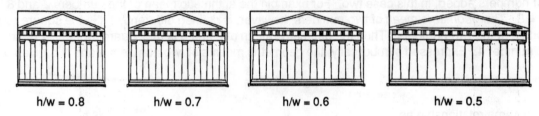

| h/w = 0.8 | h/w = 0.7 | h/w = 0.6 | h/w = 0.5 |

Introductory Problem Solutions

FIBONACCI NUMBERS. <u>IDENT PATTERNS</u>. The six sequences of numbers given are extended in bold type as shown below:

1	3	5	7	9	11	13	**15**	**17**	**19**	. . . (odd numbers)
1	4	9	16	25	36	49	**64**	**81**	**100**	. . . (squares of integers)
1	2	4	8	16	32	64	**128**	**256**	**512**	. . . (double each time)
1	3	2	4	3	5	4	**6**	**5**	**7**	. . . (add 2, subt. 1, add 2, subt.1, . . .)
1	3	2	5	4	8	7	**12**	**11**	**17**	. . . (add 2, subt. 1, add 3, subt.1, . . .)
1	1	2	3	5	8	13	**21**	**34**	**55**	. . . (add the two prior numbers)

<u>CONSIDER LAST SEQUENCE</u>. The last of these is the Fibonacci sequence whose numbers can often be found in nature. For example, the pine cone shown has 13 counterclockwise and 8 clockwise spirals. The sunflower exhibits 34 counterclockwise spirals and 55 clockwise spirals.

FLIPPING AND ROTATING A BOOK. <u>CREATE MATRIX</u>.
Pairs of operations that commute and those that do not commute can be determined from the matrix at the right.

<u>APPLY MATRIX</u>.For example, it was previously asserted that operations D and B commute. From the table we see that when these are performed in either order, the single equivalent operation is E. For operations D and A, however, their order does make a difference. Operation D first and A second is equivalent to the single operation F. On the other hand A first and D second is equivalent to the single operation G. Excluding all operations involving the identity operation I either as the first or second operation, and also excluding each operation followed by itself, there remain nine pairs of operations that commute and 12 that do not commute.   [Skip the next two pages. Reference will be made to them later].

Second operation

First operation	I	A	B	C	D	E	F	G
I	I	A	B	C	D	E	F	G
A	A	B	C	I	G	F	D	E
B	B	C	I	A	E	D	G	F
C	C	I	A	B	F	G	E	D
D	D	F	E	G	I	B	A	C
E	E	G	D	F	B	I	C	A
F	F	E	G	D	C	A	I	B
G	G	D	F	E	A	C	B	I

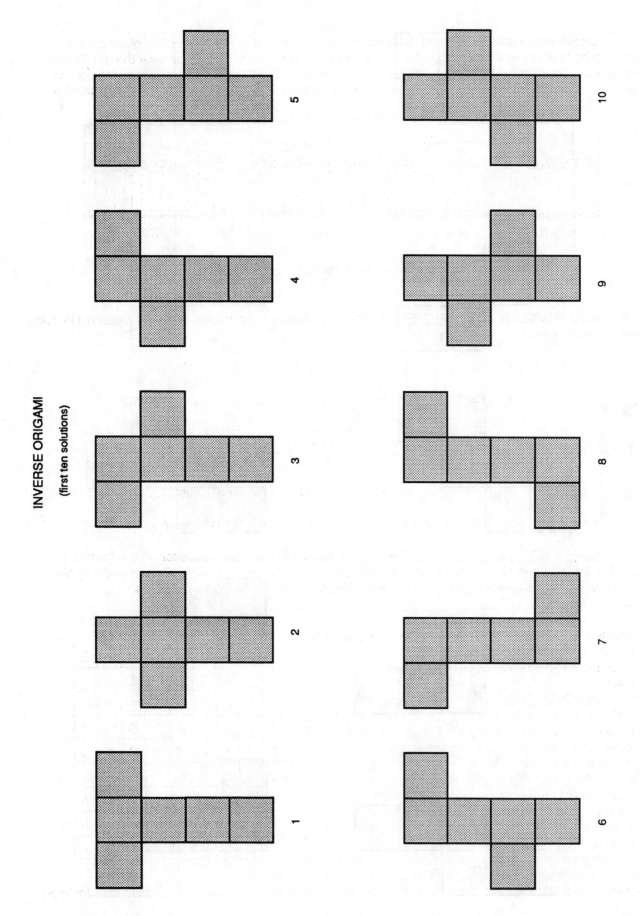

INVERSE ORIGAMI

(first ten solutions)

117

INVERSE ORIGAMI
(second ten solutions)

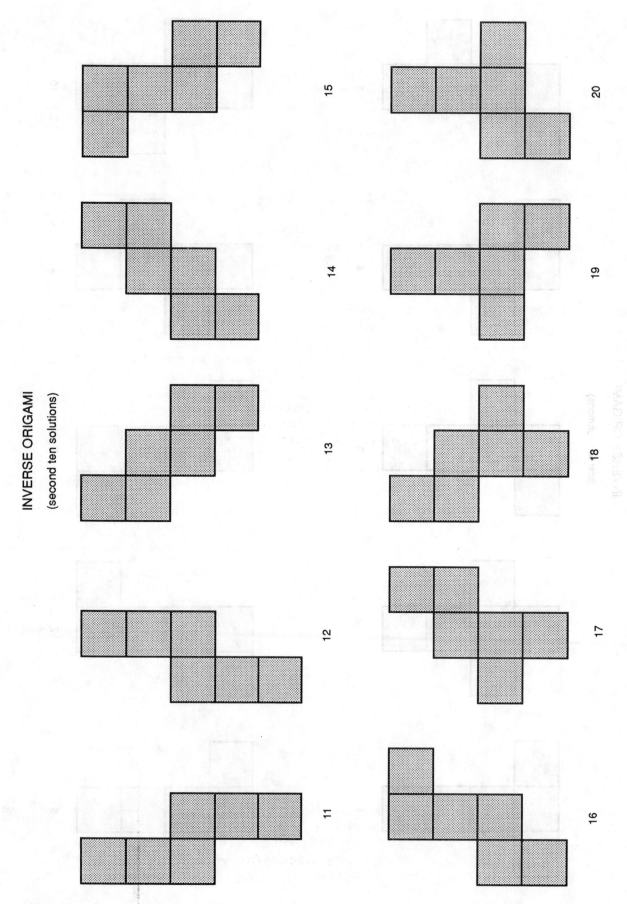

11

12

13

14

15

16

17

18

19

20

INVERSE ORIGAMI (constructing a cube). <u>RECAP PROB</u>. Twenty plane figures, each consisting of six identical squares, are shown near the beginning of this chapter. Among the twenty are two "imposter" pairs, i.e., two pairs where each figure will not fold into a cube.

  <u>IDENT IMPOSTER PAIRS</u>. Examining the 20 figures that contain the two imposter pairs and using our powers of spatial visualization one can see that it is the pairs 9,10 and 13,14 that will not fold into a cube.

  <u>IDENT VALID PAIRS</u>. New figures 9 and 10 that will fold to form a cube are shown on the immediately preceding pages. They are seen to be variations on the figures 1 through 8, each with a spine of 4 squares in a row. The new figures to fill the now vacated spots 13 and 14 are seen to be variations of patterns shown in figures 15, 16, 17, and 18.

THE EXISTENTIAL "THERE." <u>ANALYSE PATTERNS</u>. Part I. Looking first at sentences 1 and 2 we see that when *there* is inserted at the beginning of the sentence, the subject and verb are interchanged (note that this does not work for sentences 3 and 4). Inspection of sentences 5, 13, and 17 reveals that when there is a compound verb (such as *was killed*) the noun is inserted between the two parts of the verb. Part 2. The special conditions that apply are as follows: (a) examination of sentences 3 to 10 shows that there-insertion is grammatical only when the verb is a form of *to be* or a compound verb with a form of *to be*. (b) ungrammatical sentences 14, 16, and 18 show that for there-insertion the subject of the sentence cannot be a definite noun (i.e., preceded by *the*).

Additional Problems

*FIBONACCI'S PUZZLE. In the year 1202 a distinguished Italian mathematician, Leonardo of Pisa, also known as Fibonacci, published the following puzzle in his book on mathematics.

> Assume that every month a pair of rabbits produces another pair, and all new pairs begin to bear young ones two months after their own birth. If you start with one pair of one month old rabbits, how many pairs of rabbits will be born in one year?

To solve this puzzle it will be helpful to draw a tree diagram that starts with a single pair P of one month old rabbits at the beginning of the first month. At the end of the first month there will be the original rabbit pair P plus a second pair of newborn rabbits, designate them N. Continue this tree diagram noting the number of rabbit pairs, both P's and N's. The number wanted is simply the number of rabbit pairs at the end of the twelfth month. The sequence of numbers starting with the one pair of one-month old rabbits at the beginning of the year and continuing for twelve more months is a part of the famous sequence of numbers named for the author of this puzzle.

  THE CHAMBERED NAUTILUS. The shell of a chambered nautilus, when sliced in half to reveal its structure, exhibits a beautiful spiral arrangement of internal chambers. A spiral such as this can be drawn using the geometry of the golden rectangle. For a rectangle whose height h is less than its width w, the ratio h/w = 0.618. Draw such a rectangle to scale. Make the width five or six inches or so.

THE CHAMBERED
NAUTILUS

Step 1. Divide the golden rectangle into a square at the left leaving a rectangle standing on one of its narrow sides at the right. This rectangle is another golden rectangle. (Can you convince yourself that this is true?) Mark the bottom left corner and the upper right corner of the square with small dots. These will form the first and second points for a spiral figure. Now, rotate this entire figure a quarter turn counterclockwise making the new golden rectangle at the top one whose long sides are horizontal.

Step 2. Perform precisely the same operations of step 1 on this new smaller golden rectangle. (Don't forget to mark the opposite corner of the new small square and rotate the entire new figure a quarter turn counterclockwise).

Steps 3, 4, 5, and 6. Repeat the operations of the prior step.

You now have six golden rectangles in addition to the one you started with and seven points marked with small dots. Connect these seven points with a smooth curve to form a spiral. Where in nature, in addition to the chambered nautilus, can such spirals be found?

DISTINGUISHING A "Z' FROM A "2." One of the tasks that a computer does reasonably well is to digitize scanned documents containing text. The software that does this is referred to as an Optical Character Recognition (OCR) program. Once digitized, text can be sized, given a new font, or edited in whatever way is desired. This process is just one example of an important general process referred to as *pattern recognition*. To be successful the OCR software must identify each letter in a text accurately. Certain letters are more difficult to identify than others because they can be mistaken for some other letter or digit. For example, it is easy to mistake a "B" for the numeral "8," and an "8" for a "B." It may also be difficult to distinguish the letter "Z" from the numeral "2." This latter example is the subject of the present problem. Given below are fourteen fonts in which a capital letter Z and the digit 2 are shown. While not exhaustive since there are many hundreds of different fonts, the sample is large enough to make some reasonable generalizations about Z's and 2's. Identify three to five points on each character that may be used to distinguish the two. Which characteristics are the same for each character and which are different? Make a table or draw a diagram that organizes your findings. Let someone else write the software that executes a program that actually makes the distinction. Imagine how difficult it is for a computer to convert hand written (cursive) text into print. Nonetheless, there are such programs.

Basset	Z 2	Boston	Z 2
Chancery	Z 2	Chicago	Z 2
Geneva	Z 2	Gilde	Z 2
Helvetica	Z 2	Krone	Z 2
New York	Z 2	Optim	Z 2
Palamino	Z 2	Palatino	Z 2
Schoolbook	Z 2	Times	Z 2

*PATTERNS IN BRICK. One of the more common patterns that we see every day are patterns in brick. Bricks can be laid in a great many different ways. Some patterns are rather plain, some decorative. Shown below are nine patterns, some more commonly seen in sidewalls and others at ground level to form courtyards, walkways, and patios. None in this collection of patterns exhibit brick ends as all bricks are oriented with the side of the brick showing. The width to the height of all bricks is in the ratio 2:1. Identify all patterns according to their symmetry using the flow chart for two-dimensional one-color patterns. You will find six different symmetries in the collection of nine patterns.

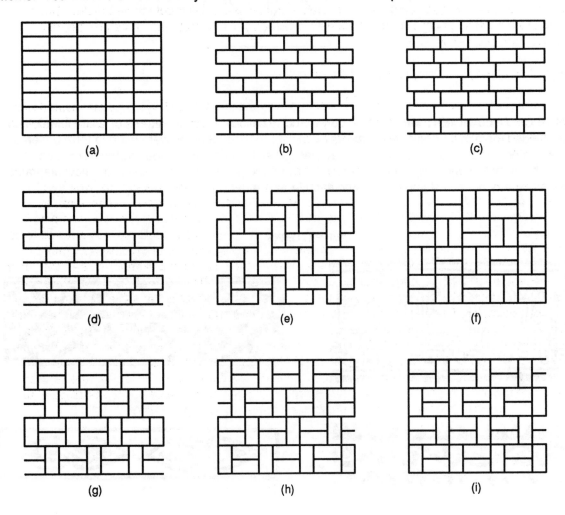

*INVERSE ORIGAMI (constructing a tetrahedron). Earlier in this chapter we saw that a hexahedron (cube) could be formed by 20 different flat patterns of six connected squares. In that problem you were given the fact that there were twenty such patterns and in addition, that only 16 of these figures were correct. Finally, you were asked to identify the incorrect figures and replace these with four that are correct, i.e., that will fold to form a cube. Here we have the same kind of a problem for a tetrahedron as we had before for the cube. A tetrahedron is a regular solid consisting of 4 sides each of which is an equilateral triangle. First, how many plane figures are there consisting of four identical equilateral triangles connected by at least one side? Having identified these, the second problem is to determine which can be folded to form a tetrahedron and which cannot. Shown below is a tetrahedron and, at the right, one of a number of figures consisting of four equilateral triangles that will fold to form a tetrahedron. Incidentally, the tetrahedron is a model for the ammonia molecule. The nitrogen atom lies at the center of a tetrahedron while the four hydrogen atoms occupy places at each of the four vertices.

THE TETRAHEDRON

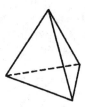 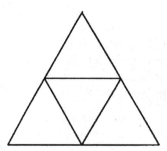

*PATTERNS OF THE ANCIENT MEXICANS. Jorge Enciso collected stamp patterns of ancient Mexicans and included them in his book *design motifs of ancient mexico.* Stamps were used to form patterns in pottery and other terra cotta items while the clay was still soft. Strip patterns generated from such stamps are shown below and wallpaper patterns in fabric on the page following. Using the flow diagrams identify the symmetry of each stamp pattern and each fabric pattern.

STAMP PATTERNS

AGREEMENT RULES IN SPANISH. The following linguistics pattern problem is taken from *Fundamentals of Linguistic Analysis* by Ronald W. Langacker.

State the agreement rules to which the data below attests. Comment on the phonological manifestation of this agreement. ["phonology" is the science of speech sounds]. Are there exceptions to these rules? A masculine noun is indicated by [m] and a feminine noun by [f].

(1)	un caballo[m] blanco	'a white horse'
(2)	las mesas[f] rojas	'the red tables'
(3)	unas casas[f] blancas	'some white houses'
(4)	el palo[m] negro	'the black stick'
(5)	los palos rojos	'the red sticks'
(6)	una mesa negra	'a black table'
(7)	la mesa blanca	'the white table'
(8)	unos caballos negros	'some black horses'
(9)	la casa roja	'the red house'
(10)	un palo rojo	'a red stick'
(11)	las casas negras	'the black houses'
(12)	unos palos blancos	'some white sticks'

MUSICAL PATTERNS. In his book *What to Listen for in Music* Copeland classifies musical forms according to five categories:

I. SECTIONAL FORM

two part, or binary form A - B

A - A - B

A - A - B - B

where A and B seem to balance one another;
B is often little more than a rearrangement of A;
B is often made up partly of a repetition of A and partly a kind of development
of certain phrases in A

three part form   A - B - A

B is often a distinct contrast to A, sometimes like an independent little piece;
can connect A to B by a bridge passage and, likewise, B to A;
return to A section made up of a combination of both A and B

rondo   A - B - A - C - A - D - A, etc.

free sectional form   A - B - B

A - B - C - A

A - B - A - C - A - B - A

II. VARIATIONS

rhythmic
contrapuntal
combinations of the preceding
variations: A - A' - A" - A'" - A "" , etc. (usual scheme), but also
A - A' - A" - A' - A'" - A"" - A' - A

III. FUGAL FORM

> the fuge proper
> concerto grosso
> chorale-prelude
> motets and madrigals

IV. SONATA FORM

> three-movement species: fast - slow - fast
> four movement: fast - slow - moderately fast - very fast
>> first movement: sonata-allegro form
>> second movement: theme and variation or slow version of rondo
>> third movement: minuet or scherzo A - B - A form
>> fourth movement: extended rondo or sonata-allegro form

V. FREE FORMS

For one movement of classical music make a thorough analysis of its musical pattern, i.e., its musical form using Copeland's classification scheme. Alternatively, analyse Scott Joplin's rags or some other less than classical music.

ACTIVITY—DESIGN YOUR OWN STRIP PATTERNS. On the following page there are seven strip patterns made by shading in certain squares in each grid. Think of the strips as designs on a belt, and each shaded square as a piece of turquoise or other semi-precious stone. Each of the seven possible strip symmetries is shown and each is labelled. Each pattern is identified through use of the flow chart for one-color one-dimensional patterns. Interestingly, only two motifs in various orientations have been used to make these patterns, one a Y-shaped arrangement of four squares and the other a fish hook shaped pattern consisting of three squares. Exclude the vertical and horizontal lines that form the grid from the patterns that are formed.

On the page after the example patterns there are seven strips with no shading in any of the squares. Use this sheet or a xerox copy of it to design your own strip patterns by shading the smaller squares as you wish. Your objective is to create seven strip patterns which together exhibit all seven of the possible strip symmetries. Label each of your patterns according to its symmetry classification. Do not repeat any of the patterns shown on the page of example patterns. You will find that there are a number of ways of creating the symmetry pm11, for example, and similarly for the other symmetries. You will of course want to use the flow chart for strip patterns to assist you. Use a regular or colored pencil to lightly shade in the squares so that these may be easily erased in case your resulting pattern is not what you desire. Label all of the patterns that you obtain.

Alternatively, use the seven strips consisting of circles to accomplish the same objective as that described above. These strips appear on the third page following. Be sure to identify each of the strip symmetries that you have drawn.

ACTIVITY—COMPUTER GENERATED PATTERNS. If you have your own computer or have access to one, you might consider generating an interesting pattern using your draw program. Starting with a pleasing motif, use the draw program's duplicate, translate, rotate, and reflection commands to create several attractive strip patterns or wallpaper patterns.

125

EXAMPLE STRIP PATTERNS

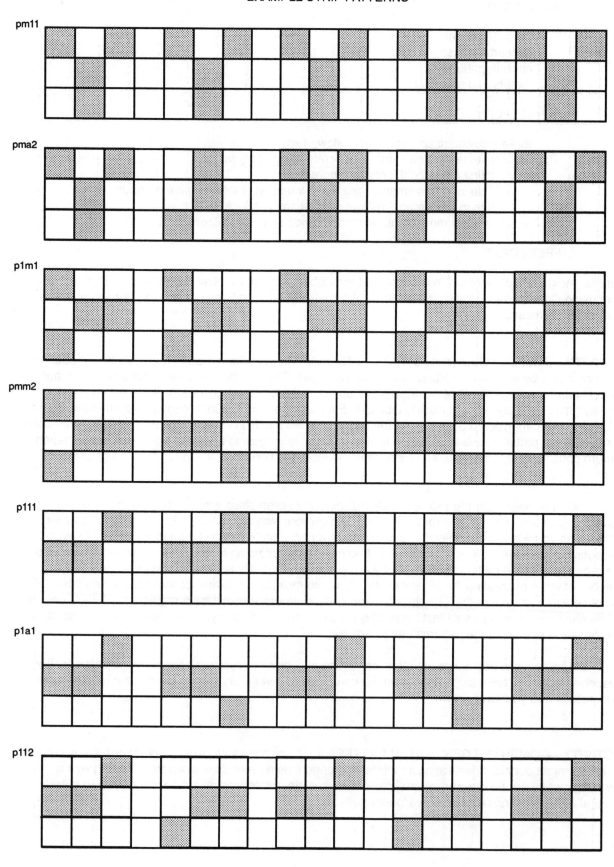

126

DESIGN YOUR OWN STRIP PATTERNS

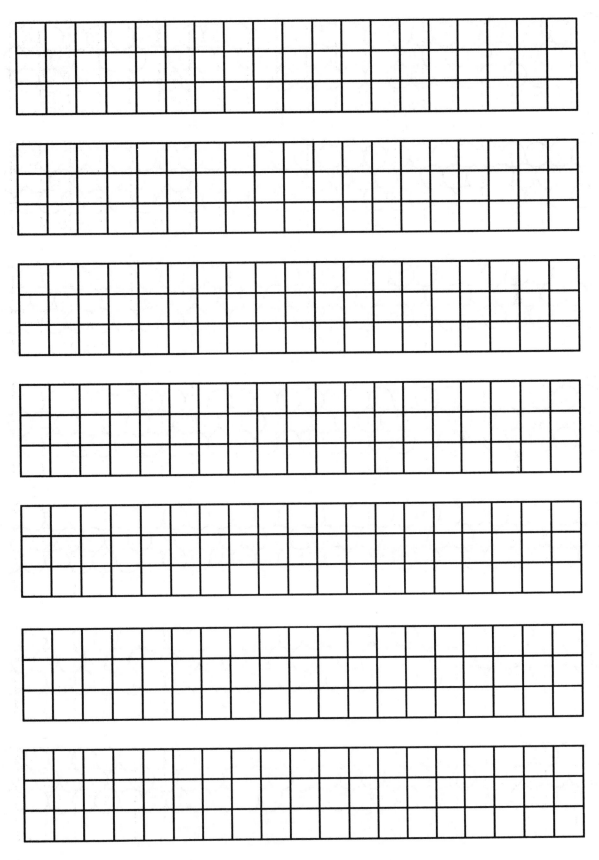

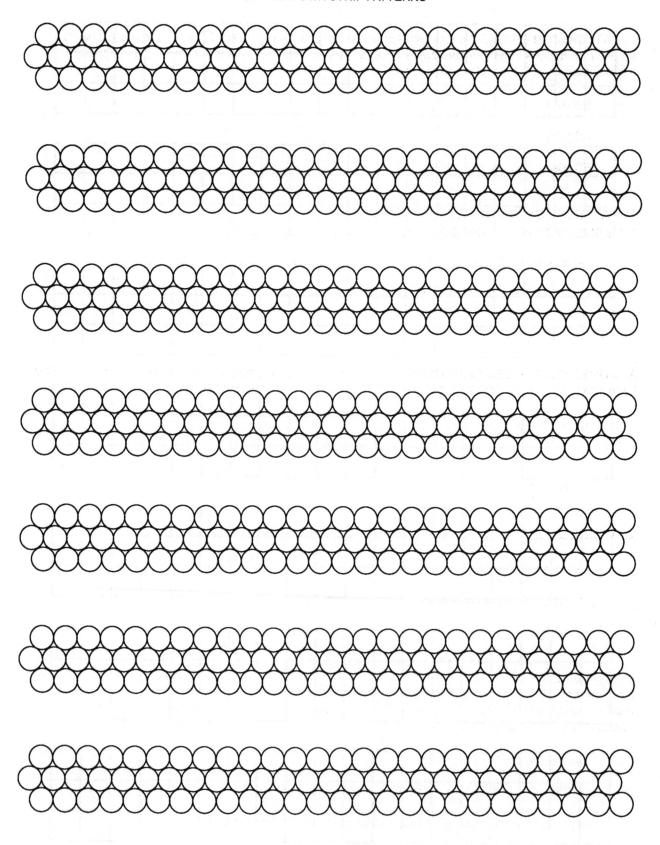

1. PATTERNS IN BRICK. If bricks with a width-to-height ratio of 3:1 (not 2:1 as it is in this problem) were laid to make a basket-weave pattern like that shown in figure (e) in the manual, the symmetry classification would be (circle correct response):

      (a) cmm

      (b) pmg

      (c) pgg

2. PATTERNS OF THE ANCIENT MEXICANS. There are six fabric patterns shown in the manual. How many of these six exhibit (ignore defects):

      (a) a vertical reflection axis? _____

      (b) a horizontal reflection axis? _____

      (c) a glide reflection? _____

3. AGREEMENT RULES IN SPANISH. The masculine singular articles (both definite and indefinite) that have special forms, i.e., are exceptions to a rule, are (circle the correct response):

      (a) *un* and *el*

      (b) *un* and *una*

      (c) *las* and *el*

4. MUSICAL PATTERNS. Patterns in music are exhibited by repetitions of

      (a) musical themes

      (b) fast and slow movements

      (c) rhythms

5. EXAMPLE STRIP PATTERNS. Seven example strip patterns are shown in the manual. These have been created by coloring certain squares in a grid 3 squares wide and 19 squares long. In each strip the motif is repeated five times. Which of the following operations leave the symmetry of all the strips unchanged? Circle all correct responses.

      (a) turning the strip end-for-end.

      (b) flipping the strip over about a horizontal axis.

      (c) rotating each motif 90° about an axis perpendicular to the plane of the strip.

Chapter VI Self Test—Bob's Strip Patterns

Place the identification of the symmetry of each strip pattern at the right.

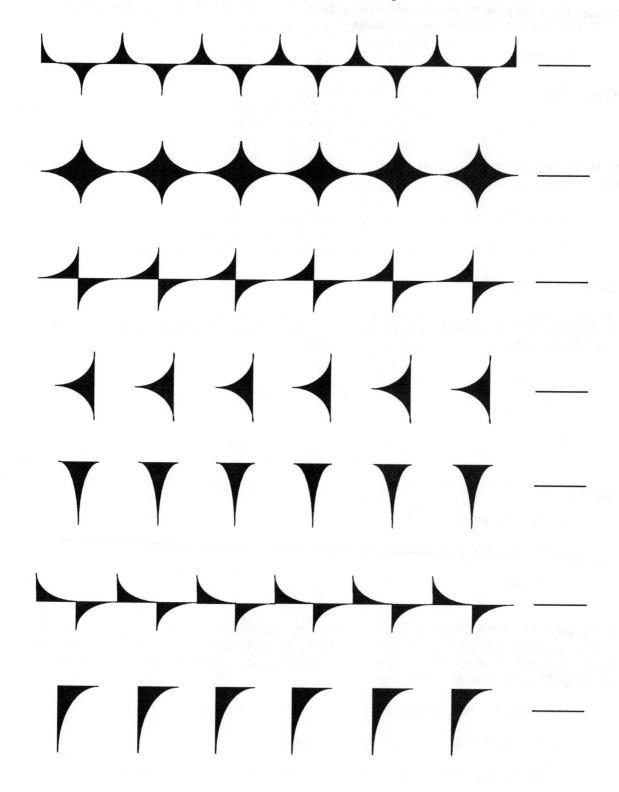

VII. PLAUSIBLE REASONING

Introductory Problems: PHASES OF VENUS
SLAVERY AND THE CIVIL WAR
ANALOGY
FOUND GUILTY / ACTUALLY GUILTY

Background: LOGIC IN LANGUAGE
LOGICAL RELATIONSHIPS
      Truth Table Representation
      2X2 Matrix Representation
      Graphical Representation
PLAUSIBLE REASONING
      Learning
      Relevance
      You are the Prosecuting Attorney
      Constructing a Bayes' Diagram
      Successive Verification / Multiple Evidence

Introductory Problem Solutions

Additional Problems: BLUE AND GREEN TAXICABS REVISITED
THE MAMMALARY CANCER PROBLEM REVISITED
THE OIL LOBBYIST
SMOKING AND LUNG CANCER
PART TIME JOBS
EINSTEIN'S PREDICTIONS
PARADOX IN DIAGNOSTICS
MR. HILLER'S MURDER
LEMPERT'S PARADOX REEXAMINED
ACTIVITY - Use of Plausible Reasoning in a Book or Newspaper Article

Self Tests: SELECTED PROBLEMS
THE INCLUSIVE "OR"

The Ptolemaic universe, an early model, as presented in Peter Apian's *Cosmographia (1539).*

VII. PLAUSIBLE REASONING

In this chapter the foundations for a structure of Plausible Reasoning are explored. By the word *plausible* is meant the kind of reasoning that is persuasive without being formal. It is the kind of reasoning most often used in everyday thinking, particularly in critical thinking. While plausible reasoning is in fact based upon formal logic this relationship is not readily apparent. Plausible reasoning is to be found in courts of law, in political campaign rhetoric, in the doctor's office, in an auto dealer's showroom, in history books, on a therapist's couch — in fact almost everywhere that people attempt to persuade others to their points of view, draw conclusions from observations, invent new social institutions, or make speculations of one kind or another. The "father" of plausible reasoning is Georg Polya who wrote the seminal works in the field, the two volume set *Mathematics and Plausible Reasoning*. He referred to his later work *How to Solve It* as a dictionary of problem solving heuristic. As in Chapter II, the name of Thomas Bayes is featured in discussions of plausible reasoning because such reasoning is based primarily upon subjective probability. It is what people generally use in communicating ideas, exchanging views, and refining both their questions and their conclusions.

To illustrate the widespread use of plausible reasoning, a Hispanic laborer was once noted to be carrying a bottle of peppermint schnapps to the checkout register. A curious person behind him in line thought this strange and asked the man why he was purchasing a bottle of peppermint schnapps. "Oh," he replied, "a friend of mine recommended it as a great "Mexican drink." The questioner responded that it is a German product which is very popular in that country. The man with the bottle appeared puzzled, perhaps thinking that information received from his informant was usually quite reliable. To his interrogator he responded, after a moment's hesitation, "How *sure* are you?"

Individuals, being only human, often reveal deficiencies in plausible reasoning. On occasion, however, reasoning that at first appears to be faulty is not, as in many cases in advertising and public relations. On other occasions deficiencies are real. In such cases there may simply be a lack of appropriate skills. Chapter VIII is devoted to an analysis of common kinds of deficiencies in reasoning, both real and supposedly real. Here, however, the emphasis is upon the characteristics of sound reasoning.

Introductory Problems

PHASES OF VENUS. In the sixteenth century the prevailing view as to the arrangement of the sun, moon, and planets was the Ptolemaic view that the earth was at the center of this system with the moon orbiting about the earth relatively close by and with the sun and planets in orbits about the earth farther out. In 1543, however, the Polish astronomer Copernicus proposed a new arrangement with the sun, not the earth, at the center of things. Copernicus thus hypothesized a heliocentric system to replace the geocentric model. Observations at the time neither contradicted nor supported one view of the planetary system or the other. Was the sun at the center of the universe or was it the earth? It wasn't until the year 1609 when the first telescope was invented that observational evidence could be brought to bear to settle the question of whether the Copernican system or the older Ptolemaic system was correct.

In the Ptolemaic universe the earth is at the center and the moon, planets, sun, and stars occupy a series of concentric rings about the earth. In the years prior to the time that Galileo first viewed the skies with a telescope, speculation was rampant regarding the two models, the earth system and the solar system. One of Galileo's students suggested to him that if the Copernican system was correct, then Venus, which lies between the sun and the earth, should show all the same phases as the moon, from a thin crescent through quarter full, to full, and back again to a waning crescent. In consequence, the student continued, if Venus actually does show phases like the Moon, the new sun-centered model must surely be correct. The problem here is whether to agree or disagree with the student that his stated conclusion is correct.

Before examining the student's conjecture one must understand that at the time the simple model with the moon, sun, planets, and stars in circular orbits about the earth had been abandoned in favor of a more sophisticated version of the Ptolemaic model in which the moon and planets did not themselves move in circles about the earth. Instead, they were presumed to be attached to giant wheels whose axles moved in circles about the earth. This modification was necessary to account for the so-called retrograde motion of the planet Mars and also, the fact that Venus never appeared in the sky at an angle greater than 48° from the direction to the sun. The motion of Venus in this model relative to the earth and to the sun is diagrammed below.

PHASES OF VENUS — PTOLEMAIC MODEL

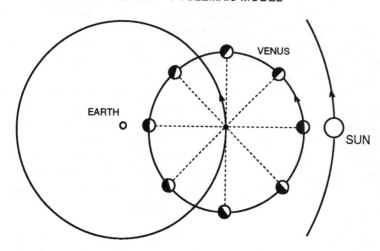

According to this model, starting with Venus nearest the sun, an observer on earth would first see the dark side of Venus and later a series of crescent shapes followed by another view of the dark side followed by the reverse sequence of crescent shapes for Venus.

The student must have realized this. Recall that he said that *if* Copernicus was right in thinking that the sun, not the earth, was at the center of things, *then* Venus would show all the phases of the moon, crescent shapes leading up to half full and gibbous shapes and from there to full. A heliocentric model showing only the earth, the sun, and Venus, is given below. This model gives moon-like phases for Venus.

PHASES OF VENUS
COPERNICAN MODEL

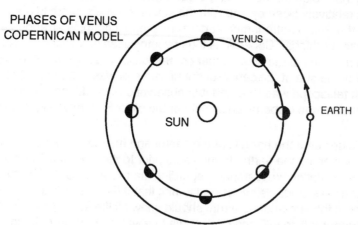

Of course the advent of the telescope did bring the moon-like phases of Venus into view. Does this mean, as the student claimed, that the Copernican model was indeed correct?

SLAVERY AND THE CIVIL WAR. The Civil War in America was a long and bloody struggle between the North and the South. There were a number of important factors that led to the beginning of the war when southern forces fired on Fort Sumter. Perhaps the most important factor contributing to the onset of war was the issue of slavery about which emotions ran extremely high. Let us assume that this single factor *strongly suggested* that military conflict was inevitable. The supposition, then, is that the issue of slavery nearly implied civil war as a consequence. A strictly hypothetical question is this: If there had been no civil war, could one have then concluded that the issue of slavery was not really considered to be of great significance? To fix ideas, let S represent the issue of slavery and CW the onset of civil war. Set the prior probability that the issue of slavery S was significant be $P(S) = 0.50$ and let $P(CW|S) = 0.90$ and $P(CW|\bar{S}) = 0.30$. Now find the value of $P(S|CW)$ and $P(S|\overline{CW})$. Can it be said that no civil war, $(\overline{CW})$, would strongly suggest that slavery was not a dominant issue, i.e., $\bar{S}$?

ANALOGY. In discussing the situation in which two properties are said to be analogous, Polya presents for comparison the data in the two tables shown below. In the table at the left are listed perimeters of certain plane figures, each figure having the same area. (This area has been set at 1.00.) At the right below are listed the fundamental frequencies of vibration of membranes stretched to cover certain plane geometric shapes, again each shape having the same area. The fundamental vibrational frequency of a circular membrane such as found in a kettle drum occurs when the entire membrane vibrates up and down in unison. In higher frequency modes of vibration part of the circular membrane moves upward at the same time that other parts are vibrating downward. Similar remarks could be made about the other shapes. What is important is that the fundamental frequency listed is the lowest possible vibrational frequency for that shape.

Perimeters		Frequencies	
Circle	3.55	Circle	4.261
Square	4.00	Square	4.443
Quadrant	4.03	Quadrant	4.551
Rectangle 3:2	4.08	Sextant	4.616
Semicircle	4.10	Rectangle 3:2	4.624
Sextant	4.21	Equilateral triangle	4.774
Rectangle 2:1	4.24	Semicircle	4.803
Equilateral triangle	4.56	Rectangle 2:1	4.967
Rectangle 3:1	4.64	Isosceles right triangle	4.967
Isosceles right triangle	4.84	Rectangle 3:1	5.736

The entries in each listing increase from top to bottom and while the first three plane figures, the circle, square, and quadrant, are the same in each table, later entries are not in the same order but not far from it. We say that the two tables are *analogous* to each other or, closely correspond to each other. While the listings are the same in many respects, they also differ in certain respects. According to the table it would seem that of all plane figures the circle has the least perimeter (circumference) for a given area. It had long been a conjecture that no other plane figure had a smaller perimeter. Later, it was **proven**, mathematically, that it was true. What can be said now about the conjecture that the circular membrane, of all plane membranes, vibrates in its fundamental mode at the very lowest frequency?

FOUND GUILTY / ACTUALLY GUILTY. One-hundred individuals are brought to trial. Some of these are found guilty (FG) and some are found innocent (FI). Some are actually guilty (AG) and some are actually innocent (AI). Given below are reasonable expectations of society for the judicial system:

$P(AG) = 0.40$
$P(FG|AG) = 0.90$
$P(FG|AI) = 0.05$

Find the values for both $P(AG|FG)$ and $P(AG|AI)$. Can it be said that the statements that an individual is AG and that he is also FG are analogous, i.e., closely correspond to one another?

LOGIC IN LANGUAGE. In ordinary language we frequently use expressions that denote logical relation-ships between statements, conjectures, or propositions. Most of us probably don't realize how often we use this kind of language. We can also find it in newspapers, magazines, on TV, in advertising, in books, and in ordinary conversation. Listed below are excerpts from Tapscott's *Elementary Applied Symbolic Logic* in a chapter he calls "A Logic-English Translation Guide."

Conjunctive Operators

and	but
although	however
. . . also . . .	whereas
both . . . and . . .	but even so
after all	for
nevertheless	besides
not only . . . but also . . .	in spite of the fact that
plus the fact that	
still (*except in the sense of* 'any more')	Note: Of the 21 entries in this list, the
even though (*but not* 'even if')	following five also do double duty as
inasmuch as *(but not* 'insofar as')	temporal indicators: *still, while, since, as,* &
while (*in the sense of* 'although')	*and (when used in the sense of* 'and then')
since (*in the sense of* 'whereas', *but not* 'after')	
as (*in the sense of* 'whereas', *not* 'at the same time as')	

Disjunctive Operators

or	either . . . or . . .
or else	or, alternatively
otherwise	with the alternative that
unless	

Conditional Operators

Forms in which the antecedent (. . .) comes before the consequent (- - -)

if . . . then - - -	if . . . , - - -
given that . . . it follows that - - -	given that . . . , - - -
not . . . unless - - -	in case . . . , - - -
insofar as . . . , - - -	so long as . . . , - - -
. . . implies - - -	. . . leads to - - -
. . . only if - - -	whenever . . . , - - -
. . . is a sufficient condition for - - -	. . . means that - - -
to the extent that . . . , - - -	

Forms in which the consequent (- - -) comes before the antecedent (. . .)

- - - if . . .	- - - in case . . .
unless - - - , not . . .	- - - whenever . . .
- - - insofar as . . .	- - - so long as . . .
- - - follows from . . .	- - - is implied by . . .
- - - is a necessary condition for . . .	only if - - - , . . .
- - - provided that . . .	- - - to the extent that . . .

Biconditional Operators

if and only if	if but only if
is equivalent to	is a necessary and sufficient condition for
just in case	just if
just insofar as	just to the extent that

This table lists phrases, called *operators,* that connect two statements or propositions. For example: The child has a high fever *and* a rash on her face. The defendant is likely to be fined *or* serve several weeks in jail *or* both. *If* we get no more rain this month *then* we'll set an all-time record for low rainfall. Getting an advanced degree *is equivalent to* a union card when it comes to getting a teaching position. Since the emphasis here is upon logical relationships among propositions and not on the propositions themselves, it is useful to denote the two propositions involved as proposition A and proposition B. The preceding statements can now be abbreviated to read as follows: A *and* B, A *or* B *or* both, *If* A *then* B, and A *is equivalent to* B.

Truth Table Representation. We start with the simplest possible kind of logic, that in which propositions are either true or false, i.e., T or F. In the truth table below the two columns at the left give all the possible combinatins of T and F. These combinations represent possible conjunctive relationships between propositions A and B. In the first row we have both A and B true, in the second row A is true while B is false, in the third row A is false and B true, and in the last row both propositions are false. These combinations lie to the left of the heavier vertical line. To the right of this line are the truth values, T's or F's, of these conjunctive combinations for the particular logical relationship indicated at the head of the column. Thus each vertical column of T's and F's forms a kind of fingerprint for a logical relationship. All T's in a column represents the relationship A*B, called complete affirmation. In the next column a T then an F followed by two T's represents A→B, etc. Symbols are used rather than words to denote logical relationships. Thus A→B stands for "if A then B," or what is the same thing, "A implies B," i.e. the truth of A implies the truth of B. A←B is written for "A if B" or "A is implied by B." A↔B represents A implies B *and* B implies A. It can also be stated as "A if and only if B" or "A is equivalent to B."

TRUTH TABLE

A	B	A*B	A→B	A←B	A↔B	A
T	T	T	T	T	T	T
T	F	T	F	T	F	T
F	T	T	T	F	F	F
F	F	T	T	T	T	F

The relationship of implication A→B gives many people difficulty when it is read as "if A then B." That relationship is evident in the first two rows where we get a T when both A and B are true but an F when A is true but B is false. What *isn't* evident is that when A is false, B can then be either true or false. The "if . . . then" language simply doesn't specify the relationship when proposition A is false. The relationship A←B can be thought of as B implies A which must be the same as A→B with A and B interchanged. The relationship A↔B can be stated not only as "A is equivalent to B," but also as "the truth of A is a necessary and sufficient condition for the truth of B." As can be seen from the truth table the relationship is T when both A and B are true and again when both are false, but is F otherwise. Heading the last column we simply have A, i.e., "A is true," which has truth values identical to those in the extreme lefthand column. A good way to look at this relationship is that A is true *no matter what* — no matter whether B is true or false.

As examples of the above logical relationships, relationships which can be described by their columns of T's and F's, consider the following translations into ordinary English:

S*W　　In April some days are sunny and warm (S.W), some are cloudy and warm ($\bar{S}$.W), some are sunny and cool (S.$\bar{W}$), while still others are cloudy and cool ($\bar{S}.\bar{W}$).

S→G　　If Henry gets the top score (S) in his psychology class he is then sure to receive a top grade (G).

B←F　　Mary's flowers will have many large beautiful blooms (B) provided that she fertilizes them regularly.

J↔M　　Janet and Mary are undecided whether they will go to the gymnastics meet. They will either both go (J.M) or neither will go ($\bar{J}.\bar{M}$).

H　　　One's height (H) is in no way influenced by one's intelligence (I).

2X2 Matrix Representation. At this point we make a significant break with the supposition that propositions can only be true or false. We now take a proposition to have a certain probability for being true and a corresponding probability for being false. For proposition A, for example, $P(A)$ is the probability it is true and $P(\bar{A})$ the probability that it is false. Recall from Chapter II that $P(A) + P(\bar{A}) = 1$. In a table similar to the one above, for each logical relationship reading from the top down the elements are $P(A.B)$, $P(A.\bar{B})$, $P(\bar{A}.B)$, and $P(\bar{A}.\bar{B})$. One example (and only one) of each of the logical relationships with which we have been working is shown in the probability table below.

PROBABILITY TABLE EXAMPLES

Conjunction	A*B	A→B	A←B	A↔B	A
$P(A.B)$	0.48	0.20	0.33	0.40	0.30
$P(A.\bar{B})$	0.22	0	0.33	0	0.70
$P(\bar{A}.B)$	0.12	0.35	0	0	0
$P(\bar{A}.\bar{B})$	0.18	0.45	0.33	0.60	0

The probability values entered in the above table for each of the five relationships shown between propositions A and B are obtained as follows. First, 0's are placed in each box if the corresponding truth table location that has an F in it. Other than this, the non-zero entries in each column must add to one. Any set of values that satisfies these two conditions is an example of the logical relationship specified at the top of the column. An immediate conclusion is that there is not just one A*B relationship, nor just one A→B relationship, nor just one of any of the others, but many relationships all qualifying as instances of a general characteristic. That general characteristic is distinguished from the others by the number and pattern of 0's contained in the column of four values. Note that in the first column there are no 0's, the next two have a single 0, and the last two columns both have two 0's. From the probability table representation it is just a small step to obtain 2X2 matrices that describe the same relationships between propositions A and B.

2X2 PROBABILITY MATRIX EXAMPLES

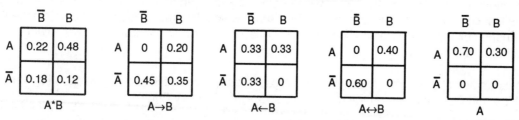

The probability values in these matrices are the same as those in the columns in the Probability Table examples. The matrices have more graphic appeal than the column arrangement because each conjunctive probability lies at the intersection of the row and column denoting the conjunction. In addition, a matrix representation of the logical relationship between two propositions is natural since observational data is often taken in this form. For example, in the Blue and Green Taxicab problem in Chapter II one row could represent a Blue taxicab and the other row not a blue taxicab, i.e. a green cab. One column could represent the eyewitness identification of the cab as blue and the other column its identification as not blue. A 2X2 matrix representation is also appropriate in the Mammalary Cancer problem. Here, the two rows in the matrix could represent having cancer and not having cancer while one column represents a test result that is positive and the other column one that is negative.

Graphical Representation. As appealing as the 2X2 matrix representation is for some purposes, it does not focus upon a number of parameters that are often of great interest. For example, what is the probability of A, i.e., what is P(A)? What is P(B)? There are in addition four conditional probabilities that enter into many problem situations. These are P(A|B), P(A|B̄), P(B|A), and P(B|Ā). As you will recall, conditional probabilities play an essential role in Bayes' equation. Each of these six parameters, let us call them *Bayes' parameters*, can be determined without too much difficulty from the four conjunctive probabilities that are entered in the 2X2 probability matrices. This has been done in obtaining the values listed below for each of the same five numerical example relationships with which we have been working.

THE BAYES'
PARAMETERS

	A*B	A→B	A←B	A↔B	A
P(A)	0.70	0.20	0.67	0.40	1.00
P(B)	0.60	0.55	0.33	0.40	0.30
P(A|B)	0.80	0.36	1	1	1
P(A|B̄)	0.55	0	0.50	0	1
P(B|A)	0.69	1	0.50	1	0.30
P(B|Ā)	0.40	0.44	0	0	—

Let's check how the values for each of the six Bayes' parameters for the relationship A*B are obtained from the conjunctive probabilities in the 2X2 matrix. P(A) is simply the sum of the two probabilities in the top row of the matrix since P(A) = P(A.B) + P(A.B̄). Likewise, P(B) is the sum of the two probabilities in the right hand column. To determine P(A|B) we focus on the right hand column since it is there that the condition B (B true) is satisfied. The upper of these two values represents proposition A being true, so P(A|B) is this value in the upper right hand corner of the matrix, P(A.B), divided P(B), the sum of the two values in the right hand column. Numerically, P(A|B) = 0.48 / (0.48 + 0.12) = 0.80. In similar fashion the remaining three conditional probabilities in the A*B column above are: P(A|B̄) = the upper left box value divided by the sum of the values in the left hand column; P(B|A) = upper right box value divided by the sum of the values in the top row; and finally, P(B|Ā) = lower right hand box value divided by the sum of the values in the bottom row.

It remains to exhibit the six Bayes' parameters in graphical form. Since we are dealing with two propositions only, each of which can assume a probability value between zero and one, it seems quite natural to create a graph that extends from 0 to 1 along a horizontal axis and also from 0 to 1 along a vertical axis. Let us plot P(A) vertically and P(B) horizontally to locate a point whose coordinates are P(B) and P(A). This is exactly the same as plotting a point whose coordinates are x and y on a sheet of graph paper. Having done this, we now recognize that the quantities P(A|B) and P(A|B̄) are simply two kinds of P(A)'s, one conditioned on the truth of B and the other on its falsity. Thus P(A|B) should represent a point plotted in the vertical direction at the location where B is true, i.e., where P(B) = 1, and P(A|B̄) another point, also plotted vertically, but from the location where B is false, i.e., where P(B) = 0. These two points therefore lie on opposite side edges of our probability square. The quantities P(B|A) and P(B|Ā) become quantities plotted to the right from the left side of the square, one along the top of the square and one along the bottom side. This procedure locates five points on our graph as illustrated below. Let us call such a graph a *Bayes' Diagram*.

BAYES' DIAGRAM

GRAPHICAL
REPRESENTATION
OF
A*B

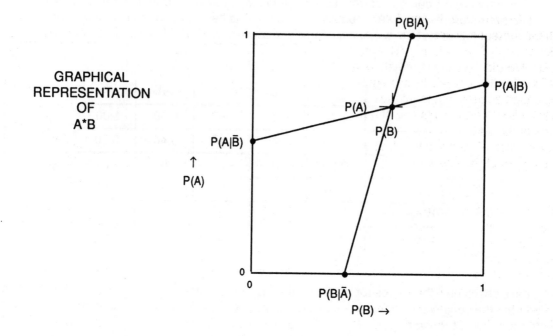

Note that when the points P(A|B) and P(A|B̄) are connected by a straight line and the points P(B|A) and P(B|Ā) are connected by a second line, these two lines intersect at the point whose coordinates are P(B) and P(A). For reasons that will be made clear later, these lines will be referred to as *relevance lines*. The locations of the five points shown above are to scale where P(A) = 0.70, P(B) =0.60,P(A|B) = 0.80, P(A|B̄) = 0.55, P(B|A) = 0.69, and P(B|Ā) = 0.40. This is the same A*B relationship that was previously represented in a probability table and again in a probability matrix. The graphical representation of the logical relationship between propositions A and B has two important features. First, the nature of a logical relationship is exhibited by the geometry of the diagram providing a new perspective to the relationship. Second, it not only represents all six Bayes' parameters in a geometrical way, but permits the analysis of the **dynamics** of a changing relationship between two propositions, conjectures, or statements.

Shown below are Bayes' diagrams for the first four logical relationships with which we have been dealing (all to the same scale) together with four additional relationships. By displaying all eight, each can readily be compared to the others. When a relevance line terminates at a corner of the square that point is marked by a large dot and labelled. In such cases the arrangement of these points serves to identify the particular logical relationship that is being represented.

Diagrams 1, 2, 3, and 4 are graphical representations of the logical relationships A*B, A → B, A ← B, and A ↔ B. A*B displays the fact that none of the conjunctive probabilities is zero in this case because neither of the relevance lines connects to any of the corners of the square. For A → B, however, each of the lines terminates at one corner of the square.

Diagram 3 shows converse implication, i.e., A is implied by B. Notice the difference between this and diagram 2. In both cases the dots anchor one end of each relevance line. In diagram 4 the two relevance lines are superimposed and become one. This diagram displays equivalence, or, A implies B **and** B implies A.

Diagram 5 shows that proposition A is independent of proposition B and consequently B also is independent of A. This diagram is related to diagram 1. The only difference is that here the relevance lines are horizontal and vertical. Diagram 6 is clearly related to diagram 4 directly above it. The single bar over the symbol shows that the entire relationship A ↔ B is negated, which, in a truth table representation would turn every T into an F and every F into a T.

Diagrams 7 and 8 are clearly related to diagrams 2 and 3. Truth table representations for the four relationships would contain three T's and one F. One conclusion from this is that every one of the four can be seen as an *or* relationship and every one of the four can also be seen as a kind of implication. The four are distinguished by that corner of the square that seems to be avoided by the two relevance lines.

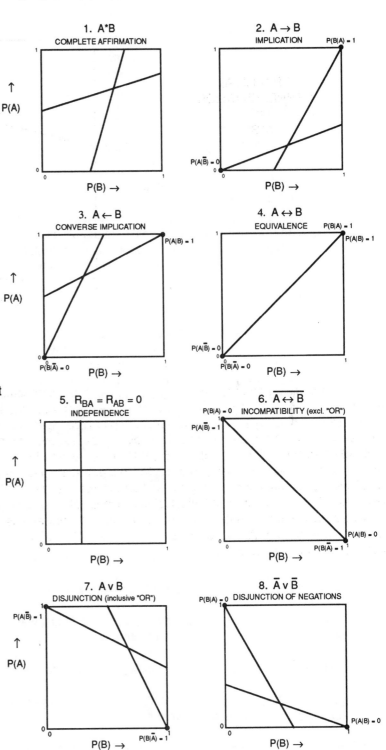

141

In summary, we now have three different kinds of probabilistic schemes to represent a logical relationship between two propositions A and B. Let us compare the three using the same logical relationship A*B that has been described previously. The three are shown below.

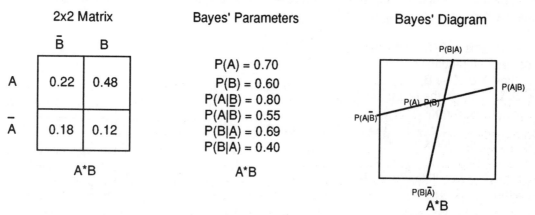

For those who are digitally inclined, either the 2x2 matrix representation or that provided by a listing of Bayes' parameters may be preferable to that of the Bayes' diagram. Of these, the 2x2 matrix accommodates data in a natural way while the Bayes' parameters may be superior in many instances of problem solving involving Bayes' equation. The geometrical representation provided by the Bayes' diagram will most likely be preferred by those who are more geometrically oriented, which includes most of us.

PLAUSIBLE REASONING

Previously displayed is Tapscott's "A Logic-English Translation Guide." It refers to logical relationships that can be described by a column of truth-table entries. Moreover, these translations into ordinary English apply to a two-value system of logic in which propositions are either true T or false F. Seldom in ordinary experience does one encounter relationships that can be described in this way. While individuals often speak in a language which seems to consist of statements that are either T or F, when pressed they will readily agree to certain qualifications. For example, "always" becomes "almost always," "never" becomes "seldom," and " true" becomes "almost always true." Qualifications of one kind or another transform deductive logic into plausible reasoning.

A partial list of words and phrases that are used to soften the absolutes of deductive logic include:

usually	rarely	relevant	is proportional to	analogous	confirms
nearly	irrelevant	probably	likely	possibly	credible
almost	approximately	affirm	unlikely	plausible	is related to
suggests	reasonably	equivalent	persuasive	similar	tends to

Qualiifiers convert the language of deductive logic into that of plausible reasoning:

S*W   qualified: Some days now are mostly sunny and fairly warm, some are mostly cloudy and fairly warm, some are mostly sunny and rather cool, while still others are rather cloudy and cool.

S→G qualified: If Henry gets the top score in his psychology class he is almost guaranteed an A.

B←F qualified: Mary's flowers will probably have many large beautiful blooms provided that she fertilizes them but doesn't overdo it.

J↔M qualified: Janet and Mary will probably both go to the gymnastics meet or neither will.

H   qualified: One's intelligence (I) in all liklihood ha s no influence on one's height (H).

Learning. Recall that Bayes' equation can be interpreted as a *learning equation.* Writing Bayes' equation as shown below,

posterior   prior

$$P(A|B) = \frac{P(B|A)}{P(B)}\ P(A)$$

P(A) is interpreted as the prior probability of proposition A, meaning that it is the appropriate value before additional information has been gained about P(B). P(A|B), on the other hand, is taken to be a revised value of P(A) having now *learned* that B is true. It is therefore called the posterior probability value for A. This same relationship can be seen using a Bayes' diagram of the relationship between A and B as shown at the left below. Take, for example, the relationship A*B with numerical values as previously given. This time, however, let us take proposition A to be proposition G, the probability that a certain defendant is guilty of the charges against him. Proposition B is now additional evidence E which tends to further incriminate the defendant. The posterior probability of guilt of the defendant is given by the learning equation below and by the Bayes' diagram shown at the left the left below.

$$P(G|E) = \frac{P(E|G)}{P(E)}\ P(G)$$

Revision. With this perspective we see from the diagram at the left that, having learned that the evidence E is true, Bayes' equation moves the point at which P(G) = 0.70 to the point P(G|E) = 0.80. This revision is indicated by the heavy arrow on the diagram. Having confirmed the evidence E to be true it can be concluded that the defendant is now more likely to be guilty than he was before. His probability of guilt has increased from 0.70 to 0.80. Of course a downward revision in P(E) would lead to a decrease in the probability that the defendant is guilty.

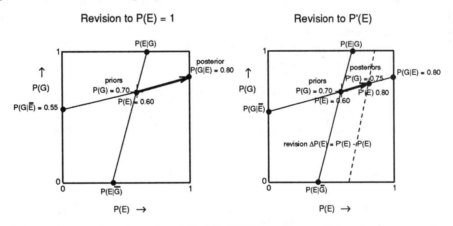

What if the evidence is not confirmed? What if the evidence E has become more credible, but not so credible as to be called "true"? Suppose P(E) increases, not from 0.6 to 1.0, but from 0.6 to 0.8? This is just half the revision in the probability of the evidence as when it was found to be completely true. This situation is illustrated in the figure at the right above where the heavy arrow indicates the result of a smaller revision in the probability for the evidence to be true. P(G) still increases as a result of this revision, but by less than when evidence E became certain. As shown to scale in the diagram at the right, the posterior probabilities are P'(E) = 0.80 and P'(G) = 0.75. The revision in the probability of the evidence has as a consequence the increase in the probability that the defendant is guilty. Other evidence could, of course, lead to a downward revision in the probability of guilt. It is by patterns such as this that we continually revise our opinions about all sorts of things based upon what we learn. We have now moved out of the realm of deductive logic into that of plausible reasoning.

Relevance. The process of revision can be better understood by introducing a quantity called *relevance*, a term appropriate to the field of plausible reasoning as well as to trial law. Referring to the graphical representation of G*E above, it is seen that the increase in P(G) as proposition B becomes more credible depends on two things. It depends on the slope of the line that connects the points P(G|E) and P(G|$\overline{E}$) and upon the amount of increase in P(E). The slope of this line can be defined by the quantity P(G|E) - P(G|$\overline{E}$), i.e., by the "rise" in the line across the square from the left side to the right side, divided by the "run." But the "run" is one since that is the width of the square. So we are left with the definition for the <u>relevance of the evidence E to the question of guilt G</u> as follows:

$$R_{EG} = P(G|E) - P(G|\overline{E})$$

It can now be understood why the line connecting the points P(G|E) and P(G|$\overline{E}$) is called a *relevance line*. In the revisions in the evidence as described on the Bayes' diagrams above the revised value of P(G), whether it be P(G|E) when P(E) has become one, or P'(G) when the revision is smaller, these new values lie on the more horizontal relevance line as did the prior values P(G) because the relevance $R_{G|E}$ is <u>constant</u>. This relevance is a property of the relationship between the evidence and the proposition of guilt. Some evidence is more relevant to Guilt than others. Relevance values range between -1 and 1. The relevance of E to G in the situations described by the Bayes' diagrams above is +0.25.

We could, of course, talk about the relevance of Guilt G to the evidence E. It is defined in an analogous fashion to that of evidence E to guilt G. Its value is given by:

$$R_{GE} = P(E|G) - P(E|\overline{G})$$

It is the slope of the more vertical relevance line in the previously given Bayes' diagrams, but only if one measures that slope relative to a vertical, not a horizontal, line. In assessing the impact of some piece of evidence E to the probability of guilt the relevance R_{GE} doesn't enter in. Nonetheless, it is clear that guilt or innocence is relevant to the truth or falsity of the evidence. A certain piece of incriminating evidence, for example, may make much more sense given that a suspect is guilty than if he's not.

Later, in the problem of resolving the PARADOX IN DIAGNOSTICS, the probability for having a certain disease D is plotted vertically on a Bayes' diagram and the probability for a positive result for a certain diagnostic test is plotted horizontally. A patient is successively given a number of independent tests for the disease all of which have the same relevance for D to a positive outcome for the test. In this case, in contrast to the situation in which evidence is relevant to guilt or innocence, it is the slope of the more vertical relevance line that remains constant. The conclusion from this is that a problem solver should assess each situation carefully to determine which relevance, if any, stays constant when revising a probability according to Bayes' equation. When such a relevance is identified Bayes' equation can be applied successively to follow the dynamics of a logical relationship.

144

LOGICAL RELATIONSHIPS IN PLAUSIBLE REASONING. Plausible reasoning involves the analysis of logical relationships that are not quite A → B, only approximately A ← B, nearly A ↔ B, or almost A (being true). These are qualitatively different from the versions of the logical relationships first presented in truth table form. These are the relationships of plausible reasoning, the kind of reasoning that characterizes ordinary discourse. Examples of strict implication, total equivalence, or certain truth of any proposition are seldom encountered. Instances in which people make sound arguments, draw plausible conclusions, and establish reasonable relationships between conjectures are found everywhere. How are these processes to be described? Certainly not by truth tables, nor by 2X2 matrix representations. Of the different representation schemes presented, only one is well adapted for the description of relationships in plausible reasoning. It is the graphical representation scheme. Except for relationships 1 and 5 in the prior display of eight logical relationships, two of the ends of the relevance lines terminate at a corner of the Bayes' diagram. At these corners a conditional probability value is either 0 or 1. There are extremely important relationships in plausible reasoning in which the ends of one or both relevance lines come close to a corner of a Bayes' diagram but do not terminate there. In such cases the conditional probabilities at these corners come close to either zero or one. It is reasonable to describe these relationships as being close to implication, close to converse implication, close to equivalence, close to complete incompatibility, close to disjunction, or close to the disjunction of negations, all of which are described three pages earlier.

On the page following, under the title YOU ARE THE PROSECUTING ATTORNEY, four relationships in plausible reasoning are illustrated by way of their Bayes' diagrams. There is no "truth" here, only relevance and credibility. Each of the four diagrams is characterized by the orientation of the pair of relevance lines it exhibits. The values of the end points of these lines and the coordinates of their intersections satisfy Bayes' equation. Since there are an infinite number of sets of six Bayes' parameters, there are likewise an infinite number of logical relationships in plausible reasoning.

On the second page following there are instructions for CONSTRUCTING A BAYES' DIAGRAM. Bayes' equation was introduced in Chapter II and used there to analyze the Blue and Green Taxicabs problem, the problem of the patient with Mammalary Cancer, the archeological problem Blasting a Hypothesis, the problem called The Diagnostic Value of Acne, the X-Linked Lethals problem, and testing for the presence of the HIV virus. A Bayes' diagram could be drawn for each of these problems to provide a graphical perspective in addition to an algebraic one.

YOU ARE THE PROSECUTING ATTORNEY

A defendant in a robbery case has been bound over for trial primarily because an eyewitness saw him leave the scene shortly after the robbery occurred. It is also possible that the defendant is the cat burglar who presumably accounts for a number of recent unsolved robbery cases. You take the prior probability of his guilt to be $P(G) = 0.4$ and the prior probability that he is the cat burglar to be $P(C) = 0.4$. Investigators have now identified three incriminating pieces of evidence E_1, E_2, and E_3.

E_1: A partial fingerprint found at the scene is consistent with the defendant's fingerprint.
E_2: The defendant is a dark complexioned Middle Easterner.
E_3: A cat burglar costume found in the defendant's trash barrel belongs to him.

As the prosecuting attorney you now sketch four Bayes' diagrams starting in each case with two prior probability values (locating the intersection of the two relevance lines) and one conditional probability. During the trial it is your job as prosecutor to convince the jury that each of the three pieces of evidence is highly credible, i.e., warrants a probability increase indicated by a heavy arrow on the diagram. You will also want to persuade the jury that the probability of the defendant being the cat burglar is very high because this will also point strongly toward the defendant's guilt. If the defendant really is the cat burglar that would suggest, i.e., nearly imply, the credibility of evidence E_3. However, as the last of the four diagrams shown below indicates, just because the costume is his by no means assures you that he is the cat burglar, for such a costume is a popular one at masked balls. Finally, you hope as prosecutor that you can convince the jury that when the evidence is compounded they will see fit to bring in a guilty verdict.

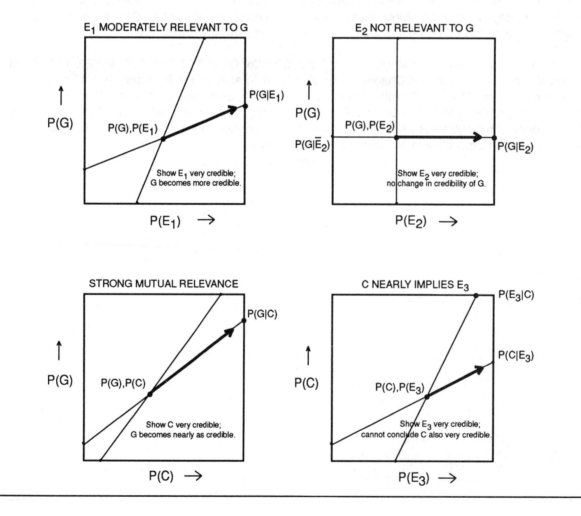

CONSTRUCTING A BAYES' DIAGRAM

Let the proposition that a certain defendant is guilty be G and a certain piece of evidence that implicates him in a crime be E. Six Bayes' parameters describe the relationship between guilt G and the evidence E. To construct a Bayes' diagram one must specify three of these six parameters before the remaining three can be determined. Shown below at the left are three ways to initiate a graphical procedure for making this determination.

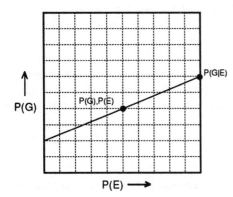

Here the three specified quantities are P(G) = 0.4, P(E) = 0.5, and P(G|E) = 0.6, each point being indicated by a heavy dot. A line connecting these two points is extended to the left side of the square where it defines the point P(G|Ē). Note that this procedure eliminates the need for finding P(G|Ē) algebraically.

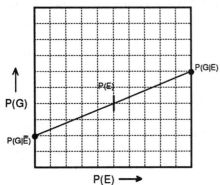

Alternatively, the two conditionals P(G|E) = 0.6 and P(G|Ē) = 0.2 can be specified together with one of the priors, in this case P(E) = 0.5. On the line drawn between these two conditionals the value of P(E) is marked by a short vertical line segment. Note that the intersection of the relevance line with the short vertical line segment graphically determines the value of P(G) to be 0.4, thus eliminating the necessity for finding P(G) algebraically.

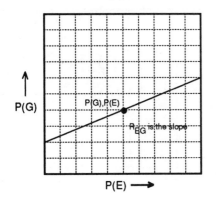

A third set of specified parameters consists of the two priors P(G) = 0.4 and P(E) = 0.5 together with the relevance of proposition E to proposition G, R_{EG} = 0.4. This relevance is the slope of the line drawn through the point P(G),P(E). Once again, the construction of the relevance line through the point representing the priors replaces algebraic methods for finding both P(G|E) and P(G|Ē).

Finally, as a second step following any one of the three beginning steps above, the value of P(E|G) is obtained using Bayes' equation:

$$P(E|G) = \frac{P(G|E)P(E)}{P(G)} = 0.75$$

The line drawn from P(E|G) through the point representing the priors and extending to the bottom of the square defines P(E|Ḡ). All six Bayes' parameters are now known.

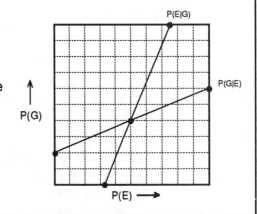

SUCCESSIVE VERIFICATIONS / MULTIPLE EVIDENCE. Researchers test a hypothesis through the examination of as many consequences of this hypothesis as can be identified. As each hypothesis is confirmed the probability that the hypothesis is true does nothing but increase. However, should any one consequent be found to be false the hypothesis is blasted, that is, is necessarily false. A second situation involves criminal cases in which the prosecuting attorney collects as many pieces of evidence as he can that implicate the defendant in the crime. So long as successive pieces of evidence point toward the guilt of the defendant, the probability that the defendant is guilty increases. The defense attorney, on the other hand, points out to the jury that certain other pieces of evidence tend to show that the defendant is innocent. The jury has the problem of assessing all the pieces of evidence. Proceedings in a criminal trial is a very special case of learning in general. In the learning process we continually revise our opinions on the basis of new information. In a third setting a person may be subject to a number of medical tests to determine whether he does or does not have a certain disease. The greater the number of tests that turn out to be positive, the more likely it is that the person has the affliction. Multiple evidence and successive verification of consequences play an extremely important role in plausible reasoning. We are not dealing here with the proposition that a defendant is 100% innocent or 100% percent guilty. Nor is it ever said that a large number of verified consequences actually *prove* a hypothesis. What is asserted in such cases is the high probability of that hypothesis.

The Copernican Model. As an example of these kinds of processes consider the evidence that tended to show that the geocentric model of the planetary system was incorrect and should be replaced with a heliocentric model as proposed by Copernicus. There was a wealth of evidence that supported the Copernican model and also a sizeable number of arguments that defended the Ptolemaic model. To simplify matters, in the analysis that follows only three pieces of evidence are considered. Two of these support the Copernican model and one does not. Let the propositions be:

C: The Copernican sun-centered model of the planetary system is correct.
E_1: Venus shows phases like the Moon.
E_2: At times Mars is observed to move relative to the backdrop of stars in a backward direction.
E_3: For the Copernican model the nearest stars, depending on the season, should appear in slightly different directions relative to more distant stars. This is called *parallax*.

Bayesian analysis involves the sequence of diagrams shown below, one for each of the relationships between proposition C and the pieces of evidence E_1, E_2, and E_3.

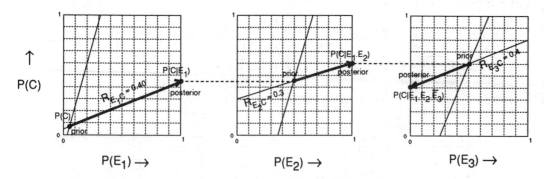

Analysis begins with the prior P(C) at the lower left corner of the first diagram. This value is low because the Copernican model went against the beliefs of the philosophers of the time and those of the Roman Catholic church. The first posterior $P(C|E_1)$ is obtained using the relevance value R_{E1C}. This revision and those to follow are shown by bolder line segments. This posterior becomes the prior in the second diagram. Using the relevance R_{E2C} one obtains the posterior $P(C|E_1.E_2)$ which in turn becomes the prior in the third diagram. Where before E_1 and E_2 were confirmed, now E_3 is found to be false—no parallax was observed. This accounts for the third posterior $P(C|E_1.E_2.E_3)$ having a lower value than its prior. Although no parallax was observed in Copernicus' time, several centuries later its very small value was in fact observed showing that the closest stars lie well beyond the limits of the solar system.

Introductory Problem Solutions

PHASES OF VENUS. <u>RECAP PROB</u>. The student's speculation was as follows: "If the Copernican system is correct, then Venus will show phases, and if Venus does actually show phases, then it can be concluded that the Copernican system is correct."

  <u>DIAGRAM RELATIONSHIP</u>. The first part of this statement contains the "if . . . then" language of implication. Let statement C be the hypothesis that the Copernican system is correct and statement Ph be the statement that Venus shows phases like the Moon. Thus the student's speculation can be written $C \rightarrow Ph$. This relationship can be represented on a Bayes' diagram as shown below. Note that the relationship between Ph and C that is shown is an example of deductive logic, not of plausible reasoning.

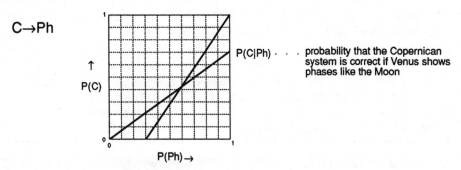

  <u>CONCLUSION</u>. Since the value of P(C|Ph) shown on the right side of the diagram need not be particularly close to one, we can by no means conclude that the Copernican system is correct. That is, if Venus does show phases like the Moon, we cannot conclude from this that the Copernican system is necessarily correct. This, of course, conflicts with the student's conclusion.

SLAVERY AND THE CIVIL WAR. <u>SET UP PROB</u>. If we let CW represent the occurrence of the civil war, and S stand for the significance of the issue of slavery, then the assumption is that slavery strongly suggested that civil war would follow. To represent this situation let $P(S) = 0.50$, $P(CW|S) = 0.90$, and $P(CW|\bar{S}) = 0.30$.

  <u>SOLVE ALGEBRAICALLY</u>. First find $P(CW) = P(CW|S)P(S) + P(CW|\bar{S})P(\bar{S})$

  <u>NUMERICALLY</u>: $P(CW) = 0.60$

Second, find both P(S|CW) and P(S|$\overline{CW}$):

$$P(S|CW) = P(CW|S)P(S) / P(CW) = (0.9)(0.5) / 0.6 = 0.75$$

$$P(S|\overline{CW}) = P(\overline{CW}|S)P(S) / P(\overline{CW}) = (0.1)(0.5) / 0.4 = 0.125$$

<u>SKETCH DIAGRAMS</u>:   (the above results are shown at the left below)

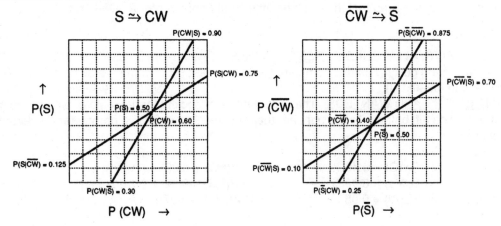

149

INTERPRET DIAGRAMS. Compare the orientation of the two relevance lines in the Bayes' diagram at the left above with the two that indicate that the Copernican model implies the statement that Venus will show phases like the earth's moon, i.e., that C → Ph. The difference here is that in expressing the relationship between slavery and the civil war these relevance lines do not terminate at a vertex of the Bayes' square. One lies at a probability value only 0.10 from a vertex and the other 0.125 from a vertex. What can be said is that the S-CW relationship approximates the C-Ph relationship. In other words, the issue of slavery **strongly suggested** it would lead to war. Alternatively, one can say that the relationship between slavery and the civil war was **nearly** that of implication. That is why the relationship as noted above the diagram is written S ⇝ CW. The arrow of implication is accompanied by a squiggle to indicate the approximate nature of the relationship.

The Bayes' diagram on the right above plots $P(\overline{CW})$ vertically against $P(\overline{S})$ horizontally. All six Bayes' parameters for this relationship are simply taken from those describing the diagram to its left. When this is done we see a pair of relevance lines, though not identically situated to those on the left, are nonetheless indicative of a relationship that is nearly one of implication, but this time it is the relationship between the absence of civil war and the absence of slavery as a significant factor in leading to war. This relationship is written, as noted above its diagram, as $\overline{CW}$ ⇝ $\overline{S}$. The answer to the question posed in this problem is now apparent. If there had been no civil war we could then conclude that the issue of slavery was not considered to be of great significance.

ASSESS PROBLEM SOLUTION. The two shorthand representations for these two diagrams obviously bear a relationship to one another. The pattern is as follows: first, A nearly implies B, and then the falsity of B nearly implies the falsity of A. A safe prediction from this result is that when A → B, then it is also true that $\overline{B} \to \overline{A}$.

ANALOGY. RECAP PROB. It has now been proven that of all plane figures the circle has the least perimeter (circumference) for a given area. Because the listing of the lowest vibrational frequencies for many plane figures is so similar to a corresponding listing of lowest perimeters for plane figures, one would like to say that in all likelihood the lowest vibrational frequency is for a circular membrane just as the lowest perimeter is for a circular membrane.

FALSE CONCLUSION. Simply because the two tables are analogous to one another does *not* mean that we can conclude with *certainty* that the circular membrane vibrates with the lowest fundamental frequency. Two things that are analogous to one another means that they are similar, that is, the same with respect to many qualities but also different in some respects. The circular membrane just might be one of the shapes that is the exception to the overall similarity. It has already been noted that the two listings are not entirely in the same order from low to higher perimeter values and from low to higher frequency values. This is sufficient to make one wary about drawing an unjustified conclusion.

JUSTIFIABLE CONCLUSION. What can be concluded is that there is a strong possibility that the very lowest vibrational frequency is for a circular membrane. One's confidence in this conclusion strengthened when it was proved that the circle had the least perimeter for a given area.

FOUND GUILTY / ACTUALLY GUILTY. RESTATE PROB. One hundred individuals are brought to trial. Some of these are found guilty (FG) and some are found innocent (FI). Some are actually guilty (AG) and some are actually innocent (AI).

IDENT GIVENS AND WANTEDS. The expectations of society for the judicial system are given by the quantities at the left below. To the right are the remaining three Bayes' parameters as found using Bayes' equation.

P(AG) = 0.40	P(FG) = 0.39
P(FG|AG) = 0.90	P(AG|FG) = 0.92
P(FG|AI) = 0.05	P(AG|FI) = 0.07

150

GRAPH RELATIONSHIP.

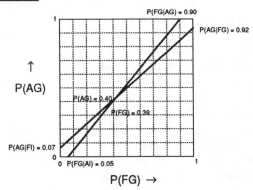

INTERPRET RELATIONSHIP. The above graph is very similar to one considered previously by the prosecuting attorney and labelled "strong mutual relevance." Also, referring to the collection of eight logical relationships given on page 141, we see that the Bayes' diagram above also closely resembles the one expressing equivalence between two propositions. In that case both relevance lines terminate in the lower left vertex of the square and in the upper right vertex. In the above, however, the relevance lines terminate fairly closely to the same vertices. We conclude that the relationship between AG and FG is nearly one of equivalence. This means that when an individual is certain to be guilty he has a high probability to be found guilty and when he is certain to be innocent he has a high probability to be found innocent. In an ideal, that is, perfect society, we would expect all those who are actually guilty to be found guilty and all those who are actually innocent to be found innocent. This would express the relationship of strict equivalence between AG and FG.

Additional Problems

BLUE AND GREEN TAXICABS REVISITED. Recall that in the Blue and Green Taxicabs problem there was a hit and run incident involving a cab. In this rather small town 85% of the cabs are blue and the remaining 15% are green. An eyewitness identified the hit and run cab as blue. This same eyewitness was given a test under similar lighting conditions to determine the probability for her to be right in this identification. When the police used a blue cab for her to identify she correctly identified the color of the cab as blue 60% of the time. When a green cab was driven by for her to identify she said it was blue 20% of the time. Thus the data available upon the conclusion of these tests was as follows:

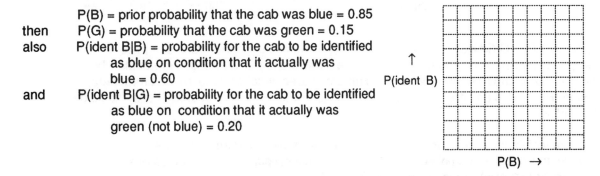

        $P(B)$ = prior probability that the cab was blue = 0.85
then $P(G)$ = probability that the cab was green = 0.15
also $P(\text{ident } B|B)$ = probability for the cab to be identified
           as blue on condition that it actually was
           blue = 0.60
and $P(\text{ident } B|G)$ = probability for the cab to be identified
           as blue on condition that it actually was
           green (not blue) = 0.20

Construct a Bayes' diagram to represent the relationship between $P(\text{ident } B)$ and $P(B)$. Label all the Bayes' parameters. What is wanted in this problem, as before, is the quantity $P(B|\text{ident } B)$, i.e., the probability that the cab really was blue on condition that it was identified as blue. What strategy should the defense attorney representing the Blue Cab Company adopt in the event this case goes to trial? What advantages and disadvantages does the graphical analysis of this problem have compared to the purely algebraic approach used earlier?

MAMMALARY CANCER PROBLEM REVISITED. The information that was supplied in this Chapter II problem consists of $P(C) = 0.10$, $P(+|C) = 0.79$, and $P(+|\bar{C}) = 0.10$. This, of course, is fictitious data. Really good data of the kind desired is simply not available.

The objective was to determine the inverse probability $P(C|+)$ which, having used Bayes' equation, turned out to be 0.48. For many individuals this set of numbers may not mean very much, particularly for those who are more graphically oriented. Repeat the analysis there, but this time find the remaining Bayes' parameters using graphical techniques where appropriate and plot these on a Bayes' diagram. The problem here is to analyse the accuracy of the tests for the presence of mammalary cancer. What is the rate for false positives? What is the rate for false negatives? Clearly, to improve the accuracy of the testing procedures both of these rates would have to be reduced. How would such reductions, if they could be accomplished, be reflected in changes in the Bayes' diagram?

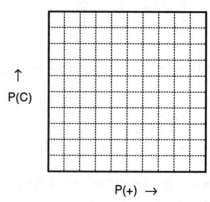

↑
P(C)

P(+) →

*THE OIL LOBBYIST. A lobbyist hired by the oil industry has taken Congresswoman Jones out to dinner, paid for her vacation to Bermuda, and arranged for her to obtain a good-sized loan from a bank at a favorable rate of interest. The lobbyist is trying to persuade the congressperson that if the oil industry is granted certain tax breaks provided by pending legislation, then benefits for all voters will result. Sketch a Bayes' diagram that represents, in a qualitative way, the relationship between tax breaks for the oil industry T and benefits for all voters B according to the lobbyist. The congressperson, however, doesn't buy the lobbyist's argument. She thinks that whether the voters benefit or not is completely independent of the passage of the pending legislation. In other words, she thinks that B is independent of T. Sketch a Bayes' diagram, also qualitatively, that represents this point of view.

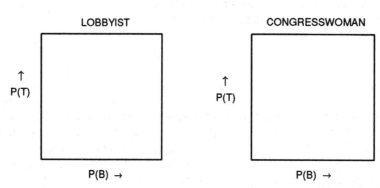

LOBBYIST

↑
P(T)

P(B) →

CONGRESSWOMAN

↑
P(T)

P(B) →

SMOKING AND LUNG CANCER. A survey of the type taken in the early 1980s sought to determine the relationship between smoking and lung cancer. The study broke the 1,000,000 individuals who were surveyed into four groups: smokers who live in an urban area, smokers who live in a rural area, non-smokers who live in an urban area, and non-smokers who live in a rural area. Let symbols be defined as follws.

U: an individual from an urban area	$\bar{U}$: an individual from a rural area
S: an individual who smoked	$\bar{S}$: an individual who is a non-smoker
L: an individual who died of lung cancer	

Let given quantities be as follows.

no.( ): the number of the quantity within the parentheses

no.(U) = 700,000	no.(S) = 170,000	no.(SU) = 140,000
no.(Ū) = 300,000	no.(S̄) = 830,000	no.(SŪ) = 30,000

Let the probabilities for dying of lung cancer for each of the four target groups be as follows.

$$P(L|S\underline{U}) = 0.000\ 85$$
$$P(L|\underline{S}U) = 0.000\ 65$$
$$P(L|\underline{SU}) = 0.000\ 15$$
$$P(L|SU) = 0.000\ 01$$

Find the following quantities, the first two of which have already been given.

no.(S\underline{U})	no.(LS\underline{U})	no.(L\underline{U})	P(L|\underline{U})	P(U|L)
no.(S\overline{U})	no.(LS\overline{U})	no.(LU)	P(L|U)	P(S|L)
no.(\overline{S}U)	no.(L\overline{S}U)	no.(LS)	P(L|S)	
no.(\overline{SU})	no.(L\overline{SU})	no.(L\overline{S})	P(L|\overline{S})	

What are the major conclusions that can be drawn from this information?

*PART TIME JOBS. In a small college 1000 students are from out of state and 3000 are state residents. One-hundred of the out-of-state students hold part-time jobs (20 hrs/wk or more) and 1500 of the in-state students have part-time jobs to help pay for textbooks, tuition, fees, and miscellaneous expenses. If a student is selected randomly from the 4000 students at the school, what is the probability for selecting a student who is both an out-of-state student and one who has a part-time job? Let S represent an in-state student and J a part-time job. Also, find the probability that a student who has a part-time job will be from out of state. Finally, construct a Bayes' diagram to describe the relationship between P(J) and P(S). What relationship in plausible reasoning does this represent?

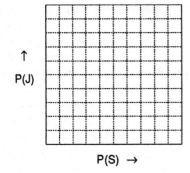

P(J) ↑

P(S) →

*EINSTEIN'S PREDICTIONS. Einstein's general theory of relativity is a theory of gravitation. It recognizes that the force of gravity cannot be distinguished from the effects produced by an acceleration through space. For example, when in an elevator accelerating upward you feel much heavier. This effect is the same as if the mass of the earth were to have been suddenly increased thereby exerting a greater gravitational pull upon your body. Not only did Einstein formulate the theory, but in addition he proposed three experiments that might be conducted that would either support the theory or refute it. One experiment had to do with the bending of starlight as it passes close to the sun on its way to earth. A second effect predicted by the theory was the reddening of light emitted by an extremely massive star as that light is attracted in a direction back toward the star while leaving that star's vicinity. A third prediction involved the orbital motion of the planet Mercury, which, being so close to the massive sun, is influenced by the sun's gravitational attraction. All three of these consequences C_1, C_2, and C_3 were eventually confirmed. The problem here is to assess changes in the probability that Einstein's theory is correct, P(T), as each of these predictions (consequences) is confirmed. Assume numerical values as necessary to sketch the three Bayes' diagrams with axes as shown below that describe the successive confirmation of the three consequences. Show that the posterior $P(T|C_1)$ is the prior for the second graph, and that the posterior of the second graph $P(T|C_1.C_2)$ is the prior for the third graph whose posterior is $P(T|C_1.C_2.C_3)$.

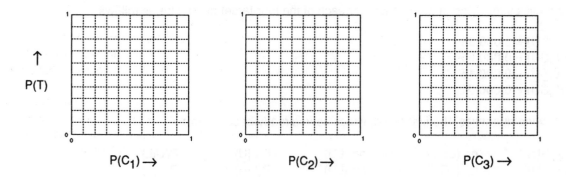

$P(T)$ $\uparrow$

$P(C_1) \rightarrow$ $P(C_2) \rightarrow$ $P(C_3) \rightarrow$

PARADOX IN DIAGNOSTICS. One of the paradoxes described in Chapter II is the "and" paradox attributed to E.A. Murphy. The paradox had to do with ten *independent* lab results that bear on a particular disease (the fictitious Murphy's anemia). Each of these ten laboratory tests is positive for 90% of those who are afflicted. Each of these tests is diagnostically important. The paradox has to do with the conclusion that the greater the number of positive test results that are obtained, the less the probability that one is afflicted. For two tests, 0.9 x 0.9 = 0.81, the probability that both will be positive. For three tests this probability is 0.9 cubed, etc. This conclusion flies in the face of common sense which tells us that with each positive test result, the probability that an individual actually has the affliction increases.

Do a proper Bayesian analysis of this situation by assuming that an individual, before he has even been tested, has a prior probability of having the disease be $P(D) = 0.1$. Assign the value for $P(+|D)$ as 0.9 denoting the probability for obtaining a positive test result for an individual with the disease. This is the value noted in the original statement of the paradox. But the probability for obtaining a false positive result must also be given. Let this be $P(+|\bar{D}) = 0.2$. These two conditional probability values set the relevance of the disease to a positive test result to be $R_{D+} = 0.7$. This relevance has the same value for all ten of the different but independent tests that can be made. Now suppose that an individual is tested. Bayes' equation will tell us what the posterior probability that the individual has the disease will be. It is the value $P(D|+)$. The individual decides to take another of the ten tests. This time the posterior probability from the first test that he has the disease becomes the prior for the second test. He takes a third test. Determine the probabilities $P(D|+)$, $P(D|++)$, and $P(D|+++)$. Plot these using three Bayes' diagrams, one for each of the three tests that were made. Plot all $P(D)$'s upward and $P(+)$'s horizontally. Does this sequence of values make sense and is the paradox resolved?

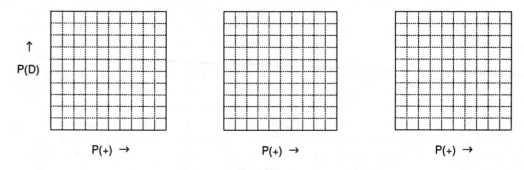

$P(D)$ $\uparrow$

$P(+) \rightarrow$ $P(+) \rightarrow$ $P(+) \rightarrow$

MR. HILLER'S MURDER. In a true story recounted by Polya in his book *Patterns of Plausible Inference* a man by the name of Hiller was shot in his home by an intruder. The police identified a suspect that they accused of the murder. The proposition is that he is guilty of murder (G). Their evidence is as follows:

B: A revolver with a smell of fresh smoke and burned powder in two chambers was found on the defendant when he was arrested. Empty cartridges still in the gun had the same factory markings as three undischarged cartridges found in Hiller's home near the dead body.

C: Fingerprints found in Hiller's house near an entry window were identified as those of the defendant and later confirmed as the defendant's by outside experts.

D: Just before the murder a prowler was seen by two women in a house next door. The man held a lighted match over his head and the two women later testified that the defendant was the prowler because he was of the same height and build and wore a shirt and suspenders that they identified.

E: The defendant lied to the police about his name and address and claimed he had no criminal record, which in fact he had. He bought the revolver that he had when arrested under a false name, then pawned it, then retrieved it from the pawn shop just five hours before the shooting.

F: The defendant could not explain the blood on his clothing nor the wound on his forearm. He had no alibi for his whereabouts at the time of the shooting.

What we are after is the degree to which the multiple evidence cited above points toward the guilt G of the defendant. This can be handled by considering the evidence piece by piece. For each of these pieces the relevance of that piece of evidence to the proposition that the defendant is guilty remains constant as the probability of that piece of evidence changes. Rather than consider all five pieces of evidence, consider only the first three pieces, B, C, and D. Presume that the prior probability of a piece of evidence is zero. Let the posterior probabilities be $P'(B) = 0.8$, $P'(C) = 0.9$, and $P'(D) = 0.7$. Assume also that, before any evidence is brought to bear upon the question of guilt, the probability that the defendant is guilty is also zero. Take $R_{BG} = 0.6$, $R_{CG} = 0.4$, and $R_{DG} = 0.05$. Use the three grids below to graph the posterior probability that the defendant is guilty based upon evidence B alone, the posterior probability of guilt based upon evidence C in addition to B, and finally, the posterior probability of guilt based upon D in addition to both B and C. Will the influence of evidence E and F be necessary to convict the defendant?

Mr. Hiller's Murder — evidence B, C, and D

$\uparrow$

$P(G)$

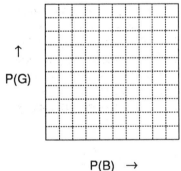 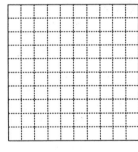 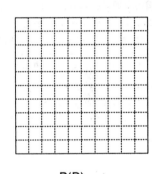

P(B) $\rightarrow$ P(C) $\rightarrow$ P(D) $\rightarrow$

*LEMPERT'S PARADOX REEXAMINED. Lempert is the individual who in Chapter II described a so-called "conjunction paradox." According to Lempert, in a civil suit in which there are a number of independent elements each existing with a probability of 0.75, a plaintiff needs only to establish this probability value for two of these elements to make his case. Since 0.75 x 0.75 = 0.56, the "preponderance of the evidence" standard is satisfied and the plaintiff should prevail (all this according to Lempert). If this ends the matter all is well for the plaintiff. But if a third element must be proved the probability for all three becomes 0.75 x 0.75 x 0.75 = 0.42 and the defendant should now win.

Conduct a Bayesian analysis of this situation to determine just how Lempert erred in stating this as a paradox. Let the elements that the plaintiff thinks he has to prove in order to win his case be designated as elements A, B, and C. Let their prior values be $P(A) = P(B) = P(C) = 0$. Interpret Lempert's probabilities $P = 0.75$ as the posterior values (the one's that the prosecutor can establish) for these elements so that $P'(A) = P'(B) = P'(C) = 0.75$. Let the prior value for making the case (before the opening statements) be $P(case) = 0$ and its posterior value be $P'(case)$ which must have some value greater than 0.50 if the plaintiff is to prevail. Finally, let the relevance of each element to the case be $R_{A\text{ to case}} = R_{B\text{ to case}} = R_{C\text{ to case}} = 0.30$. Consider the elements one by one, just as the pieces of evidence in the case of Mr. Hiller's murder were considered one by one. Use the three grids below to first, find the posterior P'(case) following the establishment of the probability of element A as P'(A) = 0.75. Next, find P'(case) after element B in addition to A has been shown to be P'(B) = 0.75. Finally, using the third grid, find P'(case) after P'(C) has been shown to likewise be 0.75. Note the sequence of values for P'(case) and compare these to the Lempert prediction. Which is more plausible?

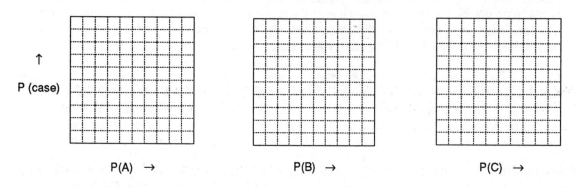

↑

P (case)

P(A) →   P(B) →   P(C) →

ACTIVITY - Use of Plausible Reasoning in a Book or Newspaper Article. Identify and describe six instances of plausible reasoning that you find in a newspaper, book, or magazine. Plausible reasoning is involved in persuasion, argumentation, and in drawing conclusions of any sort not based on formal logic. It is not necessary to cut or tear out the instances of plausible reasoning you find, simply provide a quote and state the source.

1. BLUE AND GREEN TAXICABS REVISITED.   In the problem (circle all correct responses):

   (a) P(ident B|B) + P(ident B|G) = 1.

   (b) P(B) + P($\overline{B}$) = 1.

   (c) P(B|ident B) + P(G|ident B) = 1.

2. MAMMALARY CANCER PROBLEM REVISITED. The information given in this problem is as follows: P(C) = 0.10, P(+|C) = 0.79, and P(+|$\overline{C}$) = 0.10. From this information one can learn that P(+) = _____

3. THE OIL LOBBYIST. In this problem the Bayes' diagram for the lobbyist and that for the congress-person are described in words. These two are, referring to the diagrams below (circle the two):

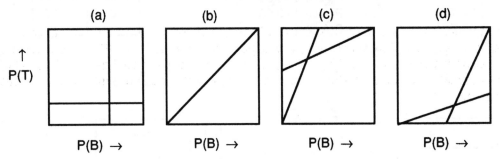

4. EINSTEIN'S PREDICTIONS. Einstein's theory of relativity predicted three consequences C_1, C_2, and C_3. (Circle all correct responses).

   (a) If all three were to be confirmed the probability that the theory is correct would be very high.

   (b) If two consequences were to be confirmed and the third found to be false, the probability that the theory is correct would be increased only a little.

   (c) If any one of the consequences were found to be false the theory must be false.

5. PARADOX IN DIAGNOSTICS. For the tests described in this problem (result + or -) for disease D it is true that (circle all correct responses):

   (a) the probability of two successive positive results for a person with the disease is greater than for a single positive result.

   (b) the probability for a person to have the disease is greater if he has received two positive results than for a single positive result.

   (c) both of the above are true.

The logical relationship of the inclusive "or" is defined by the truth table entries shown below. A particular instance of this relationship is represented by a listing of the conjunctive probabilities shown in an adjacent column together with these same probability figures given in a matrix. From this information determine the six Bayes' parameters for this same relationship and enter these values in the spaces provided. Finally, draw the Bayes' diagram on the grid provided. Afffix the labels P(A), P(B), P(A|B), P(A|B̄), P(B|A), and P(B|Ā) to each of the five points on this diagram.

truth table

A	B	A v B
T	T	T
T	F	T
F	T	T
F	F	F

conjunctions

	A v B
P(A.B̄)	0.40
P(A.B)	0.35
P(Ā.B)	0.25
P(Ā.B̄)	0

matrix

	B̄	B
A	0.35	0.40
Ā	0	0.25

A v B

P(A) = _____

P(B) = _____

P(A|B) = _____

P(A|B̄) = _____

P(B|A) = _____

P(B|Ā) = _____

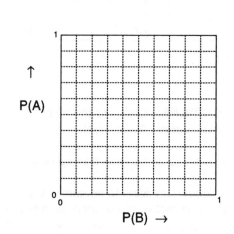

↑ P(A)

P(B) →

VIII. RATIONAL OR IRRATIONAL

Introductory Problems:

STREAK SHOOTING
DRIVE ON OR TURN BACK
DOWNSIZING A COMPUTER GIANT
DISEASE A SYMPTOM X

Background:

FRAMING
THE 2X2 DATA MATRIX
RANDOMNESS
PERCEPTION

Introductory Problem Solutions

Additional Problems:

ASIAN FLU EPIDEMIC
ANXIETY ATTACK
ADOPT OR NOT / CONCEIVE OR NOT
TESTING FOR SUCCESS
DOGS, CATS, AND CEO's
PRODUCT ENDORSEMENTS
THE B.B. KING CONCERT
DOWNSIZING SEQUEL
ACTIVITY—STREAK SHOOTING EXPERIMENT
ACTIVITY—THE SIX CIRCLES FIGURE

Self Tests:

SELECTED PROBLEMS
HOW MANY WAYS?

VIII. RATIONAL OR IRRATIONAL

Up to this point it has been implicitly assumed that problem solvers are perfectly rational individuals not subject to human frailty or weakness, that is, not intellectually disabled in any way. Of course such a person doesn't exist. We all on occasion read something into a problem situation that isn't really there, read something out of it that is there, make an implicit assumption about a problem that we aren't aware of, or in a myriad of other ways act in a manner not entirely rational or objective. Perhaps our emotions intercede. Our memory may be faulty or selective. We may be unduly influenced by a past experience that was particularly vivid. We may be influenced by the particular way a problem is worded. We may fail to recognize what we do not know as well as what we do know. Perhaps we see only what we expect to see, nothing more. Of course we all have limitations in our background knowledge and experience, but it is a disability to ignore our ignorance or to believe we know something when we don't. On the other hand, what may seem to be irrational can often be explained as entirely rational to others with a different point of view or a different knowledge base.

In this chapter some of the more common kinds of problem solving disabilities will be identified in the hope that by calling attention to them they can better be dealt with. This is not an exhortation that individuals should be totally rational at all times. Personal values or beliefs of one individual may seem irrational to another. A problem solution for one individual is not necessarily a satisfactory solution for another. Such differences, whether stemming from varying cultural backgrounds or differing personality profiles, should be acknowledged and accepted. Again, we must question whether what seems to be a disability displayed by others is in fact a disability or only appears as such.

Introductory Problems

STREAK SHOOTING. In basketball, players and fans alike recognize that players often get what is known as a "hot hand." When they are in a "streak" such players, it seems, can hardly miss. Their teammates feed them the ball when they can to take full advantage of the streak. On the other hand, players can also go "cold." No matter what they do they don't seem to be able to "buy" a bucket. A coach will often take the player out of the game hoping for better things when he rejoins the lineup. Psychologist Thomas Gilovich undertook a study of this phenomenon. At that time the only team in the NBA that kept records of their players' sequential shooting were the Philadelphia 76ers. Gilovich asked whether a player, having made his last two or three shots, was more likely to make his next shot, and whether a player, having missed his last two or three shots, was less likely to make his next shot. Data was collected on nine players during all of the 1980-81 season. After careful analysis of the data Gilovich and his colleagues concluded that the phenomenon of streak shooting simply did not exist for the 76ers, at least not during the season studied. The data Gilovich used to draw his conclusions is contained in the table below.

Player	P(x|ooo)	P(x|oo)	P(x|o)	P(x)	P(x|x)	Px|xx)	P(x|xxx)
C. Richardson	.50	.47	.56	.50	.49	.50	.48
J. Erving	.52	.51	.51	.52	.53	.52	.48
L. Hollins	.50	.49	.46	.46	.46	.46	.32
M. Cheeks	.77	.60	.60	.56	.55	.54	.59
C. Jones	.50	.48	.47	.47	.45	.43	.27
A. Toney	.52	.53	.51	.46	.43	.40	.34
B. Jones	.61	.58	.58	.54	.53	.47	.53
S. Mix	.70	.56	.52	.52	.51	.48	.36
D. Dawkins	.88	.73	.71	.62	.57	.58	.51
mean	.56	.53	.54	.52	.51	.50	.46

In this table an "x" indicates a hit and an "o" indicates a miss. Conditional probabilities for each player are placed in the seven columns. For example, in the first column the $P(x|ooo)$ means the conditional probability that the player will make his next shot on condition that he missed his three prior shots. At the bottom of each column is given the average conditional probability for that column.

Gilovich's conclusion contrasts sharply with the opinion of 100 knowledgeable basketball fans that he interviewed. These fans, considering a hypothetical basketball player who makes 50% of his shots, estimated that his shooting percentage should be 61% after having just made a shot and 42% after having just missed a shot. Who is right here, Gilovich and his colleagues or the 100 well-informed basketball fans? Carefully state the reasons for your conclusion no matter which side you agree with. Do you agree with Gilovich or with those basketball fans that disagreed so strongly with him?

DRIVE ON OR TURN BACK. As Dawes puts it in *Rational Choice in an Uncertain World* : "Would you rather pay $100 to be where you wanted to be or pay the same amount to be where you didn't want to be?" The answer to this question may seem obvious, but it wasn't to the young couple who found themselves in the following predicament. Jan and Judy have made reservations at a lodge in West Yellowstone, Montana to spend several days snowmobiling. They had to guarantee one night's stay for which they paid an advance non-refundable deposit of $100. As they drive toward "West," as it is called, they hadn't gone far when they heard over their car radio a report that there had been five inches of fresh snow overnight on the roads near the park. Jan hadn't bothered to mount his snow tires before leaving and in any event he was not anxious to drive on snowy roads that may or may not yet be plowed. Jan and Judy confer. If they go ahead to the lodge they will not have wasted the $100 deposit and the snowmobiling should be great, particularly with fresh snow. On the other hand, driving in uncertain conditions is anything but pleasurable. They might slip off the road or crash into another car. They could, however, turn around and return home along roads they know to be free of snow and ice, and this would be their choice—except for the deposit. Their dilemma is this: Should they make use of their $100 deposit for the sake of the "adventure" in driving roads to the park that are almost sure to be treacherous? Or should they give up the deposit, an amount they can ill-afford to waste, to enjoy the safety of returning home knowing there was little risk in the return trip? In brief, should Jan and Judy pay $100 (the lost deposit) to be safe at home where they have decided they really want to be, or pay the same amount (already paid) to drive on and take the risk they don't really want to take? If you were in Jan's or Judy's shoes what would you decide? What in your opinion is the wrong choice, and why?

DOWNSIZING A COMPUTER GIANT. A large computer firm with 50,000 employees and twelve plants nationwide is suffering some rather severe economic difficulties. Their products are overpriced and consequently not competing well in the marketplace. They feel that they may have to lay off about 6000 employees and close three of their plants. The executive VP would rather find more attractive alternatives. He announces two plans to meet the firm's fiscal crisis. They are as follows:

Plan No. 1. This plan will save one of the three plants and 2000 jobs.
Plan No. 2. In this plan there is a 1/3 probability to save all plants and all jobs and a 2/3 probability to save no plants or jobs.

The operations manager, however, has several plans of her own. These are:

Plan No. 3. This plan calls for the closing of two of the three plants and the loss of 4000 jobs.
Plan No. 4. For this plan there is a 2/3 probability to lose all plants and jobs and a 1/3 probability to lose no plants and jobs.

The Board of Directors decided to select one of the first two plans and one of the last two plans for final consideration. The Board's voting turned out four to one in favor of Plan 1 over Plan 2 and also four to one in favor of Plan 4 over Plan 3. Is it possible to *understand* these choices? Are they rational? Think of the *utility* of these choices to members of the Board, an idea introduced in the case of cervical cancer discussed in the Background section of Chapter III. Think of the ideas of *risk taking* and *risk aversion*.

162

DISEASE A SYMPTOM X. The following 2X2 matrix describes the relationship between individuals who do and do not have disease A with those who do and do not have a symptom of that disease, call it X. The numbers in the matrix are the *numbers of individuals* in this study in each of the four categories. The problem here is to describe as well as you can the nature of the relationship between disease A and symptom X.

DISEASE A

	A (present)	$\overline{A}$ (absent)
X (present)	20	10
$\overline{X}$ (absent)	80	40

SYMPTOM X

A student named Sam noticed that in the top row of the matrix, the row that indicates the presence of symptom X, that twice as many individuals with the symptom have the disease as don't have the disease. He therefore concluded that the presence of the symptom correlates positively with the presence of the disease. Sally, however, focused on the left side column. Here four times as many people with the disease don't have the symptom as have it. She therefore concluded that the presence of the symptom anti-correlates with the presence of the disease. Who in your opinion is right, Sam or Sally, or are they both right or both wrong? What do *you* think?

Background

The major thrust of the present chapter is to promote sensitivity to the ways a problem solving effort can appear to go wrong, or actually go wrong, because of human disabilities. There are a great many ways to make mistakes and only a few ways to avoid them. Psychologists have special names that they apply to the human disabilities that we all have. The names themselves are not important. If you wish, invent a name for a disability when you recognize it. In the background material that follows there is use made of the 2x2 matrix and a topic dealing with randomness, both of which have been previously encountered. In addition, certain aspects, both strengths and weaknesses, of our extremely important powers of visual thinking are introduced.

FRAMING. The term *framing* refers to a situation in which the language used to present a problem influences the nature of a proposed solution to that problem. Framing literally refers to a framework within which a problem solver is encouraged to approach the problem. A problem solver who is thereby constrained in his attack on a problem exhibits a kind of problem solving disability. Problems in this chapter in which framing plays a role include DOWNSIZING A COMPUTER GIANT and ASIAN FLU EPIDEMIC.

THE 2X2 DATA MATRIX. Generally speaking, people fail to accurately assess the relationship of one thing to another, more specifically, one conjecture or proposition to another. Relationships of this kind were extensively dealt with in the prior chapter. For example, one might want to assess the relationship between successful CEOs and some not-so-successful CEOs with those individuals who as children had pets and those that did not. Also, what is the relationship between performance on a certain exam where some individuals score higher than a certain score, some lower, and those individuals who later perform quite well on the job or perform poorly? For these and other binary relationships a 2X2 matrix description is extremely useful because it organizes data in a meaningful way.

Calling the two propositions, whatever they are, A and B, we let the truth of each be indicated by A and B and their falsity by $\bar{A}$ and $\bar{B}$. A and B is often indicated simply by writing the two symbols side by side and similarly for combinations with $\bar{A}$ and $\bar{B}$. The matrix that describes binary comparisons of propositions is shown below. The numbers in each box there are the *percentages* of all individuals in that category (since there are 100 individuals in all) in contrast to the Disease A Symptom X matrix above where the data refers to the *numbers* of individuals.

Proposition B

	B true	B false	
A true	AB 40	$A\bar{B}$ 20	2X2 DATA MATRIX
A false	$\bar{A}B$ 10	$\bar{A}\bar{B}$ 30	

Proposition A (label to the left of the A true / A false rows)

From this matrix we obtain the following values for the so-called Bayes' parameters:

$$P(A) = P(AB) + P(A\bar{B}) = 0.40 + 0.20 = 0.60$$

$$P(B) = P(AB) + P(\bar{A}B) = 0.40 + 0.10 = 0.50$$

$$P(A|B) = P(AB)/P(B) = 0.40 / (0.40 + 0.10) = 0.80$$

$$P(A|\bar{B}) = P(A\bar{B})/P(\bar{B}) = 0.20 / (0.20 + 0.30) = 0.40$$

$$P(B|A) = P(AB)/P(A) = 0.40 / (0.40 + 0.20) = 0.67$$

$$P(B|\bar{A}) = P(\bar{A}B)/P(\bar{A}) = 0.10 / (0.10 + 0.30) = 0.25$$

If some of the data is missing, however, the description of the relationship would be sharply curtailed.

RANDOMNESS. Events are often referred to as *random*. The position of a cloud in the sky, the places where raindrops fall on a square of sidewalk, the date a given individual will get married, the outcomes of repeated tosses of a coin — all these are made up of random events. Phenomena are random if individual outcomes are uncertain but the long term pattern of many individual outcomes is predictable. In the repeated toss of a coin, for example, we know that for a single toss the probability for heads is 0.5 and that for tails is also 0.5 (if the coin is fair). With two consecutive tosses the probabilities for HH, HT, TH, and TT are each 1/4. Thus the probability to toss two H's or two T's in a row is one-half. However, for a greater number of tosses the probability for obtaining all heads or all tails goes down markedly. For obtaining all H's or all T's in three tosses the probability is 1/4, and for six tosses it is 1/32. A more interesting question is this: What is the expected pattern of H's and T's when one tosses a coin a great many times? That is, what does random behavior really look like? Many individuals *think* they can spot random behavior when they see it, but can they really?

To attempt to answer the question about randomness consider tossing a coin six times in a row. This relatively small number will make the calculation of probabilities a reasonable chore. First, it is recognized that for a sequence of six coin tosses there are just 64 possible outcomes. This number is obtained from the realization that there are two outcomes for the first toss, two more for each of these first toss results when the second coin is tossed, two more outcomes for the third toss for each of the four possible outcomes from the first two tosses, and so on, making 2x2x2x2x2x2 = 64 total outcomes when tossing a coin six times in a row. Each of these sixty-four outcomes, taking their order into account, has a probability of occurrence of 1/2 x 1/2 x 1/2 x 1/2 x 1/2 x 1/2 = 0.015625 (the "and" rule). Finally, the number of *ways* for obtaining various results must be determined. For example, the sequence HTTHHT is one *way* for obtaining the result two sequences of two-in-a-row whether these be Ts or Hs; the sequence TTHTTH is another.

Tabulated below are the number of ways (these must total 64) to obtain certain results in the toss of a coin six times and the corresponding probabilities for each of these results (the number of ways multiplied by the probability for each way of 0.015625).

2 ways to obtain 6-in-a-row	probability	P = 0.03125
4 ways to obtain one 5-in-a-row		P = 0.06250
6 ways to obtain one 4-in-a-row		P = 0.09375
4 ways to obtain one 4-in-a-row and one 2-in-a-row		P = 0.06250
8 ways to obtain one 3-in-a-row		P = 0.12500
12 ways to obtain one 3-in-a-row and one 2-in-a-row		P = 0.18750
2 ways to obtain two 3-in-a-row's		P = 0.03125
10 ways to obtain one 2-in-a-row		P = 0.15625
12 ways to obtain two 2-in-a-row's		P = 0.18750
2 ways to obtain three 2-in-a-row's		P = 0.03125
2 ways to obtain no consecutive H's or T's		P = 0.03125
64		1.00000

We can perhaps hazard a guess as to the kinds of outcomes many people expect from random behavior exhibited by tossing a coin six consecutive times. Many individuals feel that an alternation of outcomes is a rather frequent result. They may also expect that obtaining a "run" of three or more in the coin tossing situation described above would be a rather infrequent occurrence. Let's see what the facts are. There are two ways for all six coins to alternate outcomes (no consecutive H's or T's) and four more ways for there to be an alternation involving just five of the six coins (2-in-a-row of either H or T only at the beginning or end of the string). Six ways in all gives a probability for alternation, or nearly so, of 0.09375. On the other hand, there are 38 ways to obtain a run of 3 or more in six tosses (the top seven entries in the list). This gives a combined probability of P = 0.59375. To sum up:

P for 5 or 6 coins to alternate outcomes in six tosses is approximately 1/10
P for obtaining a run of 3 or more in six tosses is approximately 6/10

It would seem that many people think the first figure to be much too low and the second much too high.

PERCEPTION. Visual information plays an extremely important role in solving many kinds of problems. As important as this is, it is also important to recognize that there are large variations in the perceptual skills of individuals. Recognition that such problems exist is the first step toward minimizing their effect. It is important to distinguish two kinds of "seeing." First, there are those direct perceptions recorded on our retinas and stored in the brain. Second, there are mental images never recorded on the retina that are somehow conjured up by the brain. These are as subject to processing and manipulation as are the images directly perceived.

Basic understanding of visual thinking is limited at best; so too is our understanding of all the ways our abilities in this area can be limited. Consider, for example, the Star of David shown below. As a composite object the mind is somehow able to disassemble it and "see" in it a pair of equilateral triangles. This is what most people see. But the Star of David can also be seen to be made up of three diamond shapes. These can readily be seen once they are pointed out. But why are the diamond shapes so slow to be perceived compared to the triangles? And what about other subpatterns? A hexagon is easy to see. Are there still other patterns?

STAR OF DAVID AND SUBPATTERNS

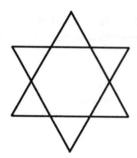  

Star of David consists of   two of these   or three of these.

There are a few generalizations that have come out of research in perception and imagery. One of these is that people tend to see what they expect to see, no doubt something familiar. An enjoyable summer pastime is to imagine various kinds of figures formed by puffy cumulus clouds. Rarely does one person say "Oh, do you see that giant lizard up there?" and the other person sees it also. Frost frozen on a window in wintertime very often forms, in some people's minds, familiar figures of one kind or another. In a bathroom floor made up of small tiles in two colors one might see a cross, letters of the alphabet, and various geometric patterns. On a Chinese mountainside sometime in late Winter, so the story goes, the pattern of splotchy snow against the darker rock formed what one person saw as a figure of Christ. The pattern was reproduced and entitled "Christ of the Chinese Mountains." It is shown on the following page. Can you see the figure of Christ? Many individuals don't see the figure at all. Others finally see it when its location and size are pointed out to them. What is the reason for this variation in a person's ability to recognize a pattern in the midst of seeming randomness?

There are many graphic illusions, some of the most famous having been drawn by M.C. Escher. A totally new illusion entitled "Twin Stairways" is shown on the second page following. The pattern itself is a tiling pattern known to the ancient Romans. What is new is the shading which creates four distinctly different illusions. In the standard view from the bottom the dark and light gray form two intersecting stairways against a white background. The dark diamond shapes are the treads and the light gray squares are the sloping risers. In a second view from either the right or left sides of the figure two more intersecting stairways are seen, but this time against a dark gray background. The white diamond shapes form the treads and the light gray squares the sloping risers. Finally, view the figure at an angle midway between the front view and the side view. The intersecting stairways have now disappeared. In their place are columns of figures consisting of flat sides which give the appearance of alternating protrusions and indentations. Take the light gray, for example. Depending on how you look at the figure, the light gray is either the top side of a protrusion or the bottom side of an indentation. How many situations have we encountered where we have simply assumed that the way we first see a figure or scene is the only way? How much have we missed in life because of this particular disability?

Christ of the Chinese Mountains

167

Twin Stairways

Introductory Problem Solutions

STREAK SHOOTING. RECAP DATA. The data Gilovich obtained is reproduced below. Each of the seven columns list conditional probabilities for each player with mean values at the bottom.

Player	P(x|ooo)	P(x|oo)	P(x|o)	P(x)	P(x|x)	Px|xx)	P(x|xxx)
C. Richardson	.50	.47	.56	.50	.49	.50	.48
J. Erving	.52	.51	.51	.52	.53	.52	.48
L. Hollins	.50	.49	.46	.46	.46	.46	.32
M. Cheeks	.77	.60	.60	.56	.55	.54	.59
C. Jones	.50	.48	.47	.47	.45	.43	.27
A. Toney	.52	.53	.51	.46	.43	.40	.34
B. Jones	.61	.58	.58	.54	.53	.47	.53
S. Mix	.70	.56	.52	.52	.51	.48	.36
D. Dawkins	.88	.73	.71	.62	.57	.58	.51
mean	.56	.53	.54	.52	.51	.50	.46

ANALYSE DATA. Looking at the mean values it is quite apparent that players were *not* more likely to make a shot after making their last one as shown by the values of P(x|x), nor less likely to make a shot after having missed the shot before as indicated by the values P(x|o). Similar remarks apply when comparing P(x|xx) to P(x|oo), and P(x|xxx) to P(x|ooo).

CREATE MODEL. Since the shooting percentages of the Philadelphia 76ers during the 1980-81 season were so close to 50%, it seems reasonable to compare their shooting to the toss of a coin. The result of a series of coin tosses is, as we say, "random." No matter how many consecutive heads (or tails) have been tossed, the probability for yet another head (tail) is precisely 0.50, no more no less. The conclusion that the shooting of the 76ers is close to random seems inescapable. A feature of this random behavior is the occurrence of streaks of both hits and misses just as there are "streaks" of both heads and tails. Basketball fans seem to remember the streaks of hits and also the streaks of misses. What they perhaps don't realize is that both are simply manifestations of random behavior.

RATIONAL CONCLUSION. It is rational to doubt a conclusion based on so little data. It is not rational, however, to simply ignore this data. Belief that the "hot hand" and "cold" streaks are attributable to something other than pure chance must be based upon evidence, not one's impressions.

DRIVE ON OR TURN BACK. RESTATE PROB. Jan and Judy found themselves in a predicament upon learning of the fresh snowfall near West Yellowstone where they had planned to spend the weekend snowmobiling. They had paid a non-refundable deposit of $100 for their accommodations there. Should they drive on in spite of what are sure to be bad road conditions, or return home and spend a pleasant stress-free weekend there?

ASSESS PROB. This situation illustrates a problem in "sunk costs" that many individuals deal with quite poorly. A fairly standard reaction to this kind of a situation is to "protect" the investment already made, in this case the $100 deposit. What many people fail to realize is that the deposit money has already been spent. There is no way that it can be returned. No matter whether Jan and Judy drive on or whether they turn back, that money has already been spent.

RATIONAL DECISION. The "rational" thing to do is to then decide whether they would rather brave the roads ahead or return home and spend a pleasant if not exciting weekend there. The mere fact that the $100 has already been spent should not influence their decision. Of course some people

169

have no desire whatsoever to behave in a rational manner. Such individuals will think it extremely unwise not to utilize the accommodations for which they have already paid. Perhaps these are the same people who, having already lost $100 at a gambling casino, invest another $100 in the hopes of winning back their losings. The alternative is, of course, to simply walk away reconciled to the $100 loss. Perhaps such individuals are likely to be the kind, having invested rather heavily in a gold mine, now face the prospect of having to invest still further in the hope of recovering their initial investment, and possibly make a killing eventually in so doing or, of course—lose everything.

ALTERNATIVE DECISIONS. The behavior described above is *presumably* rational. But is there more to it than this? There are perhaps many ways to rationalize going on to West Yellowstone in spite of snowy roads. One way that going on makes sense is as follows. Suppose the skimobiling opportunity is worth far more to both Jan and Judy than the $100 deposit. Suppose it is worth $500. Turning back then means a lost opportunity of significant value. In this case they might very well press on to West Yellowstone. Are there other rational reasons for making presumably irrational decisions?

DOWNSIZING A COMPUTER GIANT. RESTATE PROB. A large computer firm faces the prospect of closing three of their plants and laying off about 6000 employees. The executive VP's two plans to handle the situation are:
> Plan 1. This plan will save one of the three plants and 2000 jobs.
> Plan 2. In this plan there is a 1/3 probability to save all plants and all jobs and a 2/3 probability to save no plants or jobs.
The operations manager has presented her two plans. These are:
> Plan 3. This plan calls for the closing of two of the three plants and the loss of 4000 jobs.
> Plan 4. For this plan there is a 2/3 probability to lose all plants and jobs and a 1/3 probability to lose no plants and jobs.
The problem is to try to understand the Board's preference for Plan 1 over Plan 2 and its preference for Plan 4 over Plan 3. Which two plans would *you* have selected and why? Notice that, although stated differently, Plan 1 is objectively the same as Plan 3 and Plan 2 is objectively the same as Plan 4. In contrast to Plans 1 and 2, Plans 2 and 4 are probabilistic. Note that all plans are objectively the same.

PREFERENCES. In Bazerman and Neale's article appearing in Arkes and Hammond's anthology *Judgment and Decision Making* it is stated that more than 80 percent of individuals tested prefer Plan 1 to Plan 2 and 80+ percent prefer Plan 4 to Plan 3. One can assume that the Board of the computer corporation has responded in the same way, favoring Plans 1 and 4. It is to be noted that the preference for Plan 1 represents a conservative position in which a sure thing, the saving of one plant and 2000 jobs, is valued more highly than the risky 1/3 chance for saving all plants and all jobs. The preference for Plan 4 over Plan 3, however, places the value of the 2/3 chance for losing all plants and jobs higher than the value of losing 2 of the 3 plants and 4000 jobs. This is a valuation in which taking the risk of losing all plants and jobs is preferred to the outright loss of 2 plants and 4000 jobs. These preferences can perhaps be accounted for in part by the "framing" of each of the four plans.

DISEASE *A* SYMPTOM *X*. RECAP DISABILITIES. A common failing in attempting to determine the relationship between disease A and symptom X is to place an almost exclusive reliance on the "present/present" cell in the upper left corner of the 2x2 matrix no matter what the numbers might be in the other three cells. In this case the number 20 in the present/present cell tells individuals who focus their attention there that many people suffering with disease A do in fact have the symptom. Other individuals pay attention to only two of the cells such as those in the upper row or left-side column. Such people might conclude that there is a positive correlation between A and X because more people who have the disease have the symptom than those who do not have the disease and do have the symptom (the upper two cells). Others might conclude that the correlation between A and X must be negative because more people who have the disease do not have the symptom than have the disease and have the symptom (two cells at the left).

170

CHANGE DESCRIPTION. Few people understand that to fully describe the relationship between disease A and symptom X requires knowledge of all four cells. However, even for those with but a small amount of background, proper handling of fundamental statistical quantities that are determined by the entries in a 2x2 matrix should not be too difficult. For example, the relationship between disease A and symptom X can be described by the quantities $P(A)$, $P(X)$, $P(A|X)$, $P(A|\overline{X})$, $P(X|A)$, and $P(X|\overline{A})$ which are easily evaluated as shown below where the total number of individuals represented in the matrix is 150.

$$P(A) = (80 + 20)/150 = 0.67 \qquad P(A|X) = 20/(20 + 10) = 0.67 \qquad P(X|A) = 20/(20 + 80) = 0.20$$

$$P(X) = (20 + 10)/150 = 0.20 \qquad P(A|\overline{X}) = 80/(80 + 40) = 0.67 \qquad P(X|\overline{A}) = 10/(10 + 40) = 0.20$$

DRAW CONCLUSIONS. It is interesting to note that it is just as likely for one to have the disease if one doesn't have the symptom as it is to have the disease when one has the symptom. It is also just as likely for one to have the symptom if one doesn't have the disease as it is to have the symptom if one has the disease. Neither of these results is apparent by merely looking at the matrix.

Additional Problems

ASIAN FLU EPIDEMIC. Suppose that the Center for Disease Control is preparing for the outbreak of a particular strain of Asian flu this winter. If nothing is done it is expected to kill 600 people. Two alternative programs to combat the epidemic have been proposed. These have been described by the head of public relations for the Center as follows: If program A is adopted, 200 (of the 600) people will be saved, and if Program B is adopted, there is a 1/3 probability that all 600 will be saved and a 2/3 probability that nobody will be saved. Which of these two programs would you favor and why?

The Center's chief physician, however, put a different spin on the nationwide threat of a flu epidemic. He described two programs for minimizing the possible outbreak as follows. If program C is adopted 400 people will die. If Program D is adopted, there is a 2/3 probability that all 600 people will die and a 1/3 probability that nobody will die. Which of these two programs do you prefer? Compare the programs as described by the public relations office with those described by the chief physician. Which do you prefer and why? Is this problem the same as DOWNSIZING A COMPUTER GIANT or are there significant differences?

*ANXIETY ATTACK. The following problem is described by Dawes in *Rational Choice in an Uncertain World*. You are a psychiatrist who has two patients, call them Ms A and Ms B, both of whom suffer from anxiety attacks. Your attempts to identify the triggers for these attacks have been unsuccessful. You therefore decide to observe for each of these patients the onset of their attacks over a period of twenty days to determine, if you can, whether the pattern of onset is random or perhaps keyed to particular events in the lives of these patients. The result of this study gives the following sequences where an X indicates a day of an attack and an O a day free of an attack. For which patient does the sequence appear less random thus indicating that there may be factors that trigger the onset of those attacks that you've somehow overlooked?

Ms A: O X O X O X O O X O O X O X X O X O X X
Ms B: X O O X X X O O X O O O X X O O X X O O

*ADOPT OR NOT / CONCEIVE OR NOT. Gilovich describes a situation faced by many young couples wishing to start a family. There is the common belief that couples who have adopted a child because of a prior lengthy period of infertility are now more likely to have a child of their own. Evidence relevant to this belief can be represented in a 2X2 matrix. In this matrix are entered data (fictional) for 100 couples who adopt and later conceive, adopt and later do not conceive, do not adopt but later conceive, and do not adopt and later do not conceive.

	C (conceive)	$\overline{C}$ (do not conceive)	
A (adopt)	4	36	ADOPT OR NOT CONCEIVE OR NOT
$\overline{A}$ (do not adopt)	6	54	

What is your interpretation of the significance of this data? Just looking at the matrix elements, what conclusions can you draw? Now determine the probability $P(C|A)$ of conception given that the couple adopted, and also the probability $P(C|\overline{A})$ of conception given that the couple did not adopt. Reevaluate your earlier conclusion on the basis of these conditional probability values.

*TESTING FOR SUCCESS. Some highschool graduates apply for admission to small prestigious liberal arts colleges such as the Halls of Ivy. The college admissions officer of this institution considers the students' highschool records, their SAT scores, and letters of recommendation. Each student is either accepted for admission or rejected. Later, those that were accepted either graduated from the Halls of Ivy or did not. Data of this kind for 1000 applicants was collected over a period of years. The question is: What do you expect the relationship to be between admission to the College (satisfaction of the entrance criteria) and later graduation? As usual, the data is inserted into a 2X2 matrix such as the one below. What information can be gleaned from the data provided? Can one learn the probability that a rejected applicant would have been able to graduate if the applicant had been accepted rather than rejected? What other data could be collected to improve the analysis?

		Admission to Halls of Ivy		
		A (accepted)	$\overline{A}$ (rejected)	
Outcome	G (graduated)	250	0	ACCEPT OR NOT GRADUATE OR NOT
	$\overline{G}$ (did not graduate)	50	700	

*DOGS, CATS, AND CEOs. In *Rational Choice in an Uncertain World* Dawes refers to an item that appeared in the magazine *Management Focus*. This article stated that there may be a link between childhood pet ownership and future career success. Cited was the fact that 94% of a group of CEOs, all of which were employed by Fortune 500 companies, had a dog, a cat, or both as youngsters. These CEOs claimed that the ownership of a pet had instilled in them character traits that made them good managers. These traits included having empathy and respect for others, generosity, good communication skills, and the ability to handle responsibility.

Also described by Dawes, referring to another article, was the claim by a self-styled expert as to how to improve one's chances for survival in the event of an airplane accident. His tip was to learn all the emergency exits upon boarding the plane and to rehearse how to get to them. This individual had interviewed almost 200 survivors of airline accidents involving fatalities. Of this group more than 90% had in fact mentally mapped out their escape routes beforehand.

These two claims are similar in certain respects, that of the CEOs regarding pet ownership, and that of the "expert" on airline safety. The problem here is to assess these claims in each case.

PRODUCT ENDORSEMENTS. Advertising agencies typically select celebrities to huckster their products. A hall-of-fame pitcher has advice on home mortgages. An all star basketball player tells you which brand of corn flakes to buy. A Nobel laureate sells automobile tires. A well-known actress endorses health clubs. An ex-politician tells you about luggage. All that is required, it seems, is someone with a well-known name or face to sell the product to the public. Neither the ad agencies nor the public expect these individuals to possess any particular knowledge concerning the product they are endorsing. How can one justify the huge fees such celebrities are paid? Is it rational or does it represent some sort of aberration in logic?

THE B.B. KING CONCERT. Suppose a friend of yours had decided to go to a B.B. King concert. He paid the $20 price for a ticket. As he got to the gate he discovered that he had lost his ticket. There was no reserved seating and consequently he was denied admission. Should he now pay $20 for another ticket? A second situation: Another friend had planned to purchase his ticket to the concert at the gate. As he opened his billfold to buy the ticket he discovered he had lost a $20 bill. Should he still pay $20 for a ticket to the concert? Explain your response to each of these two questions. What would have been a "rational" response of your friends to each of these situations? What, in your opinion, would have been an "irrational" response in each case? Can you justify a response that some might think of as irrational as in fact being quite rational?

DOWNSIZING SEQUEL. Recall that the large computer firm with 50,000 employees and 12 plants nationwide developed four plans for downsizing. The president of the company felt that it might have to lay off about 6000 employees and close three of their plants. The executive V.P., however, had two plans which were:

> Plan no. 1. This plan would save one of the three plants and 2000 jobs.
> Plan no. 2. In this plan there was a 1/3 probability to save all plants and all jobs and a 2/3 probability to save no plants or jobs.

The two plans of the operations manager were:

> Plan no. 3. This plan called for the closing of two of the three plants and the loss of 4000 jobs.
> Plan no. 4. For this plan there was a 2/3 probability to lose all plants and jobs and a 1/3 probability to lose no plants and no jobs.

The Board of Directors favored Plan 1 four-to-one over Plan 2 and also four-to-one in favor of Plan 4 over Plan 3. A young MBA graduate newly hired by the company learned of these results. At first he couldn't understand them. In an attempt to do just that he drew what he felt would be the Board's utility curve that could describe each of these four plans in terms of the value (utility) each would have compared to the others. This curve is shown below.

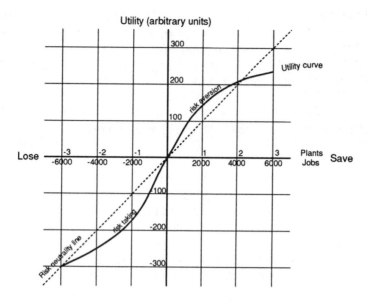

The utility curve itself is the S-shaped curve. It is a graph of the utility plotted vertically against the number of plants and jobs saved horizontally to the right of the origin (0,0 point) and horizontally to the left against the number of plants and jobs lost. Utility values in the upper right quadrant of the graph exhibit risk aversion (conservative values) since each subsequent plant and 2000 jobs saved is deemed to be worth less than the first plant saved and the first 2000 jobs saved. In the lower left quadrant the utility curve exhibits risk-taking because each additional plant and 2000 jobs that are lost is considered to be less of a disaster than the loss of the first plant and first 2000 jobs. The problem here is to mark on the utility curve six points. Two of these are the utility of saving all plants and all jobs and the utility of losing all plants and all jobs. The remaining four points mark the utilities of Plan 1, Plan 2, Plan 3, and Plan 4. Having done this can the preferences of the Board of the computer firm be better understood? Does this mean that the Board has or has not been influenced by the framing of the plans?

ACTIVITY—STREAK SHOOTING EXPERIMENT. Suppose the scoring pattern for 3-point shots of a certain player in the NBA is as shown below. Assume that from behind the 3-point line his overall success is 50 percent. Assume also that he attempts exactly eight such baskets each game. In ten games his record is as follows where "3" indicates a score (3 points) and "0" a miss.

30030003	00030003
33003303	30000333
00000303	33330330
33300303	30303333
03300333	00330300

What is this player's percentage for making 3-point shots in these ten games. How many pairs of two consecutive 3-point shots did he make in his strings of eight shots? Count 333 as two 33's. What was his percentage for making the second shot after having made the first? How many 3-in-a-row shots did he make? What was his percentage for making the third shot after having made the preceding two?

The basic question is whether this player was a streak shooter or not in these ten games. To test whether his shooting is random or not toss a coin eight times and record the succession of heads and tails. Let each head represent a successful 3-point shot and each tail a miss. Repeat this ten times to simulate hits and misses in ten games. For these results answer the same questions that were asked above. Now compare the figures for the random results for the coin tosses with the actual hits and misses as recorded above. What is your conclusion? Is the player a streak shooter? Can you be a streak flipper of heads?

174

ACTIVITY—THE SIX CIRCLES FIGURE. In the Background section a Star of David was shown together with two of the subpatterns that it can be thought to consist of. There are, of course, other subpatterns such as the six small equilateral triangles attached to each of the six sides of an imaginary interior hexagon. The imaginary hexagon is itself one of the subpatterns. Are there others? What we tend to see in any pattern is likely to be some familiar object. However, it may be important in certain situations to be able to pick out something that is not so familiar or obvious. Consider the more complicated pattern show below that is formed by six overlapping circles. This time there are many subpatterns. Which is the most obvious? Which is the next most obvious? How many symmetric subpatterns can you identify altogether? Don't forget the patterns "left behind" after you have removed from the original figure one of the subpatterns. Sketch each of the patterns of interest.

THE SIX CIRCLES FIGURE

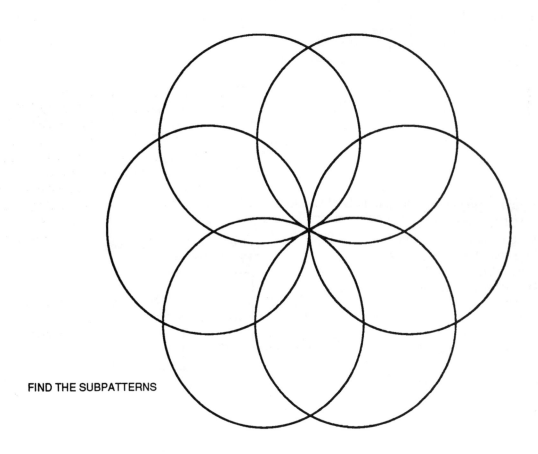

FIND THE SUBPATTERNS

Chapter VIII Self Test—Selected Problems

1. ASIAN FLU EPIDEMIC. In this problem there are four programs, A, B, C and D, to combat a possible epidemic of Asian flu. (Circle all correct statements):

    (a) Program A is objectively the same as Program C.

    (b) Program B is objectively the same as Program D.

    (c) Programs A and C (also, Programs B and D) differ only in the way the two plans are worded.

2. ADOPT OR NOT / CONCEIVE OR NOT.
Another fictitious survey of 100 couples resulted in the data in the matrix. From this data one can conclude that for this sample (Circle the correct response):

    (a) $P(C|A) > P(C|\bar{A})$

    (b) $P(C|A) < P(C|\bar{A})$

    (c) $P(C|A) = P(C|\bar{A})$

	C (conceive)	$\bar{C}$ (do not conceive)
A (adopt)	5	15
$\bar{A}$ (do not adopt)	20	60

3. DOGS, CATS, AND CEO's. Recall that 94% of successful CEO's had pets as youngsters. This figure comes from the data in the matrix. More important, however, are the two conditionals $P(S|pet)$ and $P(S|\overline{pet})$. For the data in the matrix we learn that having a dog or cat as a youngster (circle the best response):

    (a) correlates with success

    (b) anti-correlates with success

    (c) has no affect on success

	pet P — had dog or cat as youngster	no pet $\bar{P}$ — did not have dog or cat as youngster
S — most successful CEOs	470	30
$\bar{S}$ — less successful CEOs	1940	60

4. THE B.B. KING CONCERT. An acquaintance of yours is heading to the B.B. King concert at Wolf Mountain. Tickets have gone up to $30. At the entrance he discovers he has apparently lost the $30 he saved back for his ticket. Disappointed, he heads for home. His reaction should be interpreted as (circle the best response):

    (a) rational

    (b) irrational

    (c) could be either rational or irrational depending on unstated factors.

Chapter VIII Self Test — HOW MANY WAYS?

Coin tossing is an activity that is examined in the background section of Chapter II where the objective was to better understand the concept of probability. There, a coin was tossed four times in sequence. Again in Chapter VIII a coin was tossed six times in sequence in order to understand the basic idea of randomness. Here, a coin is tossed sequentially five times. It is a fair coin so that $P(H) = 0.500$ and $P(T) = 0.500$. Thus the sequence of possible results for these five tosses is completely random. In the following respond to each of the "how many ways" questions for the five-coin case.

(a) How many ways are there altogether to toss a coin five times sequentially? _____

(b) How many ways are there to toss four and only four heads in a row? _____

(c) How many ways are there to toss three and only three heads in a row? _____

(d) How many ways are there to toss exactly two heads in a row and two tails in a row in a single sequence of five tosses? _____

(e) How many ways are there to obtain a sequence in which no toss, either an H or a T, is immediately followed by the same toss? _____

IX. PROBLEMS IN ETHICS

Introduction: Three Approaches to Ethical Problems
                       Critical Analysis—Narrative Style
                       Using Problem Solving Heuristics
                       Utilitarian Analysis

Example Problems Using Each of the Three Approaches:
           TRUTH TELLING — THE PHYSICIAN   (Critical analysis - Narrative style)
           BUCKING THE SYSTEM — SHOULD NURSES STRIKE?   (Use of heuristics)
           TRUTH TELLING — THE MINISTER   (Utilitarian analysis)

Additional Problems:
           CASE NO. 1   TRUTH TELLING — THE PSYCHOTHERAPIST
                              WARNING POSSIBLE PARTNERS
           CASE NO. 2   GRADING TRUTHFULLY
           CASE NO. 3   ACCESS TO MEDICAL SERVICES
           CASE NO. 4   ACCESS TO A UNIVERSITY EDUCATION
           CASE NO. 5   BUCKING THE SYSTEM — WHISTLE BLOWING IN MEDICINE
           CASE NO. 6   PROFESSIONAL OBLIGATION — THE CLINICAL SOCIAL WORKER
           CASE NO. 7   PROFESSIONAL OBLIGATION — THE JOURNALIST
           CASE NO. 8   PROFESSIONAL OBLIGATION — A MEDICAL JOURNAL
                              "IT'S OVER, DEBBIE"

Exercises: ANALYSE any of the eight Additional Problems using any one of the three approaches.
                   Make the paper 300-500 words in length.

             ACTIVITY. Interview a professional regarding that person's experience in meeting and
                   solving problems in professional ethics. Write a 300-500 word summary of
                   your findings.

IX. PROBLEMS IN ETHICS

In our prior work we have dealt with problems that are more or less straightforward. Even if we have had difficulty with some of them, one gets the feeling that with sufficient persistence one could succeed. Let us call these *tame* problems. Now we come to problems that are significantly different. Ethical problems are not only more difficult than those we're used to, but we may not be sure whether some of them even have solutions. And if they do, there might be endless argument whether a given solution is a good or reasonable one. Many problems in ethics are societal problems, and by virtue of this fact alone are far more difficult than many other problems. Furthermore, there is little agreement as to what constitutes ethical behavior. Criteria may depend on one's religion, ethnic origin, or economic status. One can refer to problems such as these as *wicked* problems.

There are many ways to approach problems in ethics, but of these we will single out just three. The first, but not necessarily the foremost, is an assessment of a problem in narrative form using our powers of critical thinking to express ideas and draw conclusions. Let us call this a **critical analysis**. A second approach utilizes problem solving heuristics, or commands, to structure the problems and remind the problem solver that he must make conscious decisions as to his strategy for finding a problem solution. Let us call this the **heuristic** approach. Our experience with this methodology should help us to apply it to ethical problems. Finally there is a method that springs from a theory that philosophers call utilitarianism. Call this a **utilitarian analysis**. Utilitarianism will remind you of our investigation of decision making in Chapter III. The analysis here, as it did there, uses the concept of *utility* . Here, however, it is the "happiness" or, "pleasure," as the utilitarians call it, of a particular act and its consequences that is evaluated.

CRITICAL ANALYSIS (narrative style). This method of analysis employs language as the primary tool for thought. *Critical thinking*, as it is called, has received a great deal of recent attention from those in languages, in philosophy, and in communications. The "language" of critical thinking contains such words as persuasion, argumentation, reasoning, warrants, claims, grounds, fallacies, induction, deduction, syllogisms, tautologies, and rationality. Texts in critical thinking have the same broad objectives as our study here of problem solving. After all, problem solving is critical thinking, but surely not all critical thinking is problem solving. The word *critical* in association with the word *thinking* signifies the evaluation function of language and thinking in general. It can safely be concluded that critical thinking is inseparable from problem solving. However, textbook treatments of critical thinking normally exclude discussion of either symbolic or visual thinking, both of which are important aspects of critical thinking and both of which play important roles in problem solving.

ANALYSIS USING PROBLEM SOLVING HEURISTICS. Appendix C contains an extensive list of problem solving heuristics, also known as commands. One will find that many of these have little relevance to the analysis of ethical problems. One may also find that commands more appropriate in discussions of ethical problems are missing from this listing. Nonetheless, there are important overlaps between commands listed in the Appendix and those more applicable to problems in ethics. On the positive side however, attention to the use of problem solving heuristics in the analysis of any problem whatsoever forces the problem solver to structure his thinking and thus strengthen his analysis.

UTILITARIAN ANALYSIS. In the 19th century the philosophical idea of utilitarianism was described by Jeremy Bentham. The basic idea was that *values* could be quantified in much the same way as a corporation evaluates profits and losses. Desired was the Greatest Happiness for the Greatest Number (GHGN). Happiness is taken to be synonymous with pleasure. According to Bentham, and later, Mill, the dimensions of pleasure are its intensity, duration, certainty, closeness, productivity, purity, and quality. According to this philosophy, the "bottom line" for all human activity is not dollars, but pleasure. The idea that one might evaluate it numerically is reminiscent of Ben Franklin's scheme for decision making. "Weigh" a particular deed or act according to the net value of its positive and negative consequences and one can then compare it to the value of a rival deed or act and thus arrive at a decision as to which is the more desirable of the two. An evaluator can be an individual, a group, or all mankind.

Example: Critical Analysis — Narrative Style

TRUTHTELLING — THE PHYSICIAN

As a physician whose specialty is treating cancer, you have seen many kinds of misunderstandings of this disease — often for the worse. Many of your patients believe that cancer always involves extended terminal suffering, and that a diagnosis of cancer is a sentence of death. Few patients understand that more than half of the various kinds of cancer can be permanently arrested or cured.

Fortunately, the patient you are seeing on rounds today, Alex S., is quite different. He is a well-informed young man — a writer at work on his third novel — who understands that "cancer" is a catch-all term for many quite different kinds of diseases, and that for some of them, the cure rate is very good. "That word 'cancer' doesn't scare me," he says, "I know you can get well."

Alex had been brought to the hospital complaining of severe pain in the mid-abdomen, and after a complete workup, a tentative diagnosis of pancreatic mass was made. He underwent surgery, and diagnosis of cancer of the pancreas was confirmed. The surgeons removed most of the visible tumor, but some of the primary malignancy could not be contained, and distant metastases are inevitable. Radiation and chemotherapy are likely to be of little use. Pancreatic cancer is one of the worst of the cancers, with a 2-year survival rate of 1 to 2% at most; this means that after two years only 1 or 2 percent of patients are still alive. Pancreatic cancer is almost universally fatal.

But Alex, for all his knowledge, does not realize this. You have told him the diagnosis and the survival rate, but he has clearly misunderstood, and like many less knowledgeable patients, he has heard only the most optimistic diagnosis. "Oh," he says, "that's not so bad, if I have a chance of a couple of years, I'll be able to finish my new novel — that's the only thing that really counts for me, anyway. Thanks, doctor, for telling me the truth."

What do you say to Alex now?

Analysis: TRUTHTELLING — THE PHYSICIAN
Critical Analysis — Narrative Style

At the simplest possible level it is quite clear what the doctor might do after Alex tells him "Thanks, doctor, for telling me the truth." The doctor might once again attempt to explain to Alex the nature of his condition, this time with more directness and more emphasis. Simply because Alex has misunderstood what the doctor has been trying to tell him is no reason for the doctor now to change his strategy to one of "let well enough alone," or "what Alex doesn't know or realize won't hurt him."

At another level the attending physician might now, if he hasn't already, explain to Alex his alternatives. First, he can make very clear to Alex the fact that 1 or 2 percent of patients in Alex's situation *do* live as long as two years, time enough for Alex to finish his novel. The doctor can further emphasize the fact that, although radiation and chemotherapy are likely to be of little use, it is possible that such treatments might be effective in spite of the small odds for them doing so. It is Alex's choice, not the doctor's, to make. Alex knows full well how sick these treatments would make him feel. The doctor might also apprise Alex of experimental procedures that are being conducted in a number of hospitals. Again, it is for Alex to decide whether or not he would like to try to qualify for such programs. The doctor's role here is only as a source of information for Alex. It is not his role to make decisions on Alex's behalf. Another option for Alex, should his condition worsen markedly, is to elect to go the Kevorkian route, i.e., try to find someone who would assist him to commit suicide. Although this course of action is not only illegal in many states and contrary to the doctrines of some religious groups, it remains for Alex to make his own determination as to which courses of action he might take.

Nothing is mentioned in the statement of this case regarding Alex's relatives, friends, and possibly a spouse. Normal practice is for an oncologist to gather these individuals together to inform them of Alex's condition. Acting as a support team, after having gained knowledge of Alex's situation, these individuals can then counsel with Alex to help him make what for him will be the best possible decision among the available alternatives, assuming of course that by now Alex fully appreciates the gravity of his situation. Once Alex chooses his course of action, these people will then be far more satisfied with Alex's solution to his problem than they might have been if they had been left out of the decision making process entirely.

Nothing is known about the economic aspects of Alex's situation. Does he have medical insurance? If not, can either a spouse or his family pay the costs of his treatments, should he elect to take them? As sad as it is to have such considerations influence Alex's decision, it is nonetheless possible that they would loom large in Alex's mind. His care could, for example, drain his family's resources significantly.

As for obligations, it is definitely not the obligation of the attending physician to make decisions for Alex on his behalf. The patient should be autonomous in such situations. After all, it is not as if Alex has lost his mental faculties so that someone would have to make important decisions for him. Medical professionals often succumb to the temptation to advise quite strongly, or even to dictate, a certain course of action that a patient should take. What is awkward about this case is that the doctor cannot very well ask Alex if he wants it "straight from the shoulder," for Alex cannot then respond negatively. This is the reason for drawing as many as possible of the individuals who are involved in Alex's situation into a process of information sharing. As for Alex, he should realize that he has the obligation to make his own decisions once he has been fully informed of the doctor's assessment of his situation and after he fully understands that information.

Should Alex's situation worsen to the point where he is unable to rationally make his own decisions, the decision making process of course must change. Who then should make decisions on Alex's behalf presents an entirely new and difficult ethical problem.

Example: Use of Heuristics

BUCKING THE SYSTEM — SHOULD NURSES STRIKE?

As a registered nurse employed in a county-operated general hospital, you have become increasingly concerned in recent months over deteriorating working conditions and their effects on the quality of care provided to patients. Because of cutbacks in federal, state, and local funding, the administration has substantially reduced the size of the hospital's support staff, assigning many jobs usually performed by practical nurses, technicians, and even custodial personnel to the registered nurses. In addition, many of the nurses formerly employed full time have been reduced to "on-call" status, being asked to come in to work long shifts at irregular intervals and without notice, whenever they are needed. Some of your senior colleagues have resigned in response to these difficult conditions. They have been replaced by less experienced nurses who are available at lower salaries. And throughout the hospital, great pressure has been exerted to limit admissions, especially of indigent patients, and to release patients as quickly as possible in order to cut the costs further.

Nor is there improvement in sight: The budget for the hospital is not likely to increase in the near future. Thus, the laid-off employees will not soon be returned to work, and the job descriptions of the remaining staff are not likely to change. Nor will there be improvements in salaries to compensate for these increased work loads.

You are concerned about all this because your own job has been made tiresome and unpleasant, but also, and more importantly, because you believe that the quality of the hospital's work has become dangerously poor. Patients who need care are being turned away or sent home in increasing numbers. There have been some close calls with mistakes by inexperienced staff members. Extra help has become hard to find and slow in appearing, even during emergencies. And almost everyone employed in the hospital is showing the effects of fatigue and stress.

Despite a county ordinance prohibiting strikes by public employees, some of your colleagues have been urging you to participate in an institution-wide "sick day," when as many nurses as could be recruited would refuse to come to work. Should you support and participate in this protest?

Analysis: BUCKING THE SYSTEM — SHOULD NURSES STRIKE?
Use of Heuristics

LIST GIVENS: Deteriorating working conditions.
                               Lowered quality of patient care.
                               Support staff reduced.
                               Increased work load for registered nurses.
                               Shift of employment for some from full-time to part-time.
                               Lower paid replacements with less experience.
                               Pressure to limit admissions, especially of indigent patients.
                               Pressure for early release of patients to reduce costs.
                               Safety of patients in jeopardy.

WANTED: Improved conditions at hospital.

LEGAL ASPECT: County ordinance prohibits strikes by public employees.

PROPOSAL: Participation of all nurses in an institution-wide "sick day" has been proposed.

PROBLEM: Should you participate in this protest?

IDENT CONSEQUENCES:
                               Favorable: draw attention of county commissioners to hospital conditions
                                              with some hope of possible improvements.
                               Unfavorable: jeopardize well-being of hospital patients for the day; could
                                            precipitate firing of "sick day" participants resulting in replacements at
                                            even higher salaries due to market conditions.

IDENT NEEDED INFO: History of success or failure of "sick day" situations held elsewhere.

IDENT ALTERNATIVES TO A SICK DAY:
                               Ask for a grievance hearing from county commissioner.
                               Seek public airing of hospital conditions in the media.
                               Seek support from wealthy hospital patrons.

EVALUATION: Assess the success (or failure) of the sick day if held.

Example: Utilitarian Analysis

TRUTHTELLING — THE MINISTER

You are the minister of a church in a community that has a large number of elderly persons in its congregation. Over the years you have enjoyed many aspects of your calling, especially preaching and making pastoral visits to the members of your flock. You know that many members of the congregation trust you implicitly, and that the faith that you share with them and preach to them is a source of great strength, especially among those of the elderly who know that death cannot be far away.

Recently, however, a tragic, maliciously arranged "accident" has killed several members of your family and, in the process, has destroyed your faith. It now seems clear to you that the world is not just, that mankind is evil, that there is no divine plan to justify this event, and, in general, that there cannot be a God in a world with such evil. You are quite aware that your change of attitude may be associated with depression as a result of the event, and indeed your denomination has a set of doctrines and teachings concerning temporary loss of faith. At the moment, however, your loss of faith does not feel temporary; you simply no longer believe the pieties you have been preaching to your congregation, nor do you see any basis for the religious consolation you have been able to offer these people so effectively and reassuringly in pastoral counseling. Yet you cannot forget that you have been an enormous source of strength and hope to many members of your flock.

Tomorrow is Sunday. What should you say in your sermon? Can you answer this question by rereading what the doctrines and teachings of your denomination say about temporary loss of faith? If not, how should you answer this question?

Analysis: TRUTHTELLING — THE MINISTER
Utilitarian Analysis

To simplify the analysis of the minister's problem, divide his possible responses to his situation into four scenarios. These can then be compare à la Ben Franklin to determine his preference.

Scenario 1. Minister tells congregation the total truth — holds nothing back. He tells them he believes there is no divine plan, that mankind is evil, that God doesn't exist. He states his belief that his loss of faith is not temporary and therefore he feels unable to counsel the members of his church. He states that he plans to leave the ministry. Consequences of these statements are as follows: for the minister a feeling of honesty and integrity; for the congregation feelings of grief, abandonment, betrayal, sympathy, and anger.

Scenario 2. Minister tells congregation everything as in scenario 1 except that he acknowledges that his loss of faith may be only temporary. His plan is to take a leave of absence from the pulpit to avail himself of the assistance his religious superiors can provide to handle situations much like his own. A consequence for the minister is that he has regret that he has not told the total truth; for the congregation the feelings are likely to be like those expressed in scenario 1 but with the addition of some approval of the minister's doubt regarding the permanency of his loss of faith.

Scenario 3. Minister withholds from the congregation the depths of his despair concerning his loss of faith. He simply tells them he needs a period of renewal occasioned by the tragedies that have befallen members of his family. Consequently he announces that he has arranged for a substitute pastor to assume his duties for a period of time. The consequences for the minister include a loss of self respect because of his withholding of his own feelings; for the congregation the raising of many unanswered questions about the minister's plan and the reasons for it.

Scenario 4. Minister completely ignores his personal situation — pretends that nothing has happened. His hope is that over a period of time his faith will be restored in spite of his present belief that it will not return. A consequence for the minister is a severe loss of self respect because he has not told the truth; for the congregation there is the general knowledge of the death of members of the minister's family and they are left to wonder how he will be able to handle his grief.

In the utility analysis shown below the minister rates his own personal feeling on a scale of 0-10 and the happiness of his congregation on a scale of 0-100. This makes the value of their collective happiness ten times greater than his own. In consequence he rates his personal happiness greater than that of a single member of his congregation because his personal well-being clearly affects his congregation and their faith in his ministry. After entering these two utility values in the table he then adds horizontally to determine the net utility for each of the scenarios.

Scenario	Minister alone	Congregation	Net Utility
1	10	20	30
2	9	30	39
3	5	60	65
4	1	40	41

Noting that the net utility of 65 for scenario 3 is greater than that for the other scenarios he selects this as his preference. This would not be his choice were he to ignore the feelings of his congregation. Happily, this choice conforms to the maximum utility value in his estimate of the "happiness" his congregation will enjoy as a result of his decision.

CASE NO. 1   TRUTHTELLING — THE PSYCHOTHERAPIST WARNING POSSIBLE PARTNERS

As an experienced psychotherapist, you have counseled many people with sexual problems. Your client today, Rick, a young man whom you have been seeing for a considerable length of time, exhibits a severe version of a behavior pattern that you have seen frequently among patients with sexual identity confusion: Although he insists that he is heterosexual and finds "faggots" disgusting, he has sporadic episodes of aggressive homosexual activity. These episodes take the form of seductions of non-homosexual men whom Rick knows in everyday contexts, usually by getting them drunk at home when he is not drinking himself. Rick also sometimes frequents gay bathhouses. Both sorts of episodes are followed by extreme self-reproach and then virtually complete suppression; Rick does not and cannot admit that he is gay. Although his therapy sessions with you have helped Rick to make considerable progress in other areas of his life, he still cannot acknowledge, accept, or control his behavior.

Today, Rick has come to you with two bits of disturbing news. First, he has a new roommate, a young man of about the same age. "He's straight as an arrow," insists Rick, "just my kind." (You take this remark as an unwitting piece of self-revelation.) Second, as the result of some blood tests done in connection with a chronic ear infection, Rick has been told that he is seropositive for human immunodeficiency virus (HIV) antibodies. He is completely bewildered. He knows that the condition is a probable precursor to acquired immune deficiency syndrome — AIDS — and that AIDS is transmitted by, among other things, "disgusting" homosexual activity, but he cannot understand how *he* can have it. He finally remembers a bit of minor surgery he had a couple of years ago; they must have surreptitiously given him a blood transfusion, he insists, even though he was not anesthetized.

Now there is Rick's anger to deal with. Based on your past experiences with Rick, you have every reason to believe that it will not be long before his anger erupts into one of his episodic homosexual aggressive behaviors. You also expect that this is likely to take the form of Rick's seducing his new roommate; Rick is attractive and persuasive, and he seems to have a way of manipulating previously inexperienced men into homosexual sex. But while the majority of your homosexual clients are extremely responsible in the use of safer-sex practices to protect themselves and their partners, you are certain that Rick will not be. Since he cannot admit that he is gay, he cannot bring himself even to entertain the idea of taking precautions. "Fags," he says, "they should all get AIDS and die. You'd never catch me with a condom on."

You can think of no way to get Rick to assume responsibility for protecting the roommate, and you expect that the roommate will be in no condition to protect himself if and when the time comes. Rick's seropositivity could convert into full expression of AIDS at any time, and he is already capable of transmitting the AIDS virus to his sexual partners.

You know the roommate's telephone number, of course, since it is the same telephone number as Rick's. Do you warn the roommate, and if so, of what?

Note: In some states the courts have held that it is permissible in certain circumstances to break the code of confidentiality between a professional and his client.

CASE NO. 2 GRADING TRUTHFULLY

At the prestigious undergraduate college at which you teach, student suicides have averaged two a year over the last 10 or 15 years. Although the circumstances of these tragedies vary, most of them are attributed to the intensely competitive nature of the school and the anxiety that such an environment evokes for highly motivated students whose grades fall short of their own expectations.

The student now sitting beside your desk seems to fit this description perfectly. He had previously taken another course with you, and he did quite well, but that was a large lecture course in which grading was based largely on familiarity with the reading, and did not give you a real chance to perceive student' differing intellectual skills. During the course he is currently taking with you, the student has clearly revealed that he is a desperate overachiever—driven, you want to say, to a performance well beyond his actual capacities.

The student is singlemindedly intent on entering a specific graduate school. His grades, together with his letters of recommendation, will be a major factor in determining his admission. He has come to ask you to write one of these letters on his behalf, and to tell him the grade he can expect in the course.

If you write a truthful letter, you will have to say that while he is aggressive and highly motivated, his intellectual capacities do not equal those of most of the other students in your class. And if you tell him straightforwardly the grade you will be giving him—rather than offering a noncommittal response like "You'll be getting the grade you've earned," or actually changing his grade to something higher than you think he deserves—you will have to tell him it will be a C+, or maybe, at best a B-. But you know it would take an A-, at the very least, for him to be admitted to the school on which his heart is set.

You look out the window while you are considering what to do and you think about the school's average of two suicides a year. Do you tell him the grade? Do you write the letter? You know that failing to get into the graduate school he wants will be a catastrophic blow. What, in this case, should you do?

CASE NO. 3 ACCESS TO MEDICAL SERVICES

The Veterans Administration (VA) Medical Center at which you are medical director is allocated a fixed amount of money every year to be spent on patient care, and you and your staff must determine how these funds are to be apportioned and to what sorts of care. As you recognize, the VA system is a "closed" one — that is, it has a fixed pool of resources which will neither grow nor shrink. Thus, money that you spend on one sort of patient care cannot be spent on another, and savings made in one area can be used in a different one.

In this budget year, there is not enough money to go around, and there is no hope of getting the overall allocation to your medical center increased. Consequently, you must decide which kinds of patient care are to be funded, and which not. At the moment, you are considering three kinds of care — heart transplants, alcohol detoxification, and primary care in rural areas — which, given the frequency of their usage, involve approximately equal costs. You could fund two of the three in full, but not all three; or you could fund each partially but have to exclude some patients in each category.

The heart transplant program is a high-profile program for your medical center; it has a superior survival rate and is sufficiently respected to attract able surgeons to the program. Each transplant case costs about $75,000 for the testing, surgery and hospitalization; costs for immunosuppressive therapy are about $20,000 per patient for the first posttransplant year, and about $10,000 per patient for each year after that. Immunosuppressive therapy must be continued for the remainder of the patient's life. Approximately 10 cases can be done each year within the $1 million available, though supplying continuing immunosuppressive therapy to previous patients brings the figure to over $1 million. Two-year survival is 90%; this means that 2 years after their transplants, 9 of the 10 patients will still be alive, when without a transplant they would have died within a few months.

The acute alcohol detoxification program, on the other hand, makes no headlines, although it prevents a major cause of suffering when it is successful. The usual course of therapy involves 2 weeks in the hospital at a cost to you of about $150 a day; together with ancillary costs, this amounts to about $3,000 per episode. You have a 13-bed detoxification ward which, if adequately funded, would be filled year-around. This adds up to just a little over $1 million a year. Detoxification therapy has about a 20% long-term success rate, which means that of the 338 alcoholics you could treat every year, 68 would be cured.

The third of the programs that you are considering eliminating involves a series of primary-care clinics in rural areas of your state. Some 80% of the patients who use such clinics have chronic disease such as diabetes, hypertension, or chronic bronchitis. If care were not available in the rural clinics, the 20% with more severe disease would require more frequent hospitalization, and the 80% whose disease is less severe would go without treatment until their condition progresses to severe disease and hospitalization is also required. Each clinic serves about 600 patients a year, averaging 5 visits each, and there are enough clinics so that the total just happens to approximately equal the costs of either your heart transplant or detoxification programs. It is the cost of the *clinics* that happens to equal the costs of your other programs, but of course the cost of eventual hospitalization of patients who are not treated would be much, much higher.

You can fund two of the three — heart transplant, alcohol detoxification, or primary care clinics — but not all three, or you can fund some portion of each one. What is the best thing to do, and on what basis should you decide?

CASE NO. 4   ACCESS TO A UNIVERSITY EDUCATION

You are director of admissions at a large state university. Your university is the flagship of the state system, which also includes three other four-year institutions, and three two-year community colleges. Recently, the state board of regents has directed your university to begin cutting back on the number of undergraduates you admit. The regents' request is due in part to a prolonged economic recession in your state. It is also due to the regents' realization that it is more expensive to educate an undergraduate at your institution than at other institutions in the state. They have developed a master plan for the state system which will increasingly shift undergraduate education to other institutions in the state.

You firmly believe that your university offers the best undergraduate education in your state. It is the only institution that offers undergraduates the opportunity to be in advanced classes with graduate students in many fields. It has library resources and laboratory facilities that are unparalleled elsewhere in the state. Programs in many popular fields such as pharmacy and journalism are not available at the other colleges.

Up until now, your university has followed an open admissions plan: All students who have graduated from an accredited high school in your state are admitted. Over the next three years, however, you will have to reduce the size of the entering freshman class from about 5,000 to about 4,000. You know that many of the 1,000 will be able to enter other colleges in the state, but some will not. Some will find a higher education more inconvenient or impractical, because your university is the only four-year school in the state's largest urban area.

You are charged with developing a plan for achieving the reductions. The easiest method for you would be to develop an index of predicted success, based on high school grades and scores on standardized tests, but this method will disadvantage students who did not do well in high school and students who do not perform well on standardized tests. The data suggest that adopting the index will decrease the percentage of minority students in your entering class, an already small percentage. The index will also decrease the numbers of several other groups of students: students with poor high school grades who entered the military and later decided to go to college; and students, particularly women, who married early and have spent most of their young adulthood raising children. You are also concerned that the index will decrease the numbers of students from rural areas who are admitted to the university. Do you recommend adoption of the index? Should there be any exceptions to the index? If so, how should an exceptions policy be designed?

CASE NO. 5 BUCKING THE SYSTEM — WHISTLEBLOWING IN MEDICINE

You are a junior staff physician at a small community hospital in rural Nevada. You moved to this town two years ago, after the completion of your medical education and training. You and your spouse wanted to avoid raising your children in a major urban center because the family enjoys life in the mountains, and because you thought it would be worthwhile to exercise your skills in an area in which medical professionals with current training are not plentiful.

Unfortunately, your situation at the hospital has become increasingly uncomfortable as time has passed because one of your colleagues is, in your judgment, dangerously incompetent. Now approaching his 63rd birthday, this colleague is a senior member of the staff and a highly regarded practitioner in the large area served by the hospital. He was centrally involved in building the hospital more than 25 years ago; he is a prominent member of the community, quite active in civic affairs; and, as a general practitioner, he seems to have played the role of beloved family doctor to most of the town's population.

On more than 30 occasions, which you have documented in private notes, you have either observed this colleague engaging in substandard practices or seen the consequences of such practices in examining his patients. You are quite certain that you can document at least a dozen cases of serious complications that have arisen as a direct result of his work, including three instances of major birth defects. And you suspect, though you cannot prove, that four elderly patients have died in the last year because of mistaken decisions by this physician. Other members of the staff have noticed these problems, but their reactions have been either to express fear of the consequences of a scandal or to dismiss your concerns as highly exaggerated.

As your distress over this situation has increased, you have tried various remedies. You began by speaking to the physician himself, offering suggestions and help, and then urging greater caution and some retraining in current techniques. These efforts were rebuffed. Next you made informal and then formal complaints to the governing board of the hospital, and then to the regional medical society. But in each case, your colleague's long record of service and his high standing in the community prevailed over your protests. On one occasion, he was sued for malpractice in the case of an infant who suffered severe brain damage from oxygen deprivation at birth. But the litigation ended in a settlement out of court; and at the time, the board of the hospital treated the situation as a "judgment call" and backed your colleague fully, admitting nothing more than the fact that he might have been mistaken.

You have thus exhausted all the available remedies, except to take your story (and your data) to the local newspaper or the television station in the nearest city. Should you do it?

CASE NO. 6 PROFESSIONAL OBLIGATION — THE CLINICAL SOCIAL WORKER

You are a licensed clinical social worker employed by a municipal government to, among other duties, supervise the admission and retention of clients in a long-term shelter for homeless families. The people who come to your facility have usually spent at least 6 weeks moving around among various overnight shelters or even living in the streets. And because low-priced rentals are extremely scarce in your area, when clients are given rooms in your building, their average length of stay is 14 months. Families of up to four persons are assigned to single rooms. Larger families are given two rooms. Two-thirds of your residents are children under the age of 14.

According to local law and federal guidelines, preference for admission to your facility is to be given to single-parent families with young children. And because the demand for shelter is so great, all the 200 families in your building (a large and very decrepit hotel) are nominally headed by single females. But many of the frequent visitors to the facility, all of whom must sign in with a guard at the entrance, are obviously the husbands of women and the fathers of children in residence. Most of these men live in the streets or in overnight shelters, working at unskilled jobs when they can find them, and contributing whatever they can to the support of their children.

What, if anything, should you do about this situation? If you identify these men as legally involved with your clients, many of the women and children will have to leave the shelter, and most will lose other welfare entitlements in amounts much larger than the men would be able to replace. But if you ignore the problem, you will be condoning illegal activity within your area of responsibility and running some risk of losing your job.

CASE NO. 7 PROFESSIONAL OBLIGATION — THE JOURNALIST

You are a reporter employed by a metropolitan newspaper to cover events involving your state government. In recent months, public opinion has turned against the governor of the state, primarily because he has found it necessary to advocate major tax increases during a statewide economic recession. Editorials on television and in newspapers (including your own) around the state have called upon the governor not to run for reelection; opposition to his continuation has developed within his own party; and public opinion polls indicate that he is perceived as "lacking leadership qualities."

As you are going through some documents relating to his financial history, you discover that 20 years ago, the governor was involved in a dispute with the Internal Revenue Service (IRS) which ended when he paid nearly $10,000 in taxes the IRS claimed, and almost as much in penalties. The disputed taxes involved profits on some out-of-state transactions in real estate that were represented (unsuccessfully) as being tax-sheltered.

You mention this discovery to your editor, and she urges you to write the story immediately for the front page of the local section of tomorrow's paper. She sees a scoop in the story, and you see the opportunity for professional advancement in being identified as the reporter who uncovered the episode. But you are also aware of the fact that the impact of the story would derive from the suggestion, which need not be stated, that the governor had tried to evade legal responsibilities and cheat the IRS. And you are not at all sure that the facts of the case support such an inference.

Knowing that the information you have gathered is accurate, should you run the story immediately, thereby winning a round against your competition? Or should you delay instead, taking the time necessary to consult one or more tax attorneys in order to find out whether the facts really do constitute a black mark on the governor's record?

194

CASE NO. 8 PROFESSIONAL OBLIGATION — A MEDICAL JOURNAL
"IT'S OVER, DEBBIE"

The call came in the middle of the night. As a gynecology resident rotating through a large, private hospital, I had come to detest telephone calls, because invariably I would be up for several hours and would not feel good the next day. However, duty called, so I answered the phone. A nurse informed me that a patient was having difficulty getting rest, could I please see her. She was on 3 North. That was the gynecologic-oncology unit, not my usual duty station. As I trudged along, bumping sleepily against walls and corners and not believing I was up again, I tried to imagine what I might find at the end of my walk. Maybe an elderly woman with an anxiety reaction, or perhaps something particularly horrible.

I grabbed the chart from the nurses' station on my way to the patient's room, and the nurse gave me some hurried details: a 20-year-old girl named Debbie was dying of ovarian cancer. She was having unrelenting vomiting apparently as the result of an alcohol drip administered for sedation. Hmmm, I thought. Very sad. As I approached the room I could hear loud, labored breathing. I entered and saw an emaciated, dark-haired woman who appeared much older than 20. She was receiving nasal oxygen, had an IV, and was sitting in bed suffering from what was obviously severe air hunger. The chart noted her weight at 80 pounds. A second woman, also dark-haired but of middle age, stood at her right, holding her hand. Both looked up as I entered. The room seemed filled with the patient's desperate effort to survive. Her eyes were hollow, and she had suprasternal and intercostal retractions with her rapid inspirations. She had not eaten or slept in two days. She had not responded to chemotherapy and was being given supportive care only. It was a gallows scene, a cruel mockery of her youth and unfulfilled potential. Her only words to me were, "Let's get this over with."

I retreated with my thoughts to the nurses' station. The patient was tired and needed rest. I could not give her health, but I could give her rest. I asked the nurse to draw 20 mg of morphine sulfate into a syringe. Enough, I thought, to do the job. I took the syringe into the room and told the two women I was going to give Debbie something that would let her rest and say good-bye. Debbie looked at the syringe, then laid her head on the pillow with her eyes open, watching what was left of the world. I injected the morphine intravenously and watched to see if my calculations on its effects would be correct. Within seconds her breathing slowed to a normal rate, her eyes closed, and her features softened as she seemed restful at last. The older woman stroked the hair of the now-sleeping patient. I waited for the inevitable next effect of depressing the respiratory drive. With clock-like certainty, within four minutes the breathing rate slowed even more, then became irregular, then ceased. The dark-haired woman stood erect and seemed relieved.

It's over, Debbie. _____

This piece appeared in early 1988 as a reader's submission to the *Journal of the American Medical Association*. The author wished his or her name to be withheld, and the *Journal* decided that the piece was important enough to publish anyway. Prosecutors in Chicago, where the *Journal* is published, went to court to get the author's name in order to investigate the possibility of criminal prosecution. The *Journal* resisted successfully.

Should the *Journal* have published the piece? Was this a case of professional disobedience? What rules were violated? Rules of the hospital? Rules of ethics of the medical profession? State law? Were the actions of the unnamed author justified? Should any action be taken against him or her for what was done?

X. ADVANCED PROBLEM SOLVING TOPICS

VALIDATION OF ARGUMENTS
>   Exercise - Validate Syllogism Conclusions

GAME THEORY — THE NEXT STEP
>   Exercise - Analyse a 2x3 Game Matrix

TWO-COLOR STRIP AND WALLPAPER PATTERNS
>   Exercise - Identify 2-Color 2-D Patterns

THE 'BIG ONE'" — SAN FRANCISCO
>   Exercise - Analyse the "Big One" in San Francisco

VALIDATION OF ARGUMENTS

Three different representations of logical relationship between two statements (also called *propositions* or *conjectures*) is presented in Chapter VII. These are truth table, matrix, and graphical representations. The last of these was presented as the most useful representation of logical relationships in plausible reasoning. In spite of this, truth tables remain a powerful tool of analysis in deductive logic. A time honored method for establishing the validity (or lack of validity) of arguments is to put them in the form of syllogisms. Here, one or more premises is followed by a conclusion to be tested for its validity. A premise is an affirmative statement whose truth is not subject to question. Premises are assumed to be correct whether they are in fact or not. The conclusion stands or falls depending upon whether it is or is not a logical conclusion *based upon the assumption that the premises are true.*

First, let us review the symbols used for the various logical operations, their names, and examples of their use.

Operation	Name	Symbols	Examples of use		
AND	conjunction	. $\land$	$A.B$	$A \land B$	AB
OR (inclusive)	disjunction	$\lor$		$A \lor B$	
NOT	negation	~ —	$\sim A$	$\overline{A}$	$\sim(A.B)$
IMPLIES	implication	$\rightarrow$		$A \rightarrow B$	

There are additional symbols denoting other relationships between pairs of propositions. Two other symbols that are frequently encountered are $\leftarrow$ and $\leftrightarrow$. These additional symbols, and this includes $\rightarrow$ as well, are not really necessary, but are used only as a matter of convenience. All that is really necessary are the relationships of AND, OR, and NOT.

In all, there are sixteen logical relationships between two statements, propositions, or conjectures. These are shown in the table below. At the left in the two columns headed by A and B are all the combinations possible for truth values for a pair of propositions. In each of the sixteen columns that follow are listed, for each relationship, the combination of truth values for the pair of statements that occur (T) and those that do not occur (F). Thus each column provides a kind of fingerprint for the relationship labelled at the head of the column. As you will notice, no two fingerprints are alike, and all different fingerprints possible (16) are included.

A	B	A^*B	$A{\to}B$	$\overline{A}{\to}B$	$A{\leftarrow}B$	$A{\lor}B$	A	$\overline{A}$	B	$\overline{B}$	$A{\leftrightarrow}B$	$\overline{A}{\leftrightarrow}B$	$A.B$	$A.\overline{B}$	$\overline{A}.B$	$\overline{A}.\overline{B}$	$A{\circ}B$
		1	2	3	4	5	6	7	8	9	10	11	12	13	14	15	16
T	T	T	T	F	T	T	T	F	T	F	T	F	T	F	F	F	F
T	F	T	F	T	T	T	T	F	F	T	F	T	F	T	F	F	F
F	T	T	T	T	F	T	F	T	T	F	F	T	F	F	T	F	F
F	F	T	T	T	T	F	F	T	F	T	T	F	F	F	F	T	F

The significance of each column (relationship) is as follows:

1. A^*B This relationship is one of complete affirmation. All combinations of T's and F's are found, that is, are true. This relationship is important in plausible reasoning but not in deductive logic.
2. $A{\to}B$ This is the relationship of implication, A implies B, or, if A then B. What is hard for those new to the field to grasp is that if A is false, then B may be either true T or false F. The relationship is perhaps best characterized by the one false combination — A is true and B is false. $A{\to}B$ can also be written (but never is) in an equivalent way as $\overline{A}{\lor}B$.

3. A→B̄   A implies not B. If A then B̄. Can also be written in a more useful way as Ā∨B̄.
4. A←B   A is implied by B. A is a consequent of B. Can also be written as A∨B̄.
5. A∨B   Disjunction. A is true or B is true or both are true. The inclusive *or*.
6. A   A is true no matter whether B is true or not. The truth of A is independent of the truth or falsity of B. Same column of truth values as for the column at the extreme left.
7. Ā   A is false no matter whether B is true or false.
8. B   B is true no matter whether A is true or false. Same fingerprint of truth values as for the column headed by B at the left.
9. B̄   B is false no matter whether A is true or false.
10. A↔B   A implies B and B implies A. A is both a necessary and a sufficient condition for B. Also written as A≡B, A is logically equivalent to B.
11. A↔B̄   A is true or B is true but both are not true. The exclusive *or*, the relationship of incompatibility.
12. A.B   Conjunction. Both A and B are true, otherwise the relationship is F.
13. A.B̄   Conjunction. A is true and B is false.
14. Ā.B   Conjunction. A is false and B is true.
15. Ā.B̄   Conjunction. Both A and B are false.
16. A°B   Complete negation. No combinations of truth values are true. Not useful in any circumstance.

Testing for Validity. Let us test the following syllogism for the validity of its conclusion. Recall that we are **not** testing whether each of the premises is true or not. Conclusions are based on the assumption that the premises are true.

Premise 1.	If George has a new computer he will be happy.
Premise 2.	George has a new computer.
Conclusion.	George is happy.

It is traditional to draw a line under the last premise. The conclusion of the argument is written below this line. The next step is to identify and label the statements that are included in the premises and in the conclusion. Labels are commonly denoted by single letters as follows:

       G   George has a new computer
       H   George is happy

The syllogism can now be written in the following abbreviated form:

$$\frac{\begin{array}{c} G \to H \\ G \end{array}}{H}$$

Now we recognize that for the conclusion H to be a valid conclusion, the "anding" of all the premises must imply the conclusion. That is, it must be true that [(premise 1).(premise 2)] → (conclusion). This can be checked using a truth table. This table shows all the truth combinations for both G and H, has a column for G→H, another for (G→H).G and finally, one for [(G→H).G]→H. If this last column contains all T's the conclusion is a valid one. If there are one or more F's the conclusion is invalid. Often a particular column is rewritten to make it easier to identify a compound relationship. This is done below.

		1	2	3	4	5
G	H	G→H	G	(G→H).G	H	[(G→H).G]→H
T	T	T	T	T	T	T
T	F	F	T	F	F	T
F	T	T	F	F	T	T
F	F	T	F	F	F	T

Column 3 implies column 4 because there is no T in column 3 followed in the same row by an F in column 4. For this reason there are all T's in the last column indicating that the conclusion from the argument based upon the two premises is a valid one. The conclusion is implied by the conjunction of both of the premises.

There are four syllogisms in the same form as the one about George and his new computer. These are written below where the first of the four is identical to the one above. The valid conclusion is therefore written in for it. For each of the other three, however, the space below the line is left blank to give you an opportunity to see if you can identify in each case a valid conclusion from the two premises.

$$A \rightarrow B \qquad A \rightarrow B \qquad A \rightarrow B \qquad A \rightarrow B$$
$$\underline{A} \qquad\qquad \underline{B} \qquad\qquad \underline{\bar{A}} \qquad\qquad \underline{\bar{B}}$$
$$B$$
valid

The first conclusion above is valid because it is exactly the same as the syllogism involving George and his new computer. Here, A has been used in place of G and B in place of H. The second syllogism has been previously encountered in the discussion of predictions from Einstein's theory and the fourth syllogism arose in the discussion concerning slavery and the Civil War (both in Chapter VII). A possible conclusion for the second syllogism is A (A is true) which, upon using a truth table, turns out to be an invalid conclusion. $\bar{B}$ looks like a reasonable candidate as a conclusion for the third syllogism, but it too is invalid. In the fourth case, however, the conclusion $\bar{A}$ is a valid one. To illustrate this last case, the first premise could be the statement that If George has a new computer he will be happy and the second premise a statement that he does not have a new computer. A valid conclusion is that it is false that George will be happy. Of course George could be happy for other reasons, but then again he may not. Since he is not happy under *all* possible circumstances it is false in general that he is happy.

A somewhat more complicated situation arises in the following syllogism where there are not two, but three statements involved.

Premise 1.   If we drive nonstop to San Francisco we will be on the road for 13 hours.
Premise 2.   If we are on the road for 13 hours, we'll need a full day to recover from the trip.
Conclusion.   If we drive nonstop to San Francisco we'll need a full day to recover from the trip.

As before, the first task is to identify all the statements contained in the syllogism.

A: we drive nonstop to San Francisco
B: we'll be on the road for 13 hours
C: we'll need a full day to recover

The syllogism in symbolic form can now be written as follows.

$$A \rightarrow B$$
$$\underline{B \rightarrow C}$$
$$A \rightarrow C$$

Before, when we had just two different statements G and H, only four rows were required in the truth table used to verify the conclusion. This was because there are only four combinations of G or $\bar{G}$ with H or $\bar{H}$. This time, however, there are eight combinations of truth values among A or $\bar{A}$, B or $\bar{B}$, and C or $\bar{C}$. Therefore eight rows are needed in our truth table. Whatever pattern is used to write down all eight combinations in the first three columns, that pattern should be used consistently to avoid possible confusion. In the truth table below the first row in these three columns contains all T's, the next three rows contain one F only, the three after that one T only, and the final row all F's.

A	B	C	1 A→B	2 B→C	3 (A→B).(B→C)	4 A→C	5 col. 3 → col. 4
T	T	T	T	T	T	T	T
T	T	F	T	F	F	F	T
T	F	T	F	T	F	T	T
F	T	T	T	T	T	T	T
F	F	T	T	T	T	T	T
F	T	F	T	F	F	T	T
T	F	F	F	T	F	F	T
F	F	F	T	T	T	T	T

Once again, since there are all T's in column 5 the conclusion is valid. That is, the anding of the two premises does indeed imply the conclusion.

Exercise - VALIDATE SYLLOGISM CONCLUSIONS. There are four syllogisms in all that have the same form as the syllogism concerning the drive to San Francisco. These are given below. The fourth one is in the same pattern because every *or* relationship can be written as an implication.

A→B	A→B	A→C	A∨B
B→C	A→C	B→C	B∨C
A→C			
valid			

The exercise is to determine whether your proposed conclusions in these three cases are valid or invalid. These are tested using the same procedure as that used above in establishing the validity of the first conclusion. Try to find valid conclusions, if you can, for these do exist in each of these three cases. But if you don't find a valid conclusion, show that your proposed conclusion is in fact invalid since you did not obtain all T's in the last column. It might help to use the statements in the trip to San Francisco syllogism to test whether you think a particular conclusion is valid before actually testing it.

GAME THEORY — THE NEXT STEP

In Chapter IV we looked at a variety of "games" starting with that illustrated by Ray and Dotty's 4X4 matrix, proceeding to their 3X3 and 2X2 matrices, and ending up with Dotty's 2X2 "what if" matrix. In all but one of these situations we found that it was possible to simplify the game in some way. Because some strategies dominated others the 4X4 was reduced to a 3X3. The 3X3 game was made easy because the "best of the worst" strategy for Ray and the "best of the worst" for Dotty led to a single pure strategy for each. This was also the case in Ray and Dotty's 2X2 matrix game. Dotty's "what if" matrix was the first to require a mix of strategies for both Ray and Dotty. This is as complicated as things became. However, there are a very great number of game situations still more complicated and demanding of the players. In *The Compleat Strategyst* J.D. Williams goes on to describe 2Xm games (m is an integer equal to 3 or more), 3X3 games, 3Xm games, and still more complicated games requiring 4 or more active strategies. As an advanced topic here we will go only so far as 2Xm games.

As an example of a 2Xm game with m = 3 consider the game J.D. Williams describes as the Wordsmith's game. The game given below is an adaptation of the original game involving two players by the names of Goldsen and Kershaw. It was Kershaw who suggested the game, a game in which Kershaw has three letters (strategies), the consonants f, n, and m, and Goldsen has two letters (strategies), the vowels a and i. Each player selects one of his letters. Kershaw wins if a 2-letter word is formed and Goldsen wins if no word is formed.

Kershaw chooses

		f	n	m
Goldsen chooses	a	af +5	an - 2	am - 3
	i	if - 3	in - 1	im +5

Goldsen notices that there are only two ways for him to win, but each of his payoffs (+5) is relatively large. On the other hand, Kershaw has four ways to win but with smaller payoffs. Goldsen is confused. Before agreeing to play he carefully studies the payoff matrix presented by Kershaw. He knows two ways to analyse the game, the first involves a graphical procedure he once heard about, and the second involves the analysis of each of the three 2X2 games contained in the 2X3 matrix.

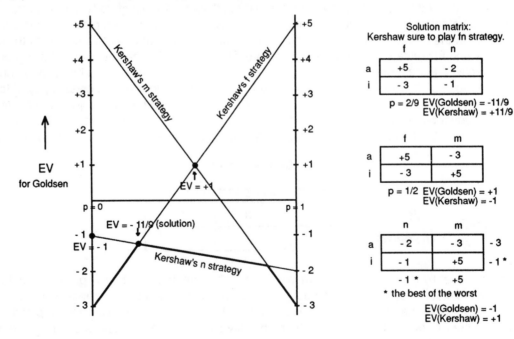

203

In the graphical scheme, shown at the left above, the probability p with which Goldsen plays his "a" strategy is plotted horizontally from 0 to 1 while the expected value of the game for Goldsen (EV) is plotted vertically. On this graph three lines are drawn representing Kershaw's f, n, and m strategies. For Kershaw's f strategy and p = 0 the payoff for Goldsen is - 3 and for p = 1 it is +5. Therefore the f line is drawn from - 3 at the left upward to +5 at the right. In similar fashion Kershaw's n strategy is a line extending from - 1 at the left to - 2 at the right. Finally, the m strategy line is drawn from +5 downward to - 3. The intersection of the f line with the n line represents both the p-value of 2/9 and an EV equal to -11/9 for a game in which Kershaw plays a mix of his f and n strategies. Compare these two values from the graph to the values obtained from the upper 2X2 submatrix shown at the right. Likewise, the intersection of the f line with the m line yields a p-value and an EV which are the same as those obtained from the middle subgraph at the right. Finally, the intersection of the n and m lines gives a solution for the lower subgraph at the right — or *would* give it if this 2X2 matrix called for a mix of strategies. Instead, this last subgraph yields a pure strategy for each of the players. For Goldsen it is his i strategy and for Kershaw it is his n strategy making p = 0 and the EV equal to - 1. Looking only at the three 2X2 matrices we see that the best Goldsen can expect, i.e., *the best Kershaw will let him do*, comes from Kershaw's mix of f and n strategies where p = 2/9 and the EV for Goldsen is -11/9, the lowest of the three possible EV values.

Looking back at the graph we see that this solution is the high point of the line segments shown by thicker lines. This too represents the best of the worst outcomes that Goldsen can manage. In addition, for purposes of comparison of the two methods, the solutions from the three matrices are indicated by the solid circles on the graph. This takes into account the pure strategies for each of the players in the one case and the mix for each in the other two cases.

Exercise - ANALYSE A 2X3 GAME MATRIX. The following game is one between the quality control people at a computer chip plant and the "Nature" of the manufacturing process that produces the chips. It is assumed that Nature is a game player out to make the quality control people pay as dearly as possible. The computer chips, some of which are rather expensive, are subject to a high degree of quality control. The quality control people have three strategies: to conduct no test whatsoever on the finished chip, to use a simple inexpensive test, or to employ a quite thorough test which, unfortunately, destroys a rather high percentage of the chips tested. The company sells most of its chips to manufacturers who use them in their computers. The chips either have a defect of some sort or they are satisfactory and without defect. If no test of any kind is made and the chips are without defects, the payoff to Nature is zero. But for chips that prove defective they have to be replaced after they have already been placed in computers by the purchasers. In the case of no test this produces for Nature a payoff of 6, a severe blow to the chip maker both in cost and in reputation. A simple test will benefit Nature by 1 if the chip is without defect but 3 if it is found defective. For a more thorough test the test cost itself is expensive in technical personnel and also costly because of the rather frequent destruction of the chips. Suppose this gives a payoff for Nature of 4 for chips without defects. These same costs are present even when the chips are defective, but is offset by the advantages in both the reputation of the firm and minimal replacement of the chips it sells. Let this payoff be 2. The resulting game matrix, call it the Computer Chip Game, is shown below.

Quality Control

		no test	simple test	destr. test
Nature	defect	6	3	2
	no defect	0	1	4

Analyse this game either by first breaking it down into three 2X2 submatrices or by the graphical method illustrated in the Wordsmith's game. If you use both methods you will have a built in check on the accuracy of your analysis. Note that this time for the graphical method of analysis you will want to plot the EV for Nature (playing the role of Goldsen) against the probability p that nature will play its defect strategy. Determine both p and the EV for Nature.

Two-Color Strip and Wallpaper Patterns

In Chapter VI both strip patterns in one color and wallpaper patterns in one color were introduced. It was learned that there were exactly seven strip patterns, sometimes called frieze patterns, and seventeen wallpaper patterns. Examples of both 1-D and 2-D patterns came primarily from ornamental designs and from fabric patterns. Such patterns are of interest to anthropologists in their studies of various cultures. More generally, the recognition of patterns is a part of perception, and skills in perception are not only important in design but in science, linguistics, psychology, and many other fields as well. Here we take the next logical step in the analysis of patterns by including two-color designs in both one dimension and in two. Consideration of 3-color and 4-color patterns lies well beyond the scope of the present discussion. We will also refrain from continuing on into the world of three dimensions where we encounter crystals, cloud formations, acoustical patterns and many others.

Let us begin with two-color one-dimensional patterns. Accompanying the flow chart for the seven one dimensional patterns in Chapter VI were examples of the seven patterns constructed from asymmetric triangles. For the two-color case some of these same strips of triangles are colored in to form the seventeen two-color one-dimensional patterns that are shown on the page following. Here the two colors are simply black and white, but they could be red and green or any other pair of colors. These designs are assumed to extend infinitely far both to the right and to the left. A word about the notation that is used to distinguish one pattern from another is in order. The symmetry of the first pattern in the first column is described as pmm2/p1m1. Each of the descriptions pmm2 and p1m1 is a description of a one-dimensional one-color pattern. (See the flow chart in Chapter VI.) The first of these describes the symmetry of the overall pattern while the second refers to the symmetry of either of the two colors taken by itself. This notation is referred to as *type/subtype*, i.e., overall pattern / one-color pattern. Note that each of the two colors taken singly exhibits the same symmetry. When this first pattern is reflected in the horizontal axis the colors of the triangles do not change. In the second pattern in the same column, however, when the upper black triangles are reflected in the horizontal axis to form those below, black changes to white, and when the white triangles below are reflected their color changes to black. Both operations are said to be "consistent with color." Note that all five of the patterns in the first column have the overall symmetry pmm2. It is the symmetry of either color taken alone that distinguishes each of the five patterns in this column from the others. In the second column the overall symmetry of the first three strips is pma2 and that of the next two is pm11. In the third column there are additional groupings according to the overall pattern. There are of course seven different overall symmetries of these 2-color patterns just as there are seven symmetries for the one-color strip patterns. Additional examples of two-color one-D patterns are given on the second page following.

The symmetries of two-color two-dimensional patterns can be designated in similar fashion. The description of the overall two-dimensional pattern comes before the slash and that of either color taken alone comes after the slash. Thus all that will be needed to classify 2-D 2-color patterns is the flow chart for the seventeen 2-D 1-color patterns. This was presented in Chapter VI and for convenience is included here on the third page following.

Exercise - IDENTIFY 2-COLOR 2-D PATTERNS. On the two pages after the flow chart examples are given of the forty-six two-color two-D patterns. There is one minor problem with the classification scheme in the case of two-color 2-D patterns that is not found for 2-color 1-D patterns. Pattern 5 can be classified as pm/pm but so also can pattern 7. To distinguish between the two patterns Washburn and Crowe label pattern 5 as pm/pm(m') and pattern 7 as pm/pm(m). Otherwise, this labelling scheme is unambiguous. While the first ten of the 46 2-color 2-D patterns are identified, the remainder are not. The problem here is to identify the ten patterns numbered 11-20.

ADDING A COLOR TO ONE-DIMENSIONAL PATTERNS

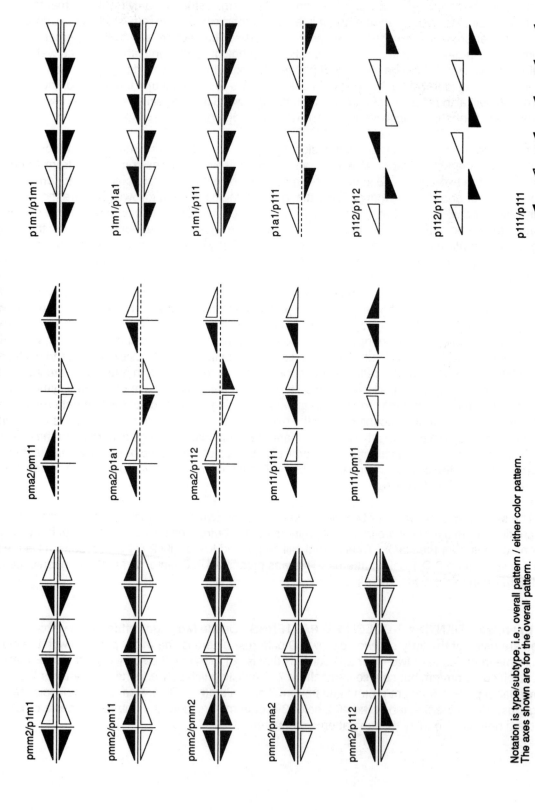

p1m1/p1m1

p1m1/p1a1

p1m1/p111

p1a1/p111

p112/p112

p112/p111

p111/p111

pma2/pm11

pma2/p1a1

pma2/p112

pm11/p111

pm11/pm11

pmm2/p1m1

pmm2/pm11

pmm2/pmm2

pmm2/pma2

pmm2/p112

Notation is type/subtype, i.e., overall pattern / either color pattern.
The axes shown are for the overall pattern.

206

The Seventeen 2-color 1-D Designs

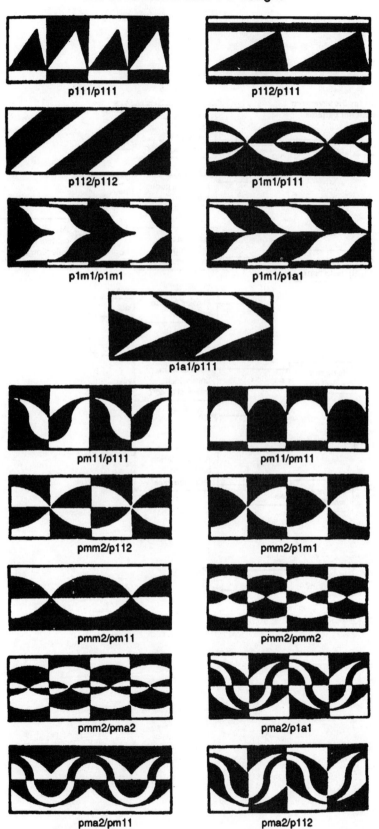

p111/p111

p112/p111

p112/p112

p1m1/p111

p1m1/p1m1

p1m1/p1a1

p1a1/p111

pm11/p111

pm11/pm11

pmm2/p112

pmm2/p1m1

pmm2/pm11

pmm2/pmm2

pmm2/pma2

pma2/p1a1

pma2/pm11

pma2/p112

**Flow chart for the seventeen
two-dimensional patterns**

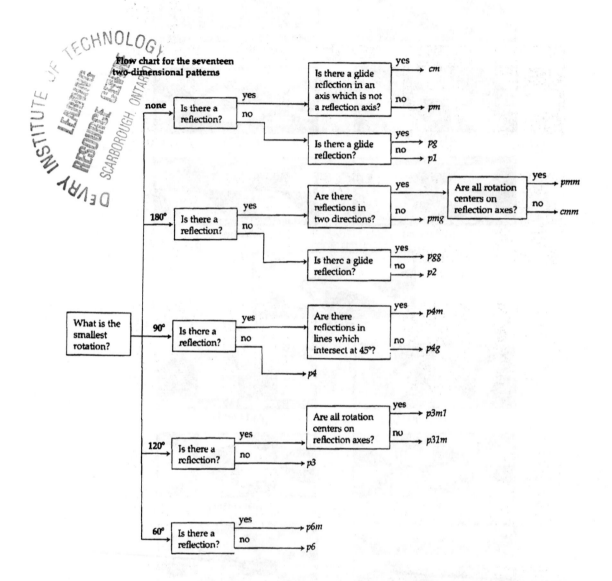

Forty-six Two-color Two-dimensional Patterns

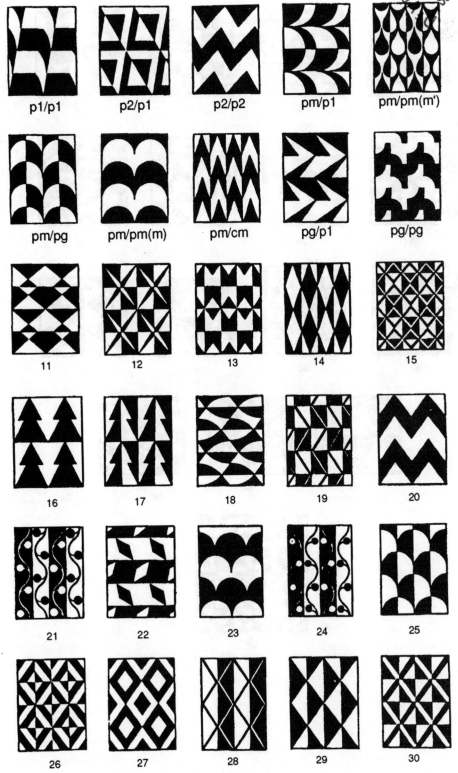

p1/p1	p2/p1	p2/p2	pm/p1	pm/pm(m')
pm/pg	pm/pm(m)	pm/cm	pg/p1	pg/pg
11	12	13	14	15
16	17	18	19	20
21	22	23	24	25
26	27	28	29	30

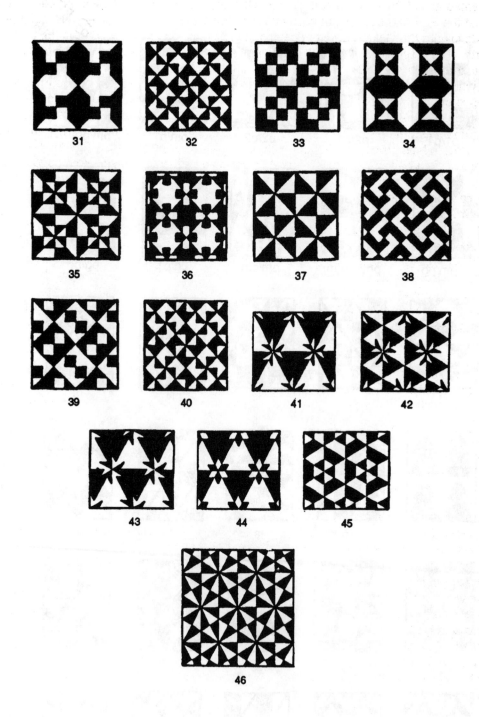

THE "BIG ONE" — SAN FRANCISCO

It is early in the 21st century. Residents of San Francisco have long awaited the "big one," the earthquake to rival or even surpass the famous 1906 quake. Severe earthquakes have come and gone, only to be deemed as not the truly big earthquake that everyone in San Francisco had feared. Everyone recognized that the San Andreas fault threads into San Francisco from the south paralleling Interstate 280 as it heads toward the Golden Gate bridge and then passes slightly seaward from the bridge as it continues north. The epicenter of the 1906 quake was along the San Andreas fault as were those of many others in the century or so since. Far to the south the San Andreas, with a number of branches only some of which are charted, becomes ill-defined in the region north and east of Los Angeles. You live in San Francisco on the 11th floor of a condominium at 10th and Market near the downtown area. The announcement has just been made that the United States Geological Survey (USGS) has issued an A-level earthquake alert, meaning that a severe earthquake in the area is imminent. The word *imminent* means that there is a high probability that the earthquake will occur within days. Residents of the city will no doubt want to evacuate to safer areas if it is at all possible for them to do so. Your condominium is in an area that is fairly close to the Bayshore Freeway, Interstate 101, heading north across the Golden Gate bridge into Marin County. Alternatively, you could head south along either I-101 or I-280 down the peninsula toward San Jose. A third option is to go east on Interstate 80 across the Bay Bridge to Oakland and beyond that perhaps to Concord where your sister lives. It seems that from where you live each of these routes is equally accessible. This assumes, of course, that you go by car. You have already rejected the idea of using mass transit. The BART (Bay Area Rapid Transit) station is very close by and in normal circumstances could take you east to Concord in about 35 minutes. Not only is BART vulnerable to earthquake damage, but so too are the freeways and bridges. The greatest problem faced by evacuees attempting to flee the earthquake before it strikes is the problem presented by all the other drivers clogging the freeways. One could be stalled in traffic for many hours. It could take days to empty the city.

How much time is there to make your escape? Nobody really knows, and that includes the geologists at the USGS. They have long examined the subject of earthquake prediction. What is the likelihood that their skills will have developed to the point that individuals can really act upon their advice? What is the state of preparedness of the city for a potential disaster. Have the residents been instructed as to what to do in a severe earthquake emergency? Even if they do remember the advice that has been given, will they actually take that advice in an emergency? As you head toward your car you wonder how long it will take you to get across the Bay Bridge to Oakland. In off hours it takes about 20 minutes; during rush hour it could take an hour or so; but now it would surely take many hours. Would you escape in time? Or, upon arriving at your sister's place in Concord, assuming you actually make it, would you be holed up there for a week or more still waiting for the predicted earthquake to occur? In that case, when would the USGS tell you it was alright to return home? How long would it take the citizens of San Francisco to recover their trust in the earthquake alert system developed by the USGS?

Such doubts had their origin back in 1982 when the USGS issued a "notice of potential volcanic hazard" in the vicinity of Mammoth Lakes, California. It was the lowest level volcanic alert then in use, but nonetheless this announcement touched off a series of misleading newspaper reports which upset the local residents who had not been prepared for such an eventuality. As a result the local economy, including that of the well known nearby ski resort, became seriously depressed. Tourism dropped off and property values sank. What the citizens of Mammoth Lakes did not realize was that their community sat on an ancient volcanic caldera. It had the shape of a giant potato about 20 miles in length, and the magma, which lay not far beneath the surface, had apparently begun to move. Residents were of course aware of the minor rumblings in the vicinity and even of the slight changes in the thermal nature of the area, but they were by no means prepared for the public relations fiasco that followed the USGS announcement. While the scientists were professionally qualified to assess the geologic situation, they were by no means qualified as to how to disseminate their information nor how to handle relationships with the townspeople. The USGS felt completely justified in making the announcement. In mid-1980 there was a series of four strong earthquakes, measuring about 6 on the Richter scale, that occurred in the vicinity within a 48-hour period. A series of aftershocks followed which lasted for months. The USGS scientists wondered whether the long slumbering volcano was beginning to stir. At this time a number of technologically advanced detection systems had been developed. The USGS people were unsure to what extent these new devices could help them predict volcanic activity. They felt that as a general rule there was a tendency to underestimate volcanic hazards. Since these new instruments had only been put in place recently, they could not tell whether the stirrings they detected were normal for the area or not. USGS officials had informed state emergency coordinators about their plans to release the notice, but no word ever reached local officials at Mammouth Lakes. Then came the media frenzy concerning the notice and the flood of misinformation that followed. At Mammouth Lakes they are still waiting for some volcanic threat to their community. As Wally Hofmann, editor and publisher of the Mammoth Times put it, "It was irresponsible of them [the USGS] to raise the fear factors of residents and traveling guests in the region on the basis of data which were incomplete and inconclusive."

"The event in 1982 was the catalyst for all parties involved to realize that we didn't want to do this again," said Richard Andrews, chief deputy director of the State Office of Emergency Services. As a result of their experience at Mammoth Lakes, both USGS and state officials began designing an earthquake prediction experiment along the San Andreas fault near the town of Parkfield in central California. Parkfield is a tiny town, population 34, that is about 50 miles northeast of San Luis Obispo and 75 miles southwest of Fresno. Parkfield, which lies on a particularly active stretch of the San Andreas, has reported a major earthquake about every 22 years. It was reasoned that since the most recent shock had come in 1966, the next one could come along fairly soon. Looking for some advance sign of earthquake activity, the USGS placed every conceivable detection device in the vicinity at a cost in the millions of dollars. It was their particular desire to learn to detect warnings that would give them hours to minutes advance notice of a major quake. The Parkfield experiment has been handled in a manner quite opposite to the handling of the Mammoth Lakes situation. A five-level alert system was established that ranges from A (the predicted quake is imminent) down to level E (situation normal). A strict set of criteria including slight surface warping or movements along the fault were to be used to determine the appropriate alert level. For example, a minor shock of magnitude 3.5 near Parkfield would initiate a C-level alert. Communication of information to various offices and agencies was keyed to the alert level. The townspeople of Parkfield were fully informed as to what was going on and appeared to take USGS warnings seriously. The Parkfield response system has yet to face an A-level alert but there have been a number of C-level alerts. During one such alert the town turned into a "media circus" according to Parkfield's chief scientist at the time, Evelyn Roeloffs. A sign advertising the Parkfield Cafe reads: PARKFIELD CAFE — EARTHQUAKE CAPITOL OF THE WORLD — BE HERE WHEN IT HAPPENS. Although the Parkfield system has not as yet been subject to a real test, officials are confident enough in it to use it as a model to be copied in other hazard-prone areas. However, Roeloffs believes that "The whole system of how to alert the public needs a lot more work."

Exercise - ANALYSE THE "BIG ONE" IN SAN FRANCISCO. Write a 300-500 word paper describing one or more of the following aspects of the problem of dealing with "the big one" in San Francisco. Alternatively, write about some other aspect of the overall problem not listed below.

(a) The problem of communication between the USGS and the public at large including the issuance of earthquake alerts at all levels.
(b) How can the full cooperation of the public with USGS recommendations be obtained?
(c) What are the chief problems to be faced if the USGS were to advise the city to be evacuated (except, of course, for basic services such as police and fire protection).

A description of both the Mammoth Lakes and Parkfield experiences was reported in an article entitled "Perils of Prediction" by Richard Monastersky that appeared in the June 15, 1991 issue of Science News.

APPENDIX A.   Selected Problem Solutions

APPENDIX A. Selected Problem Solutions

Chapter II.

CHANCES FOR PAROLE. Prisoner A is mistaken. His chance for parole remains unchanged.

BLASTING A HYPOTHESIS. $P(h|e) = 0.19$.

DIAGNOSTIC VALUE OF ACNE. $P(XYY|acne) = 0.028$ and $P(XY|acne) = 0.971$.

THE ROBBERY AND THE TORN COAT LINING. $P(G|H) = 0.54$.

TESTING FOR THE HIV VIRUS. $P(HIV|++) = 0.998$.

Chapter III.

LOCATING A NEW DRUG COUNSELING CENTER. One suspects that the numbers in columns might represent probabilities since various groupings sum to one. A better interpretation, however, is that these are relative weightings.

PHYSICIAN PASSES AN ACCIDENT SCENE. The physician does not stop because his utility for not stopping is 36 while that for stopping is 31.4.

WHICH URN IS WHICH? $P(I|R_1) = 1/3$, $P(II|R_1) = 2/3$, $P(I|W_2) = 0.6$, $P(II|W_2) = 0.4$.

A CREDIT RATING SERVICE. Percentage of those awarded loans who were given a safe rating by CRS is $P(S) = 0.810$. In addition, $P(P|S) = 0.965$ making $P(D|S) = 0.035$.

Chapter IV.

NUCLEAR CHICKEN. In this case there are two equilibrium solutions, payoffs 1,-2 and -2,1.

THE HUCKSTER. Merrill should buy for rain 5/9 of the time and buy for shine 4/9 of the time. The expected value of this strategy is $144.44.

MUTUAL POLLUTION. Both cities dump into the lake because that is the dominant strategy for each city. Only cooperation can lead to the preferred 0,0 solution.

THIRD DOWN AND SHORT. The probability that Washington should run is $p = 5/8$ and the probability that the Niners should defend against the run is $q = 3/4$. EV(for Wash) = 0.575.

Chapter V.

RECTANGULAR STREET NETWORKS. For a 4X5 square block area nine extra blocks of travel are required. For a 4X6 square block area ten extra blocks of travel are needed.

THE TRAVELING SALESMAN PROBLEM. There are 12 ways to visit the five cities in sequence. Of these the trip Chicago—Seattle—Los Angeles—Salt Lake City—Denver—Chicago, or its reverse, is shortest at 5367 miles.

MODEL HOME BUILDING. The critical path requires 34 days.

WINE BOTTLES PROBLEM. Seven pourings are required to divide the wine equally when first filling the 5 liter bottle; 8 pourings when first filling the 3 liter bottle.

Chapter VI.

FIBONACCI'S PUZZLE. 377 rabbit pairs will be born in one year.

PATTERNS IN BRICK. Identification of the symmetry of each brick pattern is:

(a) pmm	(b) cmm	(c) pmg
(d) p2	(e) pgg	(f) p4g
(g) cmm	(h) p2	(i) pmg

INVERSE ORIGAMI (tetrahedron). Including the original figure, there are but 4 plane figures consisting of four equilateral triangles. Of these, only the one that looks like 2/3 of a hexagon will not fold into a tetrahedron.

PATTERNS OF THE ANCIENT MEXICANS. Identifications are as shown below.

Strip patterns		Wallpaper patterns	
p111	p112	cmm	pmm
pma2	p112	pmg	p2
p111	p1m1	cmm	cmm

Chapter VII.

THE OIL LOBBYIST. The lobbyist is trying to persuade the congressperson than an "if. . .then" relationship exists. That is, if the oil industry can be granted certain tax breaks (T), then all voters will benefit (B). On a Bayes' diagram this is represented by T nearly implies B, i.e., T strongly suggests B. The Bayes' diagram for the congresswoman has one vertical and one horizontal relevance line.

PART TIME JOBS. $P(S|J) = 0.94$.

EINSTEIN'S PREDICTIONS. Confirmation of an additional consequence only adds to the credibility of the theory but does not *prove* it.

LEMPERT'S PARADOX REEXAMINED. The probability for making the case is P'(case) equals 0.225, 0.450, and 0.675 after one, then two, then all three elements have been shown to have posterior probability values of 0.75.

Chapter VIII.

ANXIETY ATTACK. The onset of anxiety attacks for Mrs. B is approximately random and therefore most likely not to be triggered by some non-random cause.

ADOPT OR NOT / CONCEIVE OR NOT. Using data from all four boxes in the matrix, the conditional probabilities of interest are $P(C|A) = 0.1$ and $P(C|\bar{A}) = 0.1$.

TESTING FOR SUCCESS. $P(A) = 0.30$, $P(G) = 0.25$, $P(G|A) = 0.83$, and $P(G|\bar{A}) = 0$.

DOGS, CATS, AND CEO's. Neither claim is justified because each is based on limited data. In the case of CEO's and pets, not taken into consideration were the CEO's who did not have pets as children and those who did not become CEO's, both with and without pets as children. Data lacking in the airline safety statement is that for people who died in airline accidents. Did they note where all the emergency exits were located?

APPENDIX B.   Solutions for Self Tests.

Chapter II Self Tests:
        SELECTED PROBLEMS. (1) 1/2; (2) c; (3) a; (4) false; (5) c.

        THE POLLSTER. $P(B) = 0.49$, $P(A|B) = 0.68$, $P(A|\bar{B}) = 0.43$

Chapter III Self Tests:
        SELECTED PROBLEMS.   (1) a; (2) c; (3) 35, 17, 31.4; (4) 0.5, 0.6, 0.4; (5) 0.73, 0.34, 0.42.

        SAM PONDERS DIVORCE DECISION TREE.   (A) +3.8; (B) -2.4; (C) +3.2; (D) +1.9.
          Sam should take no action.

Chapter IV Self Tests:
        SELECTED PROBLEMS. (1) c; (2) b; (3) c; (4) 0.575; (5) environmentalists, no.

        EARLY OR LATE.
          probability with which Henry should arrive early = 2/5
          probability with which Henry should arrive late = 3/5
          EV(Henry) = -7/5

Chapter V Self Tests:
        SELECTED PROBLEMS. (1) a; (2) a, b, c; (3) a, c; (4) a ,b; (5) two squares unbraced at
          one end and two unbraced squares in the middle.
        EULERIZING THE TOWN.
          least numbers: 2, 2, 1

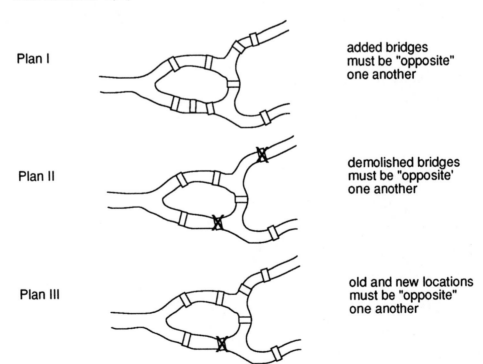

Plan I   added bridges
must be "opposite"
one another

Plan II   demolished bridges
must be "opposite'
one another

Plan III   old and new locations
must be "opposite"
one another

Chapter VI Self Tests:

      SELECTED PROBLEMS. (1) c; (2) 4, 3, 3; (3) a; (4) a, b, c; (5) a, b.

      BOB'S STRIP PATTERNS: pma2, pmm2, p112, p1m1, pm11, p1a1, p111.

Chapter VII Self Tests.

      SELECTED PROBLEMS. (1) b, c; (2) 0.17; (3) a, d; (4) a,c; (5) b.

THE INCLUSIVE "OR."

$P(A) = 0.75$
$P(B) = 0.65$
$P(A|B) = 0.615$
$P(A|\bar{B}) = 1$
$P(B|\underline{A}) = 0.53$
$P(B|\bar{A}) = 1$

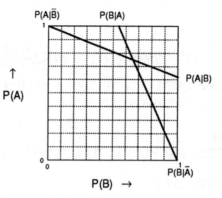

Chapter VIII Quizzes.

      SELECTED PROBLEMS. (1) a, b, c; (2) c; (3) b; (4) c.

      HOW MANY WAYS?   32, 2, 5, 4, 2.

APPENDIX C. **Problem Solving Commands**

APPENDIX C. Problem Solving Commands

I. KNOWLEDGE

IDENT RELEV KNOWLEDGE
IDENT METHODS/PROCEDURES
IDENT RELATED SOLVED PROBS
IDENT TERMINOLOGY
IDENT CONVENTIONS

IDENT THEORIES/STRUCTURES
IDENT RELEV LAWS/PRINS/EQNS
IDENT MODELS
IDENT FACTS/INFORMATION
IDENT CLASSIFICATIONS

Background Knowledge for a problem involves the recall of all information relevant, or thought to be relevant, to the problem through use of the signals, cues, and clues contained in the problem statement. At this early stage in one's attack on a problem, the problem solver may have only a general idea of the specific knowledge that will actually be utilized in arriving at a problem solution. The relationships among the various elements of relevant knowledge are a part of the overall knowledge base. The organization and reorganization of this knowledge will continue during later stages in the problem solving process. The command **IDENT RELATED SOLVED PROBS** is important in that such knowledge, also a part of the problem solver's information base, is often extremely useful in one's attack on the current problem.

II. TOOLS

USE WRITTEN LANGUAGE
USE PICTORIAL LANGUAGE
USE MATH LANGUAGE
ANALYZE PATTERNS
ANALYZE SYMMETRY
MAKE DECISIONS
CONSTRUCT MODELS

USE PROBABILISTIC REASONING
USE HEURISTICS
USE DIAGRAMS
USE ORDINARY LOGIC
EVALUATE/EMPLOY UTILITIES
EXHAUST POSSIBILITIES
LIST/CATEGORIZE

Problem solving Tools are part of the general background knowledge of the problem solver. Every problem solver will have some knowledge of the three fundamental language "tools" that are available to attack and solve problems: one's native language; the language of "pictures" including drawings, diagrams, graphs, and icons; and the language of mathematics. Note that the command **USE ORDINARY LOGIC** involves everyday language and the command **LIST/CATEGORIZE** is simply one method for imposing structure on a problem situation. **EXHAUST POSSIBILITIES** is a common-sense method that permits inspection of every conceivable problem possibility from which the desired solution path or even the solution itself may then be selected.

III. COMPREHENSION

INTERPRET PROB
CLARIFY PROB
SIMPLIFY PROB
RESTATE PROB
IDENT NATURE OF PROB SOLN

REWRITE TO WORKSPACE
IDENT STATED ASSUMPS
IDENT IMPLICIT ASSUMPS
IDENT STATED CONDITIONS
IDENT IMPLICIT CONDITIONS

Problem Comprehension refers to a level of understanding such that the individual knows what is being communicated without necessarily seeing its fullest implications. It is important for problem solvers to be able to state problems in their own words and to do so may involve interpretation, clarification, or simplification of the problem statement. It is important to **REWRITE TO WORKSPACE,** meaning that problem solvers should transcribe the problem statement to the space in which they will work out the details of their problem solutions. It is often extremely important to note that which is implicit in the problem statement by identifying both **IMPLICIT ASSUMPS** and **IMPLICIT CONDITIONS**. The command **IDENT NATURE OF PROB SOLN** comes into play whenever it is initially unclear what kind of problem solution to expect or whenever a variety of different kinds of problem solutions seems possible. Clarification of this point is a part of one's understanding of what the problem is.

IV. ANALYSIS

TRANSLATE ENG—>PICT	**ANALYZE VERBALLY**
TRANSLATE ENG—>MATH	**ANALYZE PICTORIALLY**
TRANSLATE PICT<—>MATH	**ANALYZE MATHEMATICALLY**
IDENT PROB ELEMENTS	**DRAW AND LABEL DIAGRAM**
IDENT/LABEL AUX QUANTS	**ENGAGE IN SELF DIALOG**
IDENT RELS AMONG PARTS	**WRITE THINGS DOWN**
CONCEPTUALIZE PROB	**IDENT SIMS TO PRIOR PROBS**
ANALYZE QUALITATIVELY	**IDENT DIFFS TO PRIOR PROBS**
ANALYZE QUANTITATIVELY	**IDENT PATTERNS IN PROB**
SET UP PROB	**IDENT BEGINNING AND END POINTS**
IDENT GIVENS/WANTEDS	**IDENT IRRELEVANT INFO**
IDENT KNOWNS/UNKNOWNS	**IDENT MISSING INFO**

Problem Analysis is the process of breaking down a problem into its basic elements and making explicit the relationships among those elements. It involves translation among the three languages **ENG, PICT**, and **MATH** as well as the analysis that may be made within any one language. The command **WRITE THINGS DOWN** is the admonition to commit things to paper. This relieves the burden of attempting to store too much in short term memory. **ENGAGE IN SELF-DIALOG** means that talking to oneself while attempting to solve a problem is not only permitted, but encouraged. **CONCEPTUALIZE PROBLEM** is a command that problem solvers tell themselves to execute in order to achieve a basic understanding of the problem and its parts before plunging ahead without a clear idea of the direction one is going. At this stage a closer look at relevant prior problems should be taken noting both similarities and differences to the present problem.

V. STRATEGIES

IDENT STRATEGIES/METHODS	**IDENT PROB RELATIVES**
IDENT USEFUL KNOWLEDGE	**REARRANGE PROB PARTS**
IDENT USEFUL TOOLS	**IDENT PROB STEPS**
IDENT SOLN TYPE SOUGHT	**IDENT SUB-PROBS**
VISUALIZE	**WORK PROB BACKWARD**
IDENT STANDARD STRAT	**DRAW NEW DIAGRAM**
IDENT ALT STRATS	**IDENT NEW PERSPECTIVE/INSIGHT**
IDENT APPROXIMATIONS	**INVENT METAPHORS**
USE TRIAL AND ERROR	**MODIFY/TRANSFORM**
NARROW POSSIBILITIES	**ASK 'WHAT IF"**
GENERALIZE/SYSTEMATIZE	**QUESTION**

In many cases the identification of a problem solving Strategy that will lead to a desired solution represents the highest level of cognitive skill rivaled only by a critical appraisal of the problem and its solution once that solution is found. In some cases, as in **IDENT STANDARD STRAT**, ready-made strategies are available to work certain kinds of problems. In other cases, by contrast, a particularly creative strategy may be necessary to produce a solution. Devising a problem strategy is a process whereby the problem elements identified during the stage of Analysis are put back together in a new arrangement, possibly with new elements added, to synthesize a strategy that will lead to a solution. In most cases there is no fixed recipe for finding a strategy that will work. A number of the commands listed above are merely suggestive of the various kinds of things that might be tried. Carrying on a dialog with some other person or with oneself is particularly important if one is to be successful in obtaining a workable strategy.

VI. APPLICATION

IMPLEMENT STRATEGY	APPLY KNOWLEDGE/TOOLS
FIND SOLN	SOLVE SYMBOLICALLY
FIND QUALITATIVE SOLN	SOLVE NUMERICALLY
FIND APPROX SOLN	SOLVE SUB-PROB
FIND TENTATIVE SOLN	COMPARE ALT SOLNS
GUESS SOLN	IDENT CONCLUSIONS

In this stage the problem solver undertakes the Application of the knowledge, tools, and strategies resulting from the prior stages. The process of Application does not require as high a level of cognitive skill as that in either of the two preceding stages, Analysis and Strategies. Application is the stage that students often think of as "working the problem," and as such, thought to lie at the heart of problem solving activity. As can now be seen, the stage of Application is far from being the most important part of problem solving. It is also far from requiring the greatest cognitive skill. In many cases the process of application is little more than the straightforward application of what the problem solver now knows together with the strategy selected. In problems which call for a quantitative solution the command **SOLVE SYMBOLICALLY** is particularly important. One should proceed symbolically as far as is convenient, inserting numerical values into the symbolic solution only as a final step in the problem solving process.

VII. HELP

SEEK ADDL KNOWLEDGE	CHK REASONING/ANALYSIS
EXAMINE PROB STATUS	CHK IF SOLN REASONABLE
DO SIMPLER RELATED PROB	REEXAMINE KNOWNS/UNKNOWNS
CHK USE OF ALL INFO	REEXAMINE GIVENS/WANTEDS
REEXAMINE ASSUMPS	START OVER / LET INCUBATE
IDENT ALT STRATS/STEPS	SEEK HELP FROM A FRIEND

A solution to a problem cannot be obtained if the problem solver has become stalled at one point or another. Not knowing how to proceed, the individual needs Help of some sort, either self-help or help from some outside source. The need for help usually, but not always, becomes apparent at the Application stage when a satisfactory problem solution cannot be obtained. Perhaps something has gone wrong in one or more of the preceding problem stages. Because of this, the reapplication of cognitive skills at any one of the cognitive levels may be required. The individual may simply review the work already invested in the problem. Alternatively, the person may elect to **DO A SIMPLER RELATED PROB** as a warmup for a second assault on the problem. In addition, the problem solver might explore alternative steps and strategies. The command **EXAMINE PROBLEM STATUS** is good advice with or without help being required. It says, simply, look ahead and look back from where you are in the problem to examine the terrain, so to speak, so as to better decide what step is to be taken next. Of course if all else fails, one can **START OVER / LET INCUBATE** or **SEEK HELP FROM A FRIEND**, whether that friend is a novice or an expert problem solver.

VIII. EVALUATION

INTERPRET SOLN	**GENERALIZE SOLN**
TRANSLATE MATH—>ENG	**EVAL/ASSESS PROB STRATEGY**
TRANSLATE PICT—>ENG	**EVAL/ASSESS PROB SOLN**
IDENT KNOWLEDGE GAINED	**EXAMINE SPECIAL CASES**
IDENT STRATS LEARNED	**DO NUMERICAL EXAMPLE**
IDENT NEW RELATED PROBS	**IDENT SOLN APPLICATIONS**
FIND ALTERNATIVE SOLN	**IDENT SOLN CONSEQUENCES**

Having obtained a problem solution, individuals should now undertake an Evaluation of what they have learned. If the solution is in mathematical or pictorial form one should then **TRANSLATE MATH—> ENG** or **TRANSLATE PICT—>ENG** to obtain the full meaning of that solution. Is the solution in the expected form? Is there a better solution? Are there alternative solutions? What are the applications of the solution? What are the consequences of the solution? Can the problem be generalized so that it can then be applied to a wider variety of circumstances? Does the solution check out when certain special cases are examined? And finally, are there new problems that can now be opened up for investigation that before may have been too difficult to tackle.

Above all, one should recognize that problem solving, whether this be in sociology, anthropology, medicine, law, biology, or any other academic discipline, is an exercise in critical thinking. Whatever cognitive skills are gained in one area are often applicable to other areas of intellectual thought.

References

Adams, James L. 1974. *Conceptual Blockbusting — A Guide to Better Ideas, 2nd ed.* New York: W.W. Norton & Company.

Allen, R.J. 1988. "A Reconceptualization of Civil Trials" in Tillers, P. and Green, E.D. Eds. *Probability and Inference in the Law of Evidence.* Dordrecht: Kluwer Academic Publishers.

Apian, Peter 1539 *Cosmographia.*

Baird, Bruce F. 1989. *Managerial Decisions Under Uncertainty.* New York: John Wiley & Sons, Inc.

Bazerman, M.H. and Neale, M.A. 1986. "Heuristics in negotiation: Limitations to effective dispute resolution" in Arkes, Hal R. and Hammond, K.R. Eds. *Judgment and Decision Making.* Cambridge: Cambridge University Press.

Bentham, Jeremy 1988. *The Principles of Morals and Legislation.* Amherst, N.Y.: Prometheus Books.

Bierman, A.K. and Assali, R.N. 1996. *The Critical Thinking Handbook.* Upper Saddle River, N.J. Prentice Hall

Biggs, N.L., Lloyd, E.K., and Wilson, R.J. 1976. *Graph Theory 1736-1936.* Oxford: Clarendon Press.

Bloom, Benjamin S. 1956. *Taxonomy of Educational Objectives.* New York: Longman, Green, and Co.

Brams, Steven J. 1975. *Game Theory and Politics.* New York: The Free Press.

Buchler, Ira R. and Nutini, Hugo G. 1969. *Game Theory in the Behavioral Sciences.* Pittsburgh: University of Pittsburgh Press.

Cederblom, J. and Paulsen, D.W. 1982. *Critical Reasoning.* Belmont, California: Wadsworth Publishing Company.

Chartrand, Gary 1985. *Introductory Graph Theory.* New York: Dover Publications, Inc.

Christie, A.H. 1969. *Pattern Design—An Introduction fo the Study of Formal Ornament.* New York: Dover Publications Inc.

Copeland, Aaron 1957. *What To Listen For In Music.* New York: McGraw-Hill Book Company, Inc.

Dawes, Robyn M. 1988. *Rational Choice in an Uncertain World.* San Diego: Harcourt Brace Jovanovich, Publishers.

Dawes, Robyn M. 1988. "You Can't Systematize Human Judgment: Dyslexia" in Dowie, J. and Elstein, A., Eds. *Professional judgment—A reader in clinical decision making.* Cambridge: Cambridge University Press.

deBono, Edward 1982. *deBono'sThinking Course.* New York: Facts on File Publications.

Doubilet, P. and McNeil, B.J. 1988. "Clinical Decisionmaking" in Dowie, J. and Elstein, A., Eds. *Professional judgment —A reader in clinical decision making.* Cambridge: Cambridge University Press.

Dresher, Melvin 1961. *The Mathematics of Games of Strategy — Theory and Applications.* New York: Dover Publications, Inc.

Dye, Daniel 1981. *New Book of Chinese Lattice Designs.* New York: Dover Publicationss Inc.

Eddy, David M. 1982. "Probabilistic reasoning in clinical medicine: Problems and opportunities" in Kahneman, D. and Tversky, A. Eds. *Judgment under uncertainty: Heuristics and biases.* Cambridge: Cambridge University Press.

Edwards, W. and Newman, R.J. 1986. "Multiattribute evaluation" in Arkes, Hal R. and Hammond, K.R. Eds. *Judgment and Decision Making.* Cambridge: Cambridge University Press.

Enciso, Jorge 1947. *design motifs of ancient mexico.* New York: Dover Publications, Inc.

Feynman, Richard P. 1985. *Surely You're Joking Mr. Feynman!* New York: W.W. Norton and Co., Inc.

Gardner, Martin 1978. *aha! Insight.* New York City: Scientific American, Inc. and San Francisco: W.H. Freeman and Company.

Garfunkel, Solomon, Project Director 1991. *For All Practical Purposes.* New York: W.H. Freeman and Company.

Gilovoch. Thomas 1991. *How We Know What Isn't So.* New York: The Free Press.

Gorovitz, Samuel ed. 1971. *Mill: Utilitarianism.* Indianapolis: Bobbs-Merrill.

Grünbaum, B. and Shephard, G.C. 1987. *Tilings and Patterns.* New York; W.H. Freeman and Co.

Hage, Per and Harary, Frank 1983. *Structural Models in Anthropology.* Cambridge: Cambridge University Press.

Hage, Per and Harary, Frank 1991. *Exchange in Oceania.* Oxford: Clarendon Press.

Hamburger, Henry 1979. *Games as Models of Social Phenomena.* San Francisco: Harper & Row, Publishers.

Hirschberg, Stuart 1990. *Strategies of Argument.* New York: Macmillan Publishing Company.

Huntley, I.D. and James, D.J.G. Eds.1990. *Mathematical Modeling — A Source Book of Case Studies.* Oxford: Oxford University Press.

Iannucci, David 1992. *Ling/Engl/Anth Intro to the Study of Language.* Salt Lake City: University Copy Center.

Jeffrey, R.C. 1983. *The Logic of Decision.* Chicago: The University of Chicago Press.

Jones, J. 1980. *Game Theory — Mathematical Models of Conflict.* Chichester: Halsted Press.

Kahneman, D., Slovic, P., Tversky, A. 1982. "Evidential impact of base rates" in Kahneman and Tversky, Eds. *Judgment under uncertainty: Heuristics and biases.* Cambridge: Cambridge University Press.

Kahneman, D. and Tversky, A. 1986. "Choices, values, and frames" in Arkes, H.R. and Hammond, K.R. Eds. *Judgment and Decision Making.* Cambridge: Cambridge University Press.

Kappraff, Jay 1991. *Connections.* New York: McGraw-Hill Book Company, Inc.

Kemeny, Snell, and Thompson 1974. *Introduction to Finite Mathematics, 3rd ed.* Englewood Cliffs: Prentice-Hall.

Kosslyn, Stephen Michael 1983. *Ghosts in the Mind's Machine.* New York: W.E. Norton & Company.

Krantz, Les 1992. *What the Odds Are.* New York: Harper Perennial.

Krüger, L., Daston, L.J., Heidelberger, M. Eds. 1987. *The Probabilistic Revolution, Vol. 1, Ideas in History.* Cambridge: The MIT Press.

Krüger, L., Gigerenzer, G., Morgan, M.D. Eds. 1987. *The Probabilistic Revolution, Vol. 2, Ideas in the Sciences.* Cambridge: The MIT Press.

Kyburg, H.E. and Smokler, H.E. 1964. *Studies in Subjective Probability.* New York: John Wiley & Sons, Inc.

Landsburg, Steven E. 1993. *The Armchair Economist.* New York: The Free Press.

Langacker, R.W. 1972. *Fundamentals of Linguistic Analysis.* New York: Harcourt Brace Jovanovich, Inc.

Larcher, J. 1985. *Allover Patterns With Letter Forms.* New York: Dover Publications, Inc.

Lempert, Richard 1988. "The New Evidence Scholarship: Analyzing the Process of Proof" in *Probability and Inference in the Law of Evidence,* Tillers, P. and Green, E.D., Eds. Dordrecht: Kluwer Academic Publishers.

Luce, R.D., Raiffa, H. 1957. *Games and Decisions — Introduction and Critical Survey.* New York: Dover Publications, Inc.

Malkevitch, Joseph and Meyer, Walter 1974. *Graphs, Models, & Finite Mathematics.* Englewood Cliffs: Prentice-Hall, Inc.

Mosteller, Frederick 1965. *Fifty Challenging Problems in Probability with Solutions.* New York: Dover Publications, Inc.

Murphy, Edmond A . 1979. *Probability in Medicine.* Baltimore and London: The Johns Hopkins University Press.

Newton, Lisa H. 1989. *Ethics in America Study Guide, An Annenberg CPB Project.* Englewood Cliffs: Prentice Hall Inc.

Nisbett, Richard and Ross, Lee 1980. *Human Inference: Strategies and Shortcomings of Social Judgment.* Englewood Cliffs, New Jersey: Prentice-Hall Inc.

Polya, G. 1954. *Patterns of Plausible Inference.* Princeton: Princeton University Press.

Polya, G. 1957. *How to Solve It — A New Aspect of Mathematical Method.* Princeton: Princeton University Press.

Posner, Michael I., Ed. 1989. *Foundations of Cognitive Science.* Cambridge: The MIT Press.

Poundstone, William 1992. *Prisoner's Dilemma.* New York: Doubleday.

Raiffa, Howard 1968. *Decision Analysis: Introductory Lectures on Choices Under Uncertainty.* Reading, Mass: Addison-Wesley Publishing Company.

Rieke, R.D. and Sillars, M.O. 1984. *Argumentation and the Decision Making Process.* Glenview, Ill: Scott, Foresman and Company.

Rosen, Joe 1975. *Symmetry discovered.* Cambridge: Cambridge University Press.

Ross, L., Nisbett, R. 1980. *Human Inference: Strategies and Shortcomings of Social Judgment.* Englewood Cliffs: Prentice-Hall, Inc.

Rubinstein, Moshe F. 1975. *Patterns of Problem Solving.* Englewood Cliffs: Prentice-Hall, Inc.

Rubinstein, Moshe F. 1986. *Tools for Thinking and Problem Solving.* Englewood Cliffs: Prentice-Hall, Inc.

Salmon, Merrilee 1984. *Introduction to Logic and Critical Thinking.* San Diego: Harcourt Brace Jovanovich, Publishers.

Saunders, D.L. 1990. *Amish Quilt Designs.* New York: Dover Publications, Inc.

Savage, L.J. 1972. *The Foundations of Statistics.* New York: Dover Publications, Inc.

Schumacher, E.F. 1977. *A Guide For The Perplexed.* New York: Harper & Row, Publishers.

Shubnikov, A.V. and Koptsik, V.A. 1974. *Symmetry in Science and Art.* New York: Plenum Press.

Smart, J.J.C. and Williams, Bernard 1980. *Utilitarianism: For and Against.* Cambridge: Cambridge University Press.

Stevens, P. 1981. *A Handbook of Regular Patterns: An Introduction to Symmetry in Two Dimensions.* Cambridge: M.I.T. Press.

Tapscott, Bangs L. 1985. *Elementary Applied Symbolic Logic.* Lanhal, MD: University Prsessof America Inc.

Thornton, J.G., Lilford, R.J., Johnson, N. 1992. "Decision analysis in medicine." British Journal of Medicine, 304: 1099-1103.

Toulmin, S., Rieke, R., Janik, J. 1979. *An introduction to reasoning.* New York: Macmillan Publishing Co., Inc.

Von Neuman, John and Morgenstern, Oskar 1953. *Theory of Games and Economic Behavior.* Princeton: Princeton University Press.

Washburn, D.K. and Crowe, D.W. 1988. *Symmetries of Culture — Theory and Practice of Plane Pattern Analysis.* Seattle: University of Washington Press.

Weitlaner-Johnson, Irmgard 1976. *Mexican Indian Folk Designs.* New York: Dover Publications, Inc.

West, Thomas G. 1991. *In the Mind's Eye.* Buffalo, N.Y.: Prometheus Books.

Wickelgren, Wayne A. 1974. *How to Solve Problems.* San Francisco: W.H. Freeman and Company.

Williams, J.D. 1954. *The Compleat Strategyst.* New York: McGraw-Hill Book Company, Inc.

Windt, P.Y., Appleby, P.C., Battin, M.P., Francis, L.P., Landesman, B.M. 1989. *Ethical Issues in the Professions.* Englewood Cliffs: Prentice Hall.

Young, R., Becker, A.L., Pike, K.L. 1970. *Rhetoric: Discovery and Change.* New York: Harcourt, Brace, & World.